EQUAL VALUE/COMPARABLE WORTH IN THE UK AND THE USA

Also by Elizabeth Meehan and published by Macmillan

WOMEN'S RIGHTS AT WORK

Equal Value/ Comparable Worth in the UK and the USA

Edited by

Peggy Kahn
Associate Professor of Political Science
University of Michigan–Flint

and

Elizabeth Meehan
Professor of Politics
The Queen's University of Belfast

MACMILLAN

First published 1992 by
THE MACMILLAN PRESS LTD
Houndmills, Basingstoke, Hampshire RG21 2XS
and London
Companies and representatives
throughout the world

ISBN 0–333–47506–2 hardcover
ISBN 0–333–47507–0 paperback

A catalogue record for this book is available
from the British Library

Printed in Hong Kong

To Jude Stoddart and Bob Bix (*Peggy Kahn*)

To Yolande Davidson (*Elizabeth Meehan*)

Contents

vii

List of Tables and Figure

Tables

Figure

Acknowledgements

A slightly longer version of Chapter 4, 'Comparable Worth and its Impact on Black Women', by Julianne Malveaux first appeared in *Review of Black Political Economy*, vol. 14, nos 2–3 (Fall/Winter 1985–6) pp. 54–62, and the editors of this volume are grateful to Transaction, Inc. for permission to reprint it here.

Chapter 11, 'Comparable Worth for Public Employees: Implementing a New Wage Policy in Minnesota', by Sara M. Evans and Barbara J. Nelson, was originally published under the same title in *Comparable Worth, Pay Equity and Public Policy*, edited by Rita Mae Kelly and Jane Baynes (*Contributions in Labor Studies*, no 22, Greenwood Press, Inc., Westport, CT, 1988) pp. 191–212. Copyright © 1988 by the Policy Studies Organization. Reprinted with permission).

Notes on the Contributors

Alan Arthurs lectures in industrial relations at the University of Bath. He is an independent expert on equal pay for industrial tribunals. His research interests include employer strategies in industrial relations, equal pay and managerial and professional unionism. His interest in discrimination was first aroused when he was a student at Davidson College, North Carolina, which was all-male and all-white at that time.

Linda M. Blum teaches sociology at the University of Michigan, Ann Arbor, and has recently written a book on the politics of comparable worth entitled *Between Feminism and Labour.*

Sara M. Evans is Professor of History at the University of Minnesota. She is the co-author, with Barbara J. Nelson, of *Wage Justice: Comparable Worth and the Paradox of Technocratic Reform.*

Roslyn L. Feldberg is a sociologist interested in women's employment. She has written on social and technological changes in clerical work and is now studying nursing from her position as Associate Director of the Massachusetts Nurses Association.

Jeanne Gregory teaches at Middlesex Polytechnic where she also runs an MA course on gender and society. Her research and publications are mainly on sex and race discrimination law, including *Sex, Race and the Law.* She is currently involved in setting up a campaign for pay equity in Britain.

Sue Hastings is a Research Officer at the Trade Union Research Unit, Ruskin College, Oxford. She works in the related fields of grading and pay structures, job evaluation, equal pay and, in particular, equal value – giving advice to unions affiliated to the unit, tutoring on short courses and has provided 'expert' assistance on more than 25 'equal-value' cases.

Peggy Kahn teaches Western European Politics, Political Economy and Women's Studies at the University of Michigan-

Flint. She has written previously about British industrial relations and the British coalfields and was an assistant research officer at the National Union of Mineworkers between 1982 and 1984.

Kathleen Kautzer, PhD, is Assistant Professor of Sociology and Social Work at Regis College in Weston, Massachusetts. Her current research focuses on evaluating goals and strategies of a broad range of advocacy organisations representing disadvantaged persons. Formerly a union organiser, she was employed by District 65 of the Distributive Workers of America and between 1978 and 1980 directed the successful campaign for union representation among clerical and technical workers at Boston University.

Julianne Malveaux, an economist, has written widely about black women's employment. She has held appointments at the Institute for Industrial Relations and the Department of Afro-American Studies at the University of California at Berkeley.

Elizabeth Meehan has a Chair in Politics at Queen's University, Belfast, having lectured previously at Bath University. She is the author of *Women's Rights at Work* and several articles on social rights in the European Community, one of which is in U. Vogel and M. Moran (eds), *The Frontiers of Citizenship*. She is a fellow of the Royal Society of Arts.

Fiona Neathey is a research officer for Industrial Relations Services where her features for the journal *Industrial Relations Review and Report* have included major articles on job evaluation and equal value. She has recently been involved in a project for the Equal Opportunities Commission examining the effects of different forms of pay determination on women's earnings. She previously worked as a research officer for the civil service union, the CPSA. She has a BSc in sociology from the University of Bath and an MA in industrial relations from Warwick University.

Barbara J. Nelson, a political scientist, is Professor of Public Policy at the Robert H. Humphrey Institute of Public Affairs at the University of Minnesota, where she also co-directs the Center on Women and Public Policy. She is the author, with Sara M. Evans, of *Wage Justice: Comparable Worth and the Paradox of Technocratic Reform.*

Kathy Sutton gained a PhD in Soviet studies at the University of Birmingham. She worked for the West Midlands County Council as a team leader of a welfare rights take-up team researching into social security issues and carrying out community-wide campaigns to encourage people to take up their rights to welfare benefits. She then worked in the Leicester City Council low-pay campaign as Campaign Officer, advising people on their rights and researching into low-pay issues. Thereafter she became the Women's Rights Officer for the National Council for Civil Liberties and then Wages Rights Officer at the Low Pay Unit. She now works for the Labour Party as its Equal Opportunities Researcher. She is also a member of the steering group of the Pay Equity Campaign.

List of Abbreviations

ACAS	Advisory, Conciliation and Arbitration Service
AFSCME	American Federation of State, County and Municipal Employees
AFL-CIO	American Federation of Labour–Congress of Industrial Organisations
ALA	American Library Association
AMC	Association of Minnesota Counties
ANA	American Nurses Association
APEX	Association of Professional, Executive, Clerical and Computer Staff
ASTMS	Association of Scientific, Technical and Managerial Staff (now MSF)
AT&T	The American Telephone and Telegraph Company
BIFU	Banking, Insurance and Finance Union
BNA	Bureau of National Affairs (USA)
CAC	Central Arbitration Committee
Cal.	California
CBU	Clearing Banks Union
CCC	Contra Costa County (USA)
CESW	Council on Economic Status of Women
COHSE	Confederation of Health Service Employees
DFL	Democratic–Farmer–Labour Party (USA)
DHR	Department of Human Resources (Yale University)
DOER	Department of Employee Relations (Minnesota)
DRGS	Diagnosis-related Groups
DWA	Distributive Workers of America
EAT	Employment Appeal Tribunal
ECJ	European Court of Justice
EDP	electronic data processing
EEC	European Economic Community
EEOC	Equal Employment Opportunity Commission (USA)
EOC	Equal Opportunities Commission (UK)
EOR	*Equal Opportunities Review*

ERA	Equal Rights Amendment
ESRC	Economic and Social Research Council
GMB	General, Municipal and Boilermakers (Union)
GMBATU	General, Municipal, Boilermakers and Allied Trades Union
GNP	gross national product
HERE	Hotel and Restaurant Employees International Union
HMSO	Her Majesty's Stationery Office
IDS	Incomes Data Services
ILO	International Labour Organisation
IR	Independent Republican (USA)
IRS	Industrial Relations Service
IT	Industrial Tribunal
IUE	International Union of Electrical Workers
LACSAB	Local Authorities Conditions of Service Advisory Board
LAMSAC	Local Authorities Management Services and Computer Groups
LEVEL	London Equal Value Steering Group
LSE	London School of Economics
MAMA	Metropolitan Area Management Association
Mass.	Massachusetts
MLC	Minnesota League of Cities
Mo.	Missouri
MSBA	Minnesota School Boards Association
MSF	Managerial, Scientific and Finance Union (formerly ASTMS)
NAACP	National Association for the Advancement of Colored Persons (USA)
NALGO	National Association of Local Government Officers
NCPE	National Committee on Pay Equity (USA)
NEA	National Education Association (USA)
NHS	National Health Service
NJC	National Joint Council
NOW	National Organization for Women (USA)
NRC	National Research Council of the National Academy of Sciences (USA)
NUPE	National Union of Public Employees
NY	New York

OPEIU	Office and Professional Employees International Union
PNA	Pennsylvania Nurses Association
PSI	Policy Studies Institute
RN	Registered Nurse (USA)
SCF	Save the Children Fund
SEIU	Service Employees International Union
SERTUC	South-Eastern Region, Trades Union Congress
TGWU	Transport and General Workers Union
TUC	Trades Union Congress
TURU	Trades Union Research Unit
UAW	United Auto Workers (USA)
UK	United Kingdom
USA	United States of America
USDAW	Union of Shop, Distributive and Allied Workers
WIRS	Workplace Industrial Relations Survey
Wis.	Wisconsin
WTUL	Women's Trade Union League

1 Introduction: Equal Pay for Work of Equal Value in Britain and the USA

Peggy Kahn

'Equal pay for work of equal value', often referred to as 'comparable worth' or 'pay equity' in the United States of America (USA), emerged as both a movement and an employment policy in Britain and the USA in the late 1970s and 1980s. In Britain, women in unions campaigned to introduce equal value into workplaces from banks to hospitals. Under the dual pressures of union activity and an amended Equal Pay Act, employers undertook large-scale job re-evaluation or adjusted the pay of individual women workers. In the USA, groups of women tried to establish in law the principle of comparable worth, campaigned for comparable worth as an employment policy for workers in the public sector, and educated a broader public about the principles underlying comparable worth. At the same time, rank-and-file women went on strike for comparable worth. Many states conducted comparable-worth studies of their workforces and made substantial salary adjustments as a result.

This introductory chapter begins by explaining what equal value means in general terms, describing ways in which it has been enacted as wages policy, and describing two broad types of equal value activity. The chapter then surveys empirical developments in Britain and the USA, attending to both legal/administrative and collective bargaining activity.

WHAT IS 'EQUAL PAY FOR WORK OF EQUAL VALUE'?

'Equal pay for work of equal value' or 'equal pay for jobs of comparable worth' is the proposition that women should receive equal pay for work that is not the same as men's but equally demanding. It argues that jobs that are dissimilar should

1

be paid equally when they involve comparable skill, responsibility, working conditions and effort.

The original Equal Pay Acts in both Britain and the USA, while addressing a particular and blatant form of pay discrimination, did not address the problem of low pay for the majority of women. The US Equal Pay Act (1964) and the British Equal Pay Act (1970) provided that a woman doing the same work as a man should receive the same rate of pay. Where job segregation, the division of male and female labour into different jobs and occupations, prevailed, the Acts could not be used, as they required a woman to compare her pay to that of a man doing broadly similar work. Most women, in fact, work in segregated jobs and occupations. In both countries, therefore, after an initial spurt of equal-pay claims and some identifiable improvement in women's wages relative to men's, the numbers of claims under the Acts fell rapidly (Gregory, 1987a; Snell, 1986; Tzannatos and Zabalza, 1984; National Committee on Pay Equity, 1987a). The principle of equal value goes beyond equal pay for the same work to address the problem of equal pay for equivalent but different work. It still relies upon firm-specific comparison of women's to men's work, though not on the basis of specific job titles and tasks. It relies instead upon comparison of general job demands.

In going beyond equal pay for the same work, equal value tries to address the systemic undervaluation of 'women's work'. Such undervaluation is often based upon the historical development of entire occupations. Clerical work and nursing are examples of 'feminised' jobs developed on the basis of low wages for women. Low wages were related to the fact that women were not seen as doing skilled work or as having the same need as men for a 'family wage' or 'living wage' (Phillips and Taylor, 1986; Kessler-Harris, 1990; Reverby, 1987; Davies, 1982). In addition women remained for the most part outside the unions that increased the labour-market power of male workers (Hartman, 1976; Walby, 1986). Wages systems, influenced both by ideological conceptions and the exercise of power in the economy, devalued women's work.

Equal value appears in Britain and the USA in several different forms. The general idea that women are paid less than the value of their jobs because they work in predominantly female occupations may itself motivate women to demand better pay but it need not necessarily lead to job-evaluation exercises. In some American states, for example, policymakers have recognised the principle of comparable worth and increased the wages of the lowest-paid workers, disproportionately female and people of colour, without undertaking job evaluation. Unions have also negotiated pay increases for undervalued women workers in city government using employment data but without becoming involved in formal job evaluation (NCPE, n.d.; NCPE, 1989).

However, equal-value reform usually involves job evaluation and a pay policy based upon its results. There are several available methods of job evaluation. One key distinction is between whole-job or 'felt fair' methods, such as job-ranking or paired comparisons, and analytic methods, such as '*a priori*' factor methods and 'policy capturing' approaches. In both the British and US settings, the '*a priori*' factor method has been favoured by advocates of comparable-worth and under British law whole-job comparisons have been ruled inadequate for the purposes of establishing non-discriminatory pay practices. *A priori* evaluation involves breaking jobs down into a number of factors, for example, skills, responsibility, physical and mental requirements, and working conditions. Each factor may be analysed further. Jobs are assigned points on each factor and subfactor. In order for the points on each compensable factor to add up to total points, the relative weights of the factors must be decided upon. Job-evaluation exercises typically evaluate some set of predominantly male and female job categories. The job evaluation is subsequently used to allow employers or negotiators to examine the relationship of pay to points, and readjust pay in order to establish a more consistent pay-for-points relationship across male and female jobs. The extent of job evaluation and pay adjustment varies. Large studies may examine many jobs within a jurisdiction, while others may be confined to a few occupational groups or even, as in many British legal cases, to one person's job and that of her individual comparator.

Just as 'common sense' notions and managerial assessments of skill have incorporated sex bias, so job evaluation, a technology meant systematically to capture levels of skill and provide the basis for a 'rational' pay structure, may incorporate sex bias. As Fiona Neathey points out in Chapter 3, sex bias can intrude into job evaluation at many stages of the process. The degree to which job evaluation reconstitutes sex discriminatory practices seems to be closely related to who – whether traditional management consultants or union activists trained in sex bias and job evaluation together with managers – controls the overall process of evaluation and each of its stages. In Britain both the Equal Opportunities Commission (EOC) and the Trades Union Congress (TUC) are training trade unionists and managers in job evaluation free of sex bias, while in the USA there is increasing awareness of the problem of management-controlled job evaluation (Acker, 1989; Evans and Nelson, 1989; Steinberg, 1989a; 1990a; 1990b).

Typically, men's work is paid more in relation to job scores than women's. In the USA, pay adjustments move predominantly female jobs all, or some, of the way towards either the male or average (male and female) pay-for-points formula. In the absence of a legal requirement in the USA, employers have considerable discretion regarding whether to remove fully and expeditiously discrimination revealed by job evaluation. So, for example, the Washington state case, discussed by Roslyn Feldberg in Chapter 9, involved a 1985 out-of-court settlement providing that by 1993 all undervalued jobs be moved to 5 per cent of the comparable-worth line, based not on male jobs alone but also on female and mixed job categories.

Despite Britain's clearer legal requirements, ambiguities remain. As in the case of local authority manual workers discussed in this book, pay adjustments based upon job evaluation may correct basic wage rates but not overall earnings, which continue to favour men because of men's greater access to such payments as bonus and overtime. In addition, whether and how the equal-value analysis might be applied to the benefits received by women workers is unclear. The Pennsylvania Nurses Association suit against the Commonwealth of Pennsylvania described by Feldberg is the first to raise these questions in the USA. In the British case, *Hayward* v. *Cammell Laird* ([1988] ICR 464), a woman worker succeeded in establishing that her job was of equal value to that of her comparators though she was paid less, but she also enjoyed certain more favourable terms of contract than her male comparators. The Court ruled that she was nevertheless entitled to have her pay made not less favourable, and it held that in general a successful claimant was entitled to have any term of her contract made not less favourable (Willborn, 1989).

In terms of the political process of equal value, it seems worth distinguishing two broad analytic types, a managerial–bureaucratic model and a labour–mobilisation model. In the former, managers and administrators, often in consultation with union leaders, control the definition and implementation of comparable worth. Debate over and implementation of the policy occur for the most part over the heads of union members. Management's definition of skill tends to dominate job evaluation. The more far-reaching feminist and socialist possibilities of the comparable-worth argument – that is, the questions it raises about the justice of capitalist markets and the nature of class and gender hierarchies – tend to be suppressed (Feldberg, 1986; Brenner, 1987). Achieving comparable worth is seen as a matter of readjusting the meritocratic hierarchy or obtaining wage justice for individual women rather than as a revaluation of the work of women as a group or as strengthening women workers' control over their work and its evaluation. This type of comparable worth reform is similar to what Johanna Brenner has characterised as comparable worth in a discourse of liberal equality and what Cynthia Cockburn has described as 'liberal equal opportunity policy' (Brenner, 1987; Cockburn, 1989).

On the other hand, the comparable-worth process may be used upon the mobilisation of women workers, comparable worth from below. The demand for comparable worth may come from women workers and their unions. Union members and leaders are involved in campaigning for and designing pay adjustments. In the process, women workers may become more attached to their unions as organisations and to ideas of active trade unionism. In this model, women workers are less likely to cede evaluation of their jobs to professionals and experts. Comparable worth goes beyond securing an equitable wage for the individual. It may be used to challenge differentials and hierarchy, the problem of low pay inside and beyond the immediate workforce, control over working conditions, and gendered notions of skill; it involves increasing the power of women workers to define the value of their work and practices of wage payment. As Cockburn puts it, radical equal opportunity policy argues that discrimination must be identified at the level of the group, not the individual. It seeks to politicise (or re-politicise) personnel decisions and release a struggle for power and influence by disadvantaged groups.

In practice, most cases of equal value in Britain and the USA are an admixture of comparable worth from above and below, falling short of the radical model. The US movement, particularly in state government, seems to be primarily managerial in orientation. Professionalised women's organisations, union leaders, and state policymakers and politicians often put the issue on the agenda. The detailed implementation of policy is often left to personnel managers and job evaluation consultants. This approach is clearly indicated in the Minnesota case discussed by Sara Evans and Barbara Nelson in Chapter 11. Only a few cases, such as those of Yale University and San Jose discussed in this volume, seem to involve strong mobilisation from below. However, in the USA, where women's and civil rights groups often support comparable worth initiatives, the language of comparable worth often emphasises the interests of women as a group. In Chapter 5 Linda Blum situates the US comparable-worth movement in the context of American feminism and discusses the gender and class politics of two local campaigns.

The British movement is, on the one hand, structured by a legal process that explicitly frames equal value as a problem of discrimination against individual claimants. Yet individual women are supported in the legal process by their unions, which also pursue larger-scale change through collective bargaining. In a number of cases, union members have been informed and active. Notions of skill are often scrutinised by unions, job-evaluation consultants are viewed with considerable suspicion, and job evaluation is seen as a collective-bargaining matter. Elements of the 'radical' approach are particularly evident in the case of Northern Ireland hospital ancillary workers discussed by Kathy Sutton in Chapter 8. Equal value here is understood by its protagonists to be essential to strategies for dealing with low pay and a particular regional experience of economic marginalisation. On the other hand, in Chapter 6 Alan Arthurs shows that anticipated vulnerability to legal action inspired management-led reform in Midland Bank; unions were merely consulted in the job re-evaluation exercise. The majority of British cases might be described not as 'radical' but as consistent with a pay-oriented adversarial trade unionism, which attends to lower-paid members. In both countries, there is a variation in the political process of equal value depending upon the individual case and in particular upon whether labour, management, or other groups take the initiative.

The equal-value analysis was developed in connection with the undervaluation of women's work, but in the USA comparable-worth principles have also been applied to jobs in which people of colour are disproportionately represented. Julianne Malveaux's early analysis of the impact of comparable worth on black women, which is reprinted in Chapter 4, concluded that many black women would gain from comparable worth. Because black men were overrepresented in 'typically female' jobs, black males also stood to gain. Finally, she argued, job evaluation could be used to reveal race as well as sex bias in wage payment (Malveaux, 1985/6; Malveaux, 1985; Scales-Trent, 1984). Subsequent work has shown that occupations with a disproportionate representation of people of colour are paid less than predominantly white male occupations of comparable value to the employer, and that women of colour suffer double discrimination in wage-setting systems (NCPE, 1987b). Numerous public-sector jurisdictions have studied and corrected discrimination in wage-setting based upon race (NCPE, 1989, NCPE, n.d.).

BRITISH DEVELOPMENTS – POLICY AND LAW

Perhaps the clearest contrast between developments in Britain and the USA is the existence of an equal-value provision in Britain's Equal Pay Act and the absence of any explicit equal value law in the USA. The significance of the British law is not only that it provides a possible remedy in individual cases of pay discrimination, but also that it has contributed to a broad social consensus that not paying women equally for work of equal value is a form of discrimination. The law is also an incentive to employers to correct discriminatory pay structures in advance of legal cases, which are costly and publicly embarrassing. Trade unionists, who generally prefer to negotiate rather than litigate equal-value adjustments, also benefit from the existence of the law, which may raise the awareness of their members regarding discriminatory pay practices, exert pressure upon employers to negotiate, and function as an instrument of last resort in cases of employer recalcitrance. The British Equal Opportunities Commission (EOC) has also been involved in publicising the law, evaluating its effectiveness, supporting and conducting litigation, and training management and labour in relation to its implementation.

In Chapter 2 Jeanne Gregory explores in some detail the origins of British equal-value regulations and the development of case law. She emphasises that the law was not an initiative of the Thatcher government, but the government's grudging response to the finding of the European Court of Justice that Britain was not fulfilling its obligations under the Treaty of Rome. The basic form of the regulations is partly attributable to a resistant government and partly to longer traditions of British discrimination and employment law.

The equal-value regulations allow an individual claimant to take a case to the Industrial Tribunal (IT), an informal court designed to deal expediently with employment issues. The claimant identifies individual comparators. After a preliminary screening during which the IT may dismiss a claim if it finds 'no reasonable grounds for determining that the work is of equal value', the Tribunal must commission a report from an independent expert, drawn from a roster compiled by the Advisory, Conciliation, and Arbitration Service (ACAS), as to whether the jobs being compared are of equal value. If job evaluation shows that the claimant's work is of equal value, the burden is on the employer to show that the variation in pay is genuinely due to a material factor other than sex. As Gregory shows, since 1984 there has been substantial development of case law by the various appeals courts – the Employment Appeal Tribunal (EAT), the Court of Appeals, the House of Lords, and the European Court of Justice (Bourn and Whitmore, 1989; Rubinstein, 1984; EOC, 1989b).

The incorporation of the equal-value regulations in the Equal Pay Act means that Britain's Equal Opportunities Commission (EOC), the anti-discrimination law-enforcement body, is centrally involved in legal and voluntary activity with regard to equal pay for work of equal value. The EOC is in general charged with making information about the Equal Pay and Sex

Discrimination Acts available, conducting investigations, assisting individuals in court cases (especially where major questions of legal principle are involved), and advising the government on implementation. In connection with equal value, the EOC has issued guidance booklets, conducted advertising campaigns, and engaged in other educational activities. It has also undertaken training – including training in job-evaluation free of sex bias – and development work, with such groups as the Trades Union Congress (TUC) and Law Centres. Immediately following enactment of the equal value regulations, the EOC legal strategy involved supporting a large number of cases in order to define equal value in the most expansive possible way; and it has continued to support strategic appeals cases. The EOC's latest Consultative Document also identifies two issues pertaining to the form of law and legal procedures that the Commission feel render the law ineffective in many cases. First, the Equal Pay Act as amended tends to conceptualise discrimination as individual rather than as occupational or collective and has no provision to deal with discrimination in collective agreements. Second, there continue to be procedural delays and high costs involved in legal cases. While some delays are the result of the time taken by independent experts to compile reports, others can be traced to the shift of legal argument to the preliminary hearing phase of the proceeding, where the burden of proof is on the applicant rather than the employer (EOC, 1989a).

Despite legal complexities and delays, numerous cases from both the private and public sectors have been brought under the amended Equal Pay Act. Almost 4000 'equal pay for work of equal value' applications were made between 1984 and 1989. Many of these were multiple applications from groups of women working for the same employer. Only 374 employers were directly involved in the applications. Just under a third of the claims involved British Coal, the public coal corporation, and almost 1500 applications were made by speech therapists employed by the National Health Service (NHS). Excluding these group applications, the number of equal-value claims declined from 382 in 1985 to 366 in 1986 to 343 in 1987. In 1988, 140 applications were made. By July 1989, only 20 of 4000 cases had gone through the full procedure, and on average each case took 16¹/₂ months, within a tribunal system that was intended to function informally and expediently (EOR, 1989b, 1988a and b, 1987, 1986).

BRITISH DEVELOPMENTS – UNION AND MANAGEMENT ACTIVITY

While procedural delay has deterred unions from lodging legal claims on behalf of their members, unions continue to take tribunal cases, especially where there is no prospect of successful negotiation. At the same time, unions are negotiating for equal value. The TUC lists 69 sets of negotiations undertaken mainly since 1986 (TUC, Equal Rights Department, 1990). Under the pressure of legal action and bargaining demands, managements have both unilaterally and jointly with unions engaged in job re-evaluation to remove or diminish sex bias. A 1986 survey of employers requesting copies of a Hay MSL (an influential management consultancy firm) publication on equal value showed that a majority believed that the law would necessitate some adjustment of pay structures (EOR, 1986a). Equalvalue adjustments in Britain have occurred across a range of industrial sectors and in mainly low-grade white-collar and manual occupations.

The general context of union equal-value activity is the somewhat increased priority attached to an equal opportunities or women's agenda within British unions over the past five to ten years, as patterns of employment and union membership have changed. British union capacity has been weakened not only by systematic government attacks and by high rates of unemployment, but also by economic restructuring, particularly the decrease in male manufacturing industry and an increase in disproportionately female part-time and temporary employment in the service sector. While British trade-union density has declined, it has not diminished to the level of US union density, probably because of the more deeply and widely rooted tradition of unionism, unions' emphasis upon organising, and more limited employer anti-unionism. In 1987, 81 per cent of public-sector workers, 38 per cent of private-sector workers, and 51 per cent of workers in the economy overall were union members. By 1989, women made up one-third of all trade-union members (Towers, 1989).

Unions have developed two different types of programmes directed specifically to the needs of women workers. On the one hand, union policies address a variety of practices which hinder women's full participation in unions. Represented by the *TUC Charter for Women within Trade Unions*, the internal-organisational agenda focuses on such issues as the under-representation of women on decision-making bodies and in official positions, the need for provision of child-care facilities at union functions, and the importance of women's involvement in union training and education. On the other hand, unions' workplace programmes, represented by the *TUC Charter for Women at Work*, aim to put women's issues, such as equal pay, pregnancy, maternity and parental leave, and child-care on the bargaining agenda (TUC, 1989, 1990).

Nearly all unions have made some progress on the organisational agenda, though most continue to have wide disparities between the percentages of women in membership and in leadership positions. All unions continue to have the lowest levels of women's participation among paid full-time officials. Recent research has shown that it is these women full-timers who are more likely to make a priority of issues such as equal pay, child-care, maternity leave and sexual harassment in collective bargaining and are more committed to recruiting women and developing their participation (Heery and Kelly, 1989).

As women have increased as a percentage of union members, as they have become increasingly organised and represented at most levels of the union, and as employers have looked to women to overcome current and projected skill shortages, the problems of women workers have moved onto the bargaining agenda. However, research commissioned by the EOC has shown that even where there are union and/or company declarations of commitment to equal opportunities policy, major sectors of British industry show little evidence of equality bargaining. Equality bargaining is defined as the inclusion of benefits or arrangements that facilitate women's full participation in the workforce (for example, enhanced maternity and parental leave); equality-aware handling of standard bargaining issues (for example, pay); and an equality dimension to negotiation of change (for example, reforming a grading structure) (Colling and Dickens, 1989 and 1990).

Equal-value activity is a bargaining issue often dependent upon the initiative of specific union officials or a well-developed equal-opportunity structure in the union (EOR, 1985). Equal-value bargaining may be more problematic than other equality bargaining for male negotiators, as it challenges and undoes previously negotiated agreements rather than simply adding to them. In addition, it introduces possibilities of relinquishing control to the legal process and may involve complex questions of job evaluation.

Equal-value activity undertaken by unions in the public-service sector has typically raised questions of overall job and pay structures and involved several unions. The renegotiation of the local authority manual workers' job evaluation scheme, discussed by Sue Hastings in Chapter 10, shifted the rank ordering of male and female jobs, improving the pay of largely female groups of workers such as home helps and school-meals workers. The exercise addressed basic pay levels without, however, focusing on other components of pay, such as bonus and overtime, to which male workers have greater access. Three unions, the Transport and General Workers' Union (TGWU), the National Union of Public Employees (NUPE), and the General, Municipal, Boilermakers and Allied Trades Union (GMBATU) initiated the re-evaluation in negotiations with the Local Authority Conditions of Service Advisory Board (LACSAB), which represents employers. A large-scale campaign to achieve equal pay for manual workers is underway in the National Health Service. The NHS as an employer is considerably more recalcitrant than the local authorities, however, and NUPE, TGWU, and GMBATU, and the Confederation of Health Service Employees (COHSE) are undertaking a mass campaign of registration of legal claims and worker education, while trying to initiate negotiations. The Northern Ireland health workers' case discussed by Kathy Sutton in Chapter 8 is related to this larger effort. The NHS has also fought the claims of speech therapists, whose legal case is now pending in the Employment Appeal Tribunal.

In the private-services sector, there have been major developments in both banking and finance and in retailing. Banks, a large employer of women in low-paid clerical and related jobs, have faced union and legal pressure since the early 1980s to develop equal-opportunities policies. In Chapter 6, Alan Arthurs discusses a management-led job evaluation exercise at Midland Bank. The initiative appears to be not only a response to the equal value regulations in general but also a reaction to the two legal cases brought against Lloyd's Bank in 1986 and 1989. The first Lloyds case involved female print-finishers comparing themselves with male printers (*French and others* v *Lloyds Bank*). The second case, in which female secretaries are comparing themselves to male messengers, has implications for a greater number of women workers (*Longman and others* v. *Lloyds Bank*). It is also an important legal case on the issue of separate pay structures as a material defence, an argument also invoked by the NHS against the speech therapists.

In early 1990 retailers began to respond to union activity on equal value. A legal case involving Sainsbury checkers resulted in Sainsbury's offering a joint evaluation scheme based on equality principles and an immediate wage increase of 14.5 per cent, 6 per cent above the general pay settlement. Other major retailers followed: Marks and Spencer awarded a pay rise to 44 000 sales assistants, giving them parity with warehouse workers; Tesco granted increases of 10 to 13.5 per cent to some of its women workers; and Safeway increased the pay of some workers 35 per cent (Labour Research Department, 1990). These private-sector developments suggest that equal-value gains in sectors where job structures and wage-setting are decentralised may have an effect beyond the immediate workplace or firm, an effect also noted by Feldberg in her discussion of American nurses and comparable worth.

In the first case taken under the British equal-value regulations, *Hayward* v. *Cammell Laird Shipbuilders* ([1988] ICR 464), a canteen cook claimed equal pay with tradesmen earning higher basic and overtime rates than she. Hayward involved the claim of a single worker, and cases in private manufacturing in such diverse areas as food-processing, furniture-making and upholstering, and engineering and the car industry, have typically involved limited numbers of women (TUC, 1990; Willborn, 1989).

Union strategies for winning equal value vary, depending both upon the structure of employment situations and the proclivities of union leaders. In some cases, supported by the TUC or EOC, unions aim for large-scale job re-evaluation or principle-setting legal decisions. On the other hand, especially in the private manufacturing sector, the strategy may be a small-scale intervention involving a routine tribunal claim. Routine use of tribunals aims to incorporate equal value firmly into both trade unionist and employer understandings of employment law. In many cases, union officials pursue equal-value claims as an *ad hoc* means of increasing women-members' pay and primarily as a way of increasing members' wages. Other officials, most notably Ivy Cameron during her tenure as a Banking, Insurance and Finance Union (BIFU) negotiator, pursue more integrated and systematic strategies to change women's working lives; they negotiate whole packages of career-break schemes, retraining and job desegregation measures, and large scale job re-evaluation (Cameron, n.d.; Personnel Management, 1987).

To encourage all these forms of activity, the TUC Women's Rights Department has set up an Equal Value Working Group. The Department has conducted national seminars for high-level senior negotiators. At the same time it has developed two levels of regional activity. Information-oriented seminars for regional and local officials are intended to create commitments to equal value and the possibility of inter-union work. Regional conferences for women workers, union and non-union, are more oriented towards consciousness-raising than information and are designed to create pressure from below for equal-value advances.

US DEVELOPMENTS – POLICY AND LAW

While in Britain the Equal Pay Act was amended to incorporate equal value, in the USA there has been no amendment to the Equal Pay Act. Despite some hopeful early developments, the argument that unequal pay for equally evaluated work is illegal under Title VII of the Civil Rights Act has failed repeatedly. Positive developments at the level of national law and policy in the late 1970s and early 1980s were quickly overrun by a variety of Reagan administration manoeuvres and campaigns to defeat comparable worth as a legitimate social and legal principle. Comparable-worth activity in the USA has therefore occurred despite national policy, and it is a particularly fragmented and decentralised reform.

Late in the 1977 the US Equal Opportunity Commission (EEOC), the main federal enforcement agency for employment discrimination, identified comparable worth as a priority, commissioning the National Research Council of the National Academy of Sciences, a Congressionally funded independent body, to investigate the issue. The NRC's largely favourable report, *Women, Work, and Wages: Equal Pay for Jobs of Equal Value*, was not published until 1981, however (Treiman and Hartmann, 1981). By then, the EEOC and US Civil Rights Commission, led by conservative Reagan appointees, were opposed to comparable worth. In 1985, after many years of not acting on comparable-worth complaints, the EEOC announced that it would act only on sex-based wage discrimination where there was evidence of intent to discriminate (Withers and Winston, 1989). Reagan's Department of Justice entered the *AFSCME* v. *Washington State* case, an early important legal case, on the side of the employers against the plaintiffs. In this period not only the Reagan administration but also business and political groups forced the debate onto the grounds of the costs of comparable worth and the difficulties of implementation, attacking it as a violation of *laissez-faire* market economics and individual choice and responsibility. While the structure of the debate reflected the politics of the early Reagan years, it also reflected the much longer-standing power of business to structure political debate and generalise certain values in US society (Steinberg, 1989a; Lindblom, 1977). In the USA unlike Britain, therefore, there was an organised opposition to comparable worth, which continued to influence its trajectory.

As Jeanne Gregory points out in Chapter 2 on legal developments in the USA and Britain, equal-value advocates argued that an equal-value standard was implicit in Title VII of the Civil Rights Act. While the US Equal Pay Act referred to women undertaking work that was the same as or similar to that of men, Title VII more broadly prohibited discrimination in various aspects of employment, including compensation, on grounds of sex. Following the Supreme Court ruling in *Griggs* v. *Duke Power Company* (401 US 424 [1971]) the 1964 Civil Rights Act was seen to incorporate a notion of indirect as well as direct discrimination, i.e. the idea of 'disparate impact' as well as 'disparate treatment'. An employment policy that appeared on the surface to be neutral but which in practice had an adverse impact on a group covered by Title VII was illegal. Comparable-worth advocates tried to make use of both direct and indirect discrimination arguments. They were blocked by a general reluctance of the courts to recognise this new form of wage discrimination. It became increasingly difficult to demonstrate disparate treatment where employers denied it, to demonstrate disparate impact, and to avoid employers' market-forces defences (BNA, 1984; McCann, n.d.).

Despite these legal defeats, two legal cases in the early 1980s contributed to the social and political mobilisation around comparable worth. The Supreme Court's 1981 ruling in *County of Washington* v. *Gunther* (452 US 161 [1981]) made it clear that pay cases not involving the same work could be brought under Title VII. The 1983 ruling in *AFSCME* v. *State of Washington* (578 F. Supp. 846 [W.D. Washington 1983]) found that the state, which had not paid women workers according to equal-value standards, was guilty of both direct and indirect discrimination. (This decision was later reversed on appeal, but the parties arrived at an out-of-court settlement.) (Willborn, 1989). These early legal developments publicised the idea of comparable worth as a legal rights issue and spurred legal and organising activity in California localities, Connecticut, Wisconsin and elsewhere (Blum, this volume, Chapter 5; Blum, 1991; McCann, n.d.).

EXTRA-LEGAL DEVELOPMENTS IN THE USA

As national legal developments were blocked, comparable-worth activity shifted to state and local public sectors, where gains have been achieved through a combination of state and local legislation, administrative policy, and collective bargaining. The nearly exclusive concentration of gains in the public sector is different from the British pattern where reform is spread more widely across the private and public sectors. The restriction of US efforts was due not only to the hostility of the Reagan administration and courts to the expansion of civil rights but also to patterns of unionisation.

By 1988, as employers attacked jobs, wages, unions and the social safety net, unions organized only 17 per cent of the US workforce overall, but a larger proportion of workers in the public sector. US public-sector employment grew from 1969 to 1979, and collective-bargaining rights were extended to many public employees in the 1960s and 1970s. By 1989, 57.2 per cent of public employees were union members in states that permitted them to bargain; 36 per cent of all public employees were organised (Goldman, 1989). Many of the unions that grew most quickly in the public sector, such as the American Federation of State, County and Municipal Employees (AFSCME) had a large proportion of female members. The organisation of public-sector and health-care workers created dramatic increases in women's union membership in the USA. In 1985 women accounted for 33.7 per cent of all unionised workers. Limits on the growth of women's union membership were set by the absence of unionisation in the private services sector (Needleman, 1988). In public-sector unions and others, women were working to correct the underrepresentation of women in leadership positions, on union's bargaining agendas, and in the culture of unionism (*Labor Research Review*, 1988; Bell, 1985; Roby and Uttal, 1988; Milkman, 1985). Women's union activity in the USA incorporated elements of the British programmes for women in unions and in the workplace.

Comparable-worth activity in the local public sector was also facilitated by the presence of women in state and local government. The US women's movement had a dual origin. On the one hand, women from the New Left had organised locally and somewhat informally, emphasising consciousness-raising and the development of local services, such as shelters for battered women; they had a sharp critique of gender and sometimes class relations. On the other hand, the US women's movement was a product of women who held position in or were active in national and state government or political parties. Many of these women were members of state-level Commissions on the Status of Women formed during the early 1960s (Sapiro, 1986; Harrison, 1988). State Commissions persisted into the 1970s and 1980s, as did a wing of the women's movement oriented towards working with political parties and lobbying state government. In many states and localities elected representatives and executives were committed to equal rights. These 'political insiders' were sympathetic to liberal comparable-worth arguments.

In the USA between 1979 and 1989 pay-equity initiatives yielded approximately $450 million to thousands of women and people of colour in the public sector. Twenty-three states, including the District of Columbia, began or completed pay-equity studies. Of these, New Jersey, New York, Wisconsin and Washington, DC, examined their wage-setting systems for race as well as sex bias. Twenty states made pay-equity adjustments to one or more female-dominated or minority-dominated job classification (NCPE, 1989). The State of Minnesota not only passed legislation which established equitable compensation as the primary wage-setting consideration for state employees but also required local jurisdictions to make comparable worth a primary consideration in compensation (NCPE, 1989; Evans and Nelson, 1989). Over 112 counties, including 87 in Minnesota, and over 900 municipalities, including 855 in Minnesota, were involved in pay equity. School districts, colleges and universities also reformed wages structures (NCPE, 1989).

While there has been variation among the states in the process and outcome of comparable worth, there have nevertheless been broad similarities: reliance upon élite-led or bureaucratically managed adjustment processes; the use of large-scale job evaluation schemes, often uncorrected for sex bias; and the incomplete realisation of equal pay for work of equal value. In most states, once a law was passed making equal value a factor in setting compensation or rates or appropriating money for a comparable-worth study, processes of job evaluation and pay adjustment were taken over by state administrators and policymakers. While advisory committees and task forces worked with personnel departments, initiative and control remained with administrators. Though feminists and trade-union leaders sat on these committees, representation of and accountability to their constituencies were limited. For unions, representation as a minority on the task force largely replaced collective bargaining over the terms of job evaluation and the pay policy derived from it. Feminists did not have a powerful organised base to whom they reported or from whom they commanded support. In Chapter 11 on the state of Minnesota Sara Evans and Barbara Nelson illustrate this problem of control of implementation. In addition, many state projects, especially the early precedent-setting studies in the states of Washington, Oregon, and Minnesota relied upon job-evaluation schemes which perpetuated bias against women's jobs while still revealing substantial underpayment of predominantly female job classes (Steinberg, 1990a; 1989a; Acker, 1989). Finally, in most cases, the way in which job evaluation was used and the way in which pay policy was derived from job evaluation compromised comparable-worth principles; the result was not equal pay for jobs of equal value but some amelioration of underpayment for certain groups of women and minority workers (Steinberg, 1990a; 1989a; Acker, 1989).

This pattern of activity seems related to the judgement of comparable-worth advocates that in an uncertain political climate it was 'better to get something than to get nothing'. Because comparable-worth reform was dependent upon legislative and executive activity rather than the legal system, there was always at state level the threat of an active political opposition, especially if the cost of the reform was high. The use of 'uncleansed' job evaluation schemes and the limited implementation of the equal value principle reduced the cost of reform; and they were not only actively pursued by state administrators but also assented to by pay equity advocates (Steinberg, 1990a; 1989). Despite these limits, the state reforms created substantial gains for women workers in material terms and in terms of social re-evaluation of their work.

While implementation in many smaller public jurisdictions such as those in Minnesota, has been management-dominated, elsewhere unions have either kept control of job evaluation or abandoned it, addressing women's under-valued work through collective bargaining. The San Jose case described by Linda Blum in Chapter 5 was an early example of women workers themselves mobilising around comparable worth and their union, AFSCME, insisting upon involvement in job evaluation at every stage. The National Education Association (NEA) is currently involved in large projects in Orlando, Florida, Las Vegas, Nevada and fifteen-to-twenty other school districts. Aware of the shortcomings of conventional job-evaluation schemes, the NEA commissioned its own, which positively values the skills of educational support personnel, such as teaching aides, secretaries, librarians, food-service workers, and janitorial staff. The Association has trained its own members in application of the scheme; the NEA engages in joint data-gathering with school districts, and then negotiates pay adjustments for female-dominant and minority-dominant job classes.

Other unions, such as AFSCME Council 36 in Los Angeles, negotiated pay equity without recourse to job-evaluation studies. In the early 1980s, AFSCME resorted first to negotiating

flat-rate increases to remedy underpayment in female job classifications. Subsequently the union negotiated access to the
City's EEO-4 report, information on earnings, hiring, occupations and gender and race required by Title VII of the 1964
Civil Rights Act. The union's national research department
used data in the report to demonstrate significant sex segregation and sex-based wage disparities. AFSCME re-opened negotiations with the city after having also filed a sex discrimination
charge with the EEO against the city and while drawing press
attention to sex inequities. In the City of Chicago, AFSCME's
national research department identified a pattern of strict job
segregation and wage discrimination. The union also noted the
adverse impact upon women of the City's refusal to permit
collective bargaining in female-dominated occupations. Collective bargaining rights for city employees in Illinois were at the
discretion of administrators, and the mayor of Chicago allowed
blue-collar trade workers and, later, police and fire employees
to bargain, while women were denied union rights. After a
campaign involving the filing of an EEOC complaint, large-
scale publicity, and union organising, AFSCME won representation and bargaining rights for women workers and began to
narrow the sex-based wage gap (NCPE, n.d.).

The private sector was the site of far less activity in the USA
than in Britain, due both to the absence of law to compel or
encourage such reform and to very low levels of unionisation
especially in the service sector. There is limited evidence that
large private corporations have begun to reassess job-evaluation
systems and have consequently increased salaries in female-
dominated jobs (NCPE, 1986).

Kathleen Kautzer, in Chapter 7, however, discusses one important private sector case. At Yale University, as in the city of
Chicago, organisers made the low wages of women central to
unionisation drives. The case of Yale is also an example of a
union-community mobilisation behind increasing women's
wages, a development present also in the case of Northern
Ireland health workers. In many US public-sector cases, feminists and unionists have developed general public support to
pressure elected officials to undertake reform; but the case of
Yale involved student and community support of particular
workplace mobilisations. At Yale, pay-equity arguments were a

major part of all stages of organising and bargaining, but the union postponed involvement in technical studies of the job structure until it was well organised. When employees decided to target job classification itself, the union became the dominant force on the Clerical and Technical Job Classification Study and used the job-study process to strengthen the union further. The Yale case suggests two other factors that facilitate private sector activity in the USA: employer profitability or financial surplus, and an employer culture of 'informed liberalism'. Both these factors seemed also to influence the successful equal-value initiatives of the Newspaper Guild, a union representing 40 000 Canadian and American workers in advertising, commercial, business, clerical and administrative and transport occupations in the newspaper industry (NCPE, n.d.).

There are at least two instances of comparable-worth developments in the private manufacturing sector in the USA. Perhaps the best-known early comparable-worth case was *International Union of Electrical Workers (IUE)* v. *Westinghouse* (631 F 2d 1094 3rd cir. 1980), in which the IUE won a victory in the Third Circuit Court of Appeals, which was left standing by the Supreme Court. The suit, involving a Trenton, New Jersey, plant, cited the company's practice dating to the 1930s of assigning workers to 'male' or 'female' jobs, point-rating all jobs, allocating them to labour grades, and then recompensing women's jobs at a lower rate simply because they were performed by women. This case, eventually settled out of court, resulted from a comprehensive Title VII education, research, and litigation programme launched by the union in 1972. Westinghouse agreed to upgrade jobs for 85 predominantly female jobs in assembly, subassembly, and quality control (NCPE, n.d.; Steinberg, 1989b; Steinberg, 1984). The women's committee of IUE Local 201, which organised workers in General Electric plants on the north shore of Boston, also filed a legal suit that led to a settlement in 1982. Wage rates of 353 people in predominantly female job classifications were raised an average of $2\frac{1}{2}$ rates, and the two lowest rates were eliminated. Job-posting procedures and training programmes were strengthened, as were maternity benefits and child-care leave provisions (Brown and Sheridan, 1988).

CONCLUSION

In both Britain and the USA, women's low earnings in segregated occupations in a period of changing family structures and limited social welfare provisions created a social imperative and social base for equal-value developments in the 1970s and 1980s. The political formulation and enactment of equal-value reform, however, depended upon political structures and social and political movements.

In Britain, the European Community required the Thatcher government to enact an equal-value law. Introduced from above and outside, rather than campaigned for from below, the law provides limited remedies for women doing work of equal value. It was not until the late 1980s that the equal-value movement developed momentum, as both the EOC and TUC took both strategic legal, educational and organisational initiatives; an independent Pay Equity Campaign, loosely associated with Liberty (formerly the National Council for Civil Liberties), emerged only in 1990. The law has had an impact well beyond individual legal cases themselves; it has contributed to a growing consensus about equal pay for work of equal value and spurred negotiating activity.

No law or legal amendment was enacted in the USA, and during the Reagan administration the EEOC declined to investigate and litigate comparable-worth cases, despite the possibility that equal-value standards were implied in existing civil rights legislation. As women's groups, unions and the National Committee on Pay Equity (NCPE) – a broad-based advocacy group – began to organise in the 1980s, so did the political opponents of comparable worth. The existence of a powerful opposition had a continuing impact upon the implementation of pay equity in the USA. Present prospects for enactment of equal-value law or for favourable interpretation of existing civil rights laws are nil.

Because equal value is a workplace issue with costs to employers, unions and collective bargaining are central to securing equal-value adjustments. While the enactment of equal-value regulations in Britain was not due to union activity, legal cases are nearly always initiated and supported by unions. In both the public and private sectors, unions negotiate equal value. Elected public officials are mainly absent from specific wage-setting reforms. In Britain, the union movement has remained an important presence in most employment sectors and so has been able to pursue equal value fairly widely. In the USA, a considerably weaker and more localised labour movement has been active mainly in the public sector. While women in state government and women's groups have played an important role, state-level comparable worth has been confined to states where workers have collective bargaining rights and strong unions. Unions have also been critical in smaller public jurisdictions and in the private sector.

Other characteristics of British and American unions seem to have shaped the path of equal value in each country. The majority of British equal-value cases might be described as consistent with pay-oriented adversarial unionism. Furthermore, while unions in British industry have often insisted upon wage differentials rather than wage solidarity, equal-value developments in the 1980s and 1990s suggest some attention to the needs of lower-paid women workers, who are also often part-timers. These efforts are consistent with national union organising campaigns, such as the TGWU's 'Link-Up Campaign' and USDAW's 'Reach Out' project, which seek to target unorganised part-time workers. Assisted by the existence of equal-value law and a structure of voluntary organisations, such as Law Centres and Advice Bureaus, the EOC, TUC and the new independent pay equity campaign have all called attention to the needs of unorganised low-paid women and their potential gains from equal-value adjustments. Although many lower-paid women workers have benefited from comparable-worth reform in the USA, the emphasis of the reform does not seem to be so strongly on lower-paid and part-time workers.

British unions have worked to educate female and male members about equal value and argued that such reform was in the interests of all union members. While such efforts have been undertaken in some US unions, it is also true that male workers have sometimes vigorously opposed comparable-worth adjustments and that unions have pursued administrative rather than more public comparable-worth strategies in order not to antagonise male members. The emphasis upon organised and unorganised lower-paid workers as an important part of the trade-union constituency and the emphasis upon a shared interest across male and female workers suggest a degree of class solidarity on wages in the British union movement. Unions in the USA seem to define their interests in equal value in somewhat more restricted ways that reflect group rather than more broadly defined class interests.

British unions have from an early stage of equal-value reform harboured suspicions of management consultants undertaking job evaluation, although union counter-expertise has developed only recently. In the USA, partly because of the need to legitimate a contested reform and to compromise with actual or anticipated opposition, unions cooperated with management-defined implementation. The rather long period of union cooperation with management-defined reform may also reflect a tradition of business unionism, which concedes that profitability of enterprises and management-led success in market competition are the necessary and legitimate grounds upon which union gains rest. Furthermore, the US labour movement has long existed in a system of highly regulated and bureaucratised labour–management relations in which internal and external experts have played a prominent role. British unionism has pursued a more adversarial strategy within a tradition of limited legal regulation of management–labour relations. Unions have historically defended themselves and their members through unmediated, direct collective bargaining and organised social power, rather than by relying upon experts or third parties in a highly legalistic industrial relations system.

Both in Britain and the USA, the prospect of equal-value gains for large numbers of women, including lower-paid women, is tied to the strength of unions across the economy. In addition, equal-value gains depend upon unions addressing the needs of women, both as a general priority and with concrete strategies, often involving technical knowledge.

Note

1. I would like to thank the following for their assistance: Elizabeth Meehan, Roz Feldberg, Ronnie Steinberg, Linda Blum, Jude Stoddart, Jo Morris, Heather Wakefield, Ivy Cameron, Donna Haber, Kathy Dickson, Sheila Wild, Frank Spencer, Peter Allen, Sue Hastings, Lisa Hubbard, Anna Padia, Cathy Collette, Marilyn Johnston, Claudia Withers, and DeAn McDaniel.

References

Acker, Joan (1989) *Doing Comparable Worth: Gender, Class, Pay Equity* (Philadelphia: Temple University Press).

Bell, Deborah (1985) 'Unionized women in state and local government', in Ruth Milkman (ed.) *Women, Work and Protest* (Boston: Routledge & Kegan Paul) pp. 280–99.

Blum, Linda (1987, December) 'Possibilities and Limits of the Comparable Worth Movement', *Gender and Society, I*(4) pp. 381–99.

Blum, Linda (1991) *Between Feminism and Labor: The Significance of the Comparable Worth Movement* (Berkeley: University of California Press).

Bourn, Colin and Whitmore, John (1989) *Discrimination and Equal Pay* (London: Sweet & Maxwell).

Brenner, Johanna (1987, December) 'Feminist Political Discourses: Radical versus Liberal Approaches to the Feminization of Poverty and Comparable Worth', *Gender and Society, I*(4) pp. 447–65.

Brown, Alex and Sheridan, Laurie (1988, Spring) 'Pioneering Women's Committee Struggles with Hard Times', *Labor Research Review*, 11, pp. 63–78.

Bureau of National Affairs (BNA) (1984) *Pay Equity and Comparable Worth* (Washington: BNA).

Cameron, Ivy (n.d.) *Equal Opportunities for Women: A Challenge for the Finance Industry and BIFU*, unpublished manuscript.

Charles, Nicola (1986) 'Women and Trade Unions', in *Feminist Review* (ed.) *Waged Work: A Reader* (London: Virago) pp. 160–85.

Cockburn, Cynthia (1989, Autumn) 'Equal Opportunities: The Short and Long Agenda', *Industrial Relations Journal, 20*(3) pp. 213–25.

Colling, Trevor and Dickens, Linda (1989) *Equality Bargaining – Why Not?* (London: HMSO).

Colling, Trevor and Dickens, Linda (1990, April) 'Why Equality Won't Appear on the Bargaining Agenda', *Personnel Management*, pp. 48–53.

Davies, Margery (1982) *Women's Place is at the Typewriter: Office Work and Office Workers 1870–1930* (Philadelphia: Temple University Press).

Dex, Shirley and Walters, Patricia (1989, Autumn) 'Women's Occupational Status in Britain, France, and the USA', *Industrial Relations Journal, 20*(3) pp. 203–12.

Dickens, Linda (1989, Autumn) 'Women – A Rediscovered Resource?', *Industrial Relations Journal, 20*(3) pp. 167–75.

Dickens, Linda, Townley, Barbara and Winchester, David (1988) *Tackling Sex Discrimination through Collective Bargaining* (London: HMSO).

Equal Opportunities Commission (EOC) (1989a) *Equal Pay . . . Making it Work. Review of the Equal Pay Legislation: Consultative Document* (Manchester: EOC).

Equal Opportunities Commission (EOC) (1989b) *Towards Equality: A Casebook of Decisions on Sex Discrimination and Equal Pay 1976–1988* (Manchester: EOC).

Equal Opportunities Review (EOR) (1985, November–December) 'Unions' Experience of Equal Value', *Equal Opportunities Review* (4) pp. 12–17.

Equal Opportunities Review (EOR) (1986a, March–April) 'Two Years of the Equal Value Law', *Equal Opportunities Review* (6) pp. 6–16.

Equal Opportunities Review (EOR) (1986b, March–April) 'Equal Value Survey', *Equal Opportunities Review* (6) p. 2.

Equal Opportunities Review (EOR) (1987a, January–February) 'Equal Value: The Union Response', *Equal Opportunities Review* (11) pp. 10–19.

Equal Opportunities Review (EOR) (1987b, November–December) 'Equal Value: A Union Update', *Equal Opportunities Review* (22) pp. 9–15.

Equal Opportunities Review (EOR) (1988, March–April) 'Equal Value Update', *Equal Opportunities Review* (18) pp. 8–17.

Equal Opportunities Review (EOR) (1989a, November–December) 'Attracting and Retaining Women Workers in the Finance Sector', *Equal Opportunities Review* (18) pp. 10–20.

Equal Opportunities Review (EOR) (1989b, July–August) 'Equal Value Update', *Equal Opportunities Review* (26) pp. 10–25.

Equal Opportunities Review (EOR) (1989d, January–February) 'Profile: Kay Carberry, Head, Equal Rights Department, TUC', *Equal Opportunities Review* (23) pp. 26–7.

Evans, Sara and Nelson, Barbara (1989) *Wage Justice: Comparable Worth and the Paradox of Technocratic Reform* (Chicago: University of Chicago Press).

Feldberg, Roslyn (1986) 'Comparable Worth: Toward Theory and Practice in the United States', in Barbara Gelp, Nancy C. M. Hartsock, Clare Novak and Myra Strober (eds) *Women and Poverty* (Chicago: University of Chicago Press) pp. 163–80.

Flammang, Janet (1987) 'Women Made a Difference: Comparable Worth in San Jose', in M. F. Katzenstein and C. M. Mueller (eds) *The Women's Movements of the United States and Western Europe* (Philadelphia: Temple University Press) pp. 290–312.

Freeman, Jo (1987) 'Whom You Know versus Whom You Represent: Feminist Influence in the Democratic and Republican Parties', in M. F. Katzenstein and C. M. Mueller (eds) *The Women's Movements of the United States and Western Europe* (Philadelphia: Temple University Press) pp. 215–44.

Goldman, Debbie (1989, Summer–Fall) 'Women in the Public Sector', *The Illinois Public Employee Relations Report*, 6(3–4) pp. 4–9.

Gregory, Jeanne (1987) *Sex, Race and the Law: Legislating for Equality* (London: Sage).

Harrison, Cynthia (1988) *On Account of Sex: The Politics of Women's Issues 1945–1968* (Berkeley: University of California Press).

Hartmann, Heidi (1976) 'Capitalism, Patriarchy, and Job Segregation by Sex', in Martha Blaxall and Barbara Reagan (eds) *Women and the Workplace: Implications of Occupational Segregation* (Chicago: University of Chicago Press) pp. 137–70.

Heen, Mary (1984) 'A Review of Federal Court Decisions under Title VII of the Civil Rights Act of 1964', in H. Remick (ed.) *Comparable Worth and Wage Discrimination* (Philadelphia: Temple University Press).

Heery, Edmund and Kelly, John (1989, Autumn) '"A Cracking Job for a Woman" – A Profile of Women Trade Union Officers', *Industrial Relations Journal*, 20(3) pp. 192–202.

Huws, Ursula (1989, November) 'Negotiating for Equality', *Studies for Trade Unionists*, 15(59) (London: Workers' Education Association).

Kessler-Harris, Alice (1990) *A Woman's Wage: Historical Meanings and Social Consequences*. Lexington, Kentucky: The University Press of Kentucky.

Labor Research Review (1988, Spring), Issue on *Feminizing unions, 11.*

Labour Research Department (1989, March) 'Unions and Part-timers – Do they Mix?', *Labour Research*, pp. 19–22.

Labour Research Department (1989, October) 'TUC Reports: Congress Looks Forward to the 1990s', *Labour Research*, 78(1) p. 5.

Labour Research Department (1990, March) 'Union Reserved Seats – Creating a Space for Women', *Labour Research*, 79(3) pp. 7–8.

Labour Research Department (1990, June) 'Equal Pay Claims on the Move', *Bargaining Report*, pp. 12–17.

Lindblom, Charles (1977) *Politics and Markets* (New York: Basic Books).

Malveaux, Julianne (1985, Summer) 'The Economic Interests of Black and White Women: Are They Similar?', *Review of Black Political Economy*, pp. 5–27.

Malveaux, Julianne (1985–6, Fall–Winter) 'Comparable Worth and its Impact on Black Women', *Review of Black Political Economy*, 14(2–3) pp. 47–62.

McCann, Michael (n.d.) *Gaining Even When Losing: Litigation, Legal Mobilization, and Pay Equity Politics*, unpublished manuscript.

Milkman, Ruth (1985) 'Women Workers, Feminism, and the Labor Movement', in Ruth Milkman (ed.) *Women, Work, and Protest: A Century of US Women's Labour History* (Boston: Routledge & Kegan Paul) pp. 300–22.

Mueller, Carol (1987) 'Collective Consciousness, Identity Transformation, the Rise of Women in Public Office in the United States', in M. F. Katzenstein and C. M. Mueller (eds) *The Women's Movements of the United States and Western Europe* (Philadelphia: Temple University Press).

National Committee on Pay Equity (NCPE) (n.d.) *Bargaining for Pay Equity: A Strategy Manual* (Washington, DC: NCPE).

National Committee on Pay Equity (NCPE) (1987a, February) *Pay Equity: An Issue of Race, Ethnicity, and Sex* (Washington, DC: NCPE).

National Committee on Pay Equity (NCPE) (1987b, September) *Briefing Paper on the Wage Gap* (Washington, DC: NCPE).

National Committee on Pay Equity (NCPE) (1989, October) *Pay Equity Activity in the Public Sector 1979–1989* (Washington, DC: NCPE).

Needleman, Ruth (1988, Spring) 'Women Workers: A Force for Rebuilding Unionism', *Labor Research Review* (11) pp. 1–14.

O'Donovan, Katherine and Szyszczak, Erika (1988) *Equality and Sex Discrimination Law* (Oxford: Blackwell).

Personnel Management (1987, October) 'Realising the Dividends from Positive Action', *Personnel Management*, pp. 62–7.

Phillips, Anne and Taylor, Barbara (1986) 'Sex and Skill', in *Feminist Review* (ed.) *Waged Work: A Reader* (London: Virago) pp. 54–66.

Remick, Helen (ed.) (1984) *Comparable Worth and Wage Discrimination: Technical Possibilities and Political Realities* (Philadelphia: Temple University Press).

Reverby, Susan (1987) *Ordered to Care: The Dilemma of American Nursing, 1840–1945* (Cambridge: Cambridge University Press).

Roby, Pamela and Uttal, Lynet (1988) 'Trade Union Stewards: Handling Union, Family and Employment Responsibilities', in Barbara Gutek, Ann Stromberg and Laurie Larwood (eds) *Women and Work: An Annual Review, Vol. 3* (pp. 215–48) (Newbury Park: Sage Publications).

Rubinstein, Michael (1990) *Discrimination: A Guide to the Relevant Case Law on Race and Sex Discrimination and Equal Pay* (London: Eclipse Publications) 3rd edn.

Rubinstein, Michael (1984) *Equal Pay for Work of Equal Value: The New Regulations and their Implications* (London: Macmillan).

Sapiro, Virginia (1986) 'The Women's Movement, Politics and Policy in the Reagan Era', in Drude Dahlerup (ed.) *The New Women's Movement: Feminism and Political Power in Europe and the USA* (London: Sage).

Scales-Trent, Judy (1984, Winter) 'Comparable Worth: Is this a Theory for Black Workers?', *Women's Rights Law Reporter, 8*(1–2) pp. 51–8.

Snell, Mandy (1986) 'Equal Pay and Sex Discrimination', in *Feminist Review* (ed.) *Waged Work: A Reader* (pp. 12–39) (London: Virago).

South East Region TUC (SERTUC) Women's Committee (n.d.) *Still Moving Towards Equality: A Survey of Progress Towards Equality in Trade Unions* (London: SERTUC).

Steinberg, Ronnie (1984) '"A Want of Harmony": Perspective on Wage Discrimination and Comparable Worth', in Helen Remick (ed.) *Comparable Worth and Wage Discrimination: Technical Possibilities and Political Realities* (Philadelphia: Temple University Press) pp. 3–27.

Steinberg, Ronnie (1987, December) 'Radical Challenges in a Liberal World: The Mixed Success of Comparable Worth', *Gender and Society, 1*(4) pp. 466–75.

Steinberg, Ronnie (1989a) *Mainstreaming Comparable Worth: Re-forming Wage Discrimination to Palatable Pay Equity,* unpublished manuscript.

Steinberg, Ronnie (1989b) 'The Unsubtle Revolution: Women, the State and Equal Employment', in Jane Jensen *et al.* (eds) *The Feminization of the Labour Force* (New York: Oxford University Press) pp. 189–213.

Steinberg, Ronnie (1990a) *Job Evaluation and Managerial Control: The Politics of Technique and the Technique of Politics,* unpublished manuscript.

Steinberg, Ronnie (1990b) *Social Construction of Skill: Gender, Power, and Comparable Worth,* unpublished manuscript.

Towers, Brian, (1989, January) 'Running the Gauntlet: British Trade Unions Under Thatcher, 1979–1988', *Industrial and Labor Relations Review, 42*(2) pp. 163–88.

Trades Union Congress (TUC) (1989, January) *Equality for Women Within Trade Unions* (London: TUC).

Trades Union Congress (TUC) (1990, August) *TUC Charter for Women at Work* (London: TUC).

Trades Union Congress (TUC), Equal Rights Department (1990, August) *Equal Pay for Work of Equal Value: Claims Lodged with an Industrial Tribunal and Negotiated Settlements Using Equal Value Arguments* (London: TUC).

Treiman, Donald and Hartman, Heidi (1981) *Women, Work and Wages: Equal Pay for Jobs of Equal Value* (Washington, DC: National Academy Press).

Tzannatos, P. Z. and Zabalza, A. (1984, July) 'The Anatomy of the Rise of British Female Relative Wages in the 1970s: Evidence from the New Earnings Survey', *British Journal of Industrial Relations*, *XXII*(2) pp. 177–94.

Walby, Sylvia (1986) *Patriarchy at Work* (Cambridge: Polity Press).

Willborn, Steven (1989) *A Secretary and a Cook: Challenging Women's Wages in the Courts of the United States and Britain* (Ithaca: LR Press, Cornell University).

Withers, Claudia and Winston, Judith (1989) 'Equal Employment Opportunity', in *One Nation Divided* (Washington: Citizen's Commission for Civil Rights) pp. 190–214.

Part I

Major Themes Relating to Equal Value and Comparable Worth

2 Equal Value/Comparable Worth: National Statute and Case Law in Britain and the USA
Jeanne Gregory

In both Britain and the USA, campaigns around equal value and comparable worth have from the outset been very much concerned with legal concepts and the legal process. The campaigns have developed largely in response to the failure of earlier legal provisions to remedy the problems of women's low pay and sex discrimination in employment, despite the presence (either explicitly or implicitly) of anti-discrimination and equal-value concepts in national statutes and case law. While equal-pay advocates have struggled to make ambiguous or resistant law responsive to their notions of equal value, other activists have concentrated their efforts on pursuing local collective bargaining and political strategies. All these initiatives have played an important role in challenging gender-based differences in pay, as the other contributions to this book demonstrate. The central task of this particular chapter, however, is to trace key developments in national statute and case law in Britain and the USA and to assess their actual and potential impact on rectifying pay inequalities.

The general legal arguments of equal pay advocates are grounded in a number of propositions. The first is that wage rates are affected by the sex composition of the occupational group, so that predominantly female occupations are underpaid in comparison with those in which men predominate. Second, even where specific jobs are evaluated as involving similar skill, effort, responsibility and working conditions, female job-holders are paid less than male job-holders. In other words, there are compensation differences between women workers and male workers which can only be explained in terms of gender. The final step is to argue that these differences are sex discrimination and therefore prohibited by employment discrimination laws.

This line of argument has proved to be problematic in both Britain and the USA. In the USA, there is no unambiguous legal doctrine or concept of comparable worth in relation to discrimination. Advocates have argued that as a form of sex discrimination, unequal pay for work of comparable worth is addressed by Title VII of the Civil Rights Act 1964. The courts have usually declined this interpretation, defending the fairness of the 'free market' and gendered compensation systems linked to its operation. In Britain, the Equal Pay Act has been amended to include a legal concept of equal value, but employers' defences are robust, the law is inordinately complex with litigation restricted to individual employees and the notion of adequate job evaluation remains problematic.

THE ORIGINS OF SEX EQUALITY LEGISLATION IN THE USA AND BRITAIN

In both countries, early lobbyists for equal pay drew attention to the wording of Convention 110 of the International Labour Organisation (ILO), which referred to 'equal pay for work of equal value'. In the event, both governments backed away from the equal-value principle and enacted laws which could be used to redress only the most blatant forms of wage discrimination: those where women were paid less than men although employed on the same or similar tasks. The American Equal Pay Act, passed by Congress in 1963 as an amendment to the Fair Labor Standards Act, provided for equal pay for equal work on jobs requiring 'equal skill, effort and responsibility' and performed under similar working conditions. The courts subsequently interpreted this to mean that the jobs compared had to be 'substantially equal'.[1] The first British Equal Pay Act, passed by Parliament in 1970 and taking effect in 1975, covered those situations where a woman was employed on 'like work' or 'broadly similar' work with a man in the same employment, or where her work had been rated as equivalent to his in a job-evaluation scheme.

These laws did force employers to abandon the widespread

practice of operating separate pay scales for male and female manual workers and paying the women less than the men for essentially the same work. However, for the vast majority of women workers, concentrated in all-female areas of employment, the legislation was irrelevant, as there were no men performing similar tasks with whom comparisons could be made. If anything, the laws ensured that job segregation became more rigid as employers reduced the risks of litigation by avoiding overlap between the jobs performed by women and by men.

In the USA, the discussions in Congress on equal pay paved the way for the inclusion of women in Title VII of the Civil Rights Act, passed in 1964. Following hard on the heels of the Equal Pay Act, the Civil Rights Act was by comparison a wide-ranging and comprehensive measure, the chief objective of which was the ending of racial discrimination. In its original formulation, Title VII of the Act, the section dealing with employment discrimination, did not apply to women at all. The amendment to include 'sex' alongside 'race' was introduced as a divisive tactic by a Congressman who sought to undermine support for the Bill. The tactic misfired and after numerous amendments and extensive compromises, Title VII, complete with the category 'sex', became law (Meehan, 1985, p. 62).

In Britain also, the destinies of the sex and race discrimination laws were intertwined. The Sex Discrimination Act 1975 was used to test the climate of opinion before an almost identical set of measures on racial discrimination was introduced in Parliament the following year.[2] Furthermore, certain sections of the British Sex Discrimination Act were explicitly modelled on the US experience. The most notable of these is the concept of 'disparate impact', derived from the Supreme Court decision in the case of *Griggs* v. *Duke Power Co.* (401 US 424 [1971]) and enshrined in British law as the concept of 'indirect discrimination'. In the Griggs case the Court held that an employment policy which appeared to be neutral on the surface, but which in practice had an adverse impact on a group covered by Title VII (in this case, black job applicants), was illegal. The employer's motive was irrelevant:

> absence of discriminatory intent does not redeem employment procedures or testing mechanism that operate as 'built-in headwinds' for minority groups and are unrelated to measuring job capacity (*Griggs* v. *Duke Power Co.*, p. 432).

Once the plaintiffs had demonstrated that a particular employment practice had a disparate impact on them, the burden of proof shifted to the employer to justify the practice in terms of business necessity. Adopting this principle, the British law makes it possible to challenge a requirement or condition which is ostensibly the same for all employees but is such that only a small proportion of women can comply with it in practice. The requirement or condition is illegal unless the employer can justify it.

Pay equity advocates in America and in Britain saw the potential usefulness of the concepts disparate impact and indirect discrimination; the difficulty lay in persuading the courts to apply them to cases of wage-based discrimination in the absence of any reference to these concepts in the Equal Pay Acts themselves.

DEVELOPMENTS IN THE UNITED STATES

Using the US Equal Pay Act

Despite the limited scope of the US Equal Pay Act, a useful body of case law has evolved under this statute. By contrast, attempts to use Title VII to rectify pay inequalities beyond the scope of the equal-pay law have been beset with difficulties.

Under the Equal Pay Act, it is not necessary to show that the discrimination was intentional. Once the plaintiff has established that the jobs compared are 'substantially equal' but paid at different rates, the burden of proof shifts to the employer to show that the differential is due to a seniority system, a merit system, a system which measures earnings by quantity or quality of production, or any factor other than sex. These are known as the Equal Pay Act's four defences. The case law has established that 'the burden of proof is a heavy one' and that 'factors other than sex' do not include:

> 'red circle' rates which perpetuate past wage discrimination, merit or seniority systems based solely on the subjective evaluations of the employer [or] "labor market" conditions which reflect the fact that women can be hired for less than men (Barnett 1982).[3]

To the members of the Supreme Court who adjudicated in the case of *Corning Glass Works* v. *Brennan* (417 US 188 [1974]), equal pay for men and women was 'a matter of simple justice'. The ruling was unequivocal:

> The [pay] differential arose simply because men would not work at the low rate paid women inspectors, and it reflected a job market in which Corning could pay women less than men for the same work. That the company took advantage of such a situation may be understood as a matter of economics, but its differential nevertheless became illegal once Congress enacted into law the principle of equal pay for equal work (*Corning Glass Works* v. *Brennan* at 205).

Using Title VII: *County of Washington* v. *Gunther*

As soon as we move outside the straitjacket of equal pay as enshrined in the Equal Pay Act and interpreted in case law, in order to challenge pay inequalities between women and men employed on different work, we find that the courts have not employed the same strict standards of review. Indeed, for some years it was unclear whether Title VII widened the scope of the Equal Pay Act at all. Recognising that a potential conflict existed between the two laws, Congress had added an amendment, known as the Bennett amendment, to Title VII, permitting an employer to differentiate on the basis of sex if the differentiation was 'authorised' by the Equal Pay Act. However, legal opinion divided on the question of whether the 'substantially equal' work standard applied to sex-based wage discrimination cases filed under Title VII or whether it was merely the Equal Pay Act's four defences that were imported into the new law.

The Supreme Court resolved this dilemma in 1981 in the case of *County of Washington* v. *Gunther* (452 US 161 [1981]). The plaintiffs in the case were female prison guards, employed by Washington County, Oregon, and paid substantially less than male prison guards. The women claimed intentional discrimination on the part of the County, because it had ignored the recommendations of its own survey, that female guards be paid at 95 per cent of the men's salaries, and continued to pay them 70 per cent of the male rate. The district court decided that, as the women guarded fewer prisoners than the male guards and, unlike them, spent time on clerical duties, the jobs were not 'substantially equal'. The court ruled that the case was therefore precluded by the Bennett amendment. On appeal, the Ninth Circuit Court of Appeals took a different view of the Bennett amendment and reversed the decision,[4] holding that the women did have a case even 'though the work of male and female guards was not substantially equal'. In a landmark decision, the Supreme Court confirmed the Court of Appeal's interpretation of the law: the Bennett amendment imported the employer's defences but not the 'equal work' standard into Title VII.

The Gunther decision opened the door to claims of sex-based wage discrimination in cases where the women's and men's jobs were different in content. At the same time, the Supreme Court left many questions unanswered, emphasising the narrowness of the issue to be decided in the Gunther case:

> Respondents' claim is not based on the controversial concept of 'comparable worth' . . . Rather, respondents seek to prove, by direct evidence, that their wages were depressed because of intentional sex discrimination (*County of Washington* v. *Gunther*, ibid, at 166).

The Court therefore gave judgement for the women, without pronouncing either for or against the concept of comparable worth and without delineating 'the precise contours of lawsuits challenging sex discrimination in compensation under Title VII' (ibid p. 181).

Developments since Gunther: the supremacy of market forces

Although supporters of comparable worth took heart from these developments, the courts have shown a marked reluctance to venture into the uncharted waters beyond Gunther. In an authoritative review of key judicial decisions since Gunther, the Bureau of National Affairs concluded that 'most courts have expressed great hostility to the comparable worth concept' (BNA, 1984). The Fifth Circuit Court of Appeals, for example, regarded the Gunther decision as restricted to 'blatant cases of sex discrimination'. Dismissing a claim by a woman who argued that the pay differential between herself and a male employee could not be justified by the differences between their jobs, the court declared: 'It is not the province of the courts . . . to value the relative worth of different duties and responsibilities.'[5]

The district court that adjudicated in the case of *Power* v. *Barry County* encapsulated the views of many judges when it suggested that:

> the Supreme Court's recognition of intentional discrimination may well signal the outer limits of the legal theories cognizable under Title VII. There is no indication in Title VII's legislative history that the boundaries of the Act can be expanded to encompass the theory of comparable worth.[6]

By and large, the courts had no wish to meddle with existing pay structures, nor to become involved in job-evaluation exercises of their own. Even where there was clear evidence of sex-based wage discrimination, perhaps due to the non-implementation of an agreed evaluation study, the courts would listen sympathetically to any defence couched in terms of the operation of market forces. A number of key cases decided in the early 1980s revealed a deep-seated judicial reluctance to punish employers merely for operating pay structures that reflected sex-based wage differentials commonly found in the labour market.[7]

The concept of disparate impact: *AFSCME* v. *Washington State*

Long-standing employment practices cannot easily be reduced to the motives of individuals and yet in all the Title VII cases considered so far, this is precisely what the plaintiffs were required to do. This is because they were all 'disparate treatment' cases, argued under that part of discrimination law in which it is essential to prove discriminatory intent.

There is, however, a well-established body of Title VII case law which treats the employer's motives as irrelevant; instead, the central concern is the discriminatory effects of particular employment practices. This is the concept of 'disparate impact' (see above, p. 35) which, if it were to be used successfully in pay equity cases, would open up a range of litigation strategies not available to plaintiffs in disparate treatment cases. Statistical evidence could be presented to demonstrate the historical and structural roots of job segregation within the particular company or organisation and its continuing impact on the earnings of women workers. Evidence that predominantly female areas of work within the organisation were undervalued and underpaid could be judged on its own merits; plaintiffs would not carry the additional burden of showing discriminatory intent on the part of the employer. The burden of proof would then shift to the employer, who would be required to justify the disparities in pay in terms of business necessity, a more stringent test than a simple appeal to 'market forces'.

The case of the *American Federation of State, County and Municipal Employees (AFSCME)* v. *Washington State* provided an opportunity to test the disparate impact argument. This was a massive case, involving 15 000 workers employed by Washington State in occupations in which 70 per cent or more of the employees were women. The main evidence presented on behalf of the plaintiffs consisted of a series of studies commissioned by the State itself. These studies revealed that female job classifications were paid approximately 20 per cent less than male classifications shown to be of comparable worth. Although several million dollars had at one stage been earmarked for beginning the process of implementing comparable worth, the State had dragged its feet on this issue on grounds of cost. The district court came to the conclusion that:

> The evidence is overwhelming that there has been historical discrimination against women in employment in the State of Washington, and that discrimination has been, and is, manifested by direct, overt and institutionalized discrimination (*AFSCME* v. *State of Washington*, 578 F. Supp. 846 (W. D. Wash. 1983).

The court held that the State's pay system had a disparate impact on workers in predominantly female job classifications and that this could not be justified as it was insufficient to override 'national interest in eliminating employment discrimination'. The court also found the State guilty of disparate treatment and intentional discrimination, particularly by failing to rectify the pay disparities which it had itself commissioned. The court believed that the State had acted in bad faith and ordered immediate relief at an estimated cost of one billion dollars.

Test case strategies experience a setback

Two years later, the Ninth Circuit Court of Appeals dealt a major blow to comparable-worth litigation strategies. It overturned the district court's decision with regard to both disparate impact and disparate treatment and at the same time reinstated the market forces defence (an issue not really considered by the district court) to its former glory.

The disparate impact finding was reversed on the grounds that decisions about pay structures are too complex to make such an analysis appropriate:

> Disparate impact analysis is confined to cases that challenge a specific, clearly delineated employment practice applied to a single point in the job selection process. (*AFSCME* v. *State of Washington*, 770 F. 2d. 1401 9th Cir. 1985 at 1405)

The disparate treatment finding was reversed on the grounds that the plaintiffs had failed to prove intent to discriminate:

> Job evaluation studies and comparable worth statistics alone are insufficient to establish the requisite inference of discriminatory motive critical to disparate treatment theory (ibid, p. 1407).

The court believed that it would be wrong to penalise employers who commissioned such studies merely because they failed to implement them:

> While the Washington legislature may have the discretion to enact a comparable worth plan if it chooses to do so, Title VII does not obligate it to eliminate an economic inequality that it did not create (ibid, p. 1407).

Although AFSCME's immediate response to the judgement was to set the wheels of the appeals process in motion once more, an out-of-court settlement provided for substantial pay awards to employees in female-dominated job classifications. For the plaintiffs then, as a result of political mobilisation, a satisfactory outcome was achieved despite the adverse judgement.

Six months later, the Seventh Circuit Court confirmed the conservative approach to comparable worth in the case of *American Nurses Association (ANA)* v. *The State of Illinois* (783 F.2d. 716 [7th Cir. 1986]). The ANA claimed that the State of Illinois discriminated against nurses by paying them less than workers in predominantly male job classifications and that the wage differentials could not be justified by any differences in relative worth. In the wake of the AFSCME decision, the ANA played down the 'comparable worth' and 'disparate impact' aspects of their case at the appeal stage and concentrated on proving intentional disparate treatment on the part of the State. The Association's worst fears were confirmed when the Court of Appeals ruled that Title VII placed no obligation on employers to base their wage rates on the principle of comparable worth and went on to dismiss the disparate impact claim because it did not fit the usual pattern of such claims. Turning to the disparate treatment claim, the ANA court followed the approach adopted by the circuit court in AFSCME, maintaining that an intention to discriminate cannot be inferred merely from a failure to implement the findings of a comparable-worth study.

These two decisions raise a number of unanswered questions which make it difficult to accept that they represent the outer limits of the potential development of wage-based discrimination claims under Title VII. To begin with, there seems to be no logical reason for limiting disparate impact claims to those which closely resemble past successful claims. Nor is it clear why the burden of proving discriminatory intent in disparate treatment claims should have become so much heavier than the courts had required in earlier Title VII cases.[8] Finally, if the four Equal Pay Act defences are imported into Title VII, why is it that the market-forces defence is allowed in claims under Title VII but not in claims under the Equal Pay Act?

The judicial reluctance to interfere with particular pay structures or with the operation of the labour market in general has to be seen in its political context. In the late 1970s Eleanor Holmes Norton, then Chair of the Equal Employment Opportunity Commission (EEOC),[9] played a major role in identifying comparable worth as a priority issue. She commissioned a feasibility study and also brought together academics and practitioners interested in employment discrimination, thereby providing a vital catalyst to the growing pay-equity movement.

Under the Reagan Administration, instead of producing a bold and comprehensive set of policy guidelines on comparable worth and taking the lead in bringing cases to court and filing *amicus curiae* briefs,[10] the Commission preferred to take a back seat. The Gunther decision precipitated an increase in the number of pay-equity claims submitted to the Commission and a considerable backlog of cases began to accumulate. After being severely reprimanded in 1984 by a House of Representatives subcommittee for its inaction, the EEOC was unable to sit on the fence any longer and openly rejected the concept of comparable worth as a viable legal doctrine.[11] The US Civil Rights Commission also issued a report in which it described the concept of comparable worth as 'fundamentally flawed' (US Commission on Civil Rights 1984) and the Justice Department filed an *amicus curiae* brief in the use case of *ANA* v. *The State of Illinois*, also opposing the concept.

Hope then gloom: *Bazemore* v. *Friday* and *Wards Cove* v. *Atonio*

In the short term then, the prospects for comparable-worth litigation seem fairly bleak, although a ray of hope shone briefly in the Supreme Court decision in the case of *Bazemore* v. *Friday* (106 S. Ct. 3000 [1986]).

The Bazemore case involved allegations of race-based wage discrimination. It did not raise the issues of comparable worth or disparate impact, but it did reduce the burden of proof required to bring a successful disparate treatment claim, specified the kinds of evidence required and introduced another category of discrimination. On the general issue of the evidentiary burden, the Court held that the plaintiff

> need not prove discrimination with scientific certainty; rather, his or her burden is to prove discrimination by the preponderance of the evidence (*Bazemore* v. *Friday*, p. 3009).

In this case, the evidence which impressed the Court included job-evaluation studies conducted by both parties, the employer's knowledge of the discriminatory effects of its pay system and its failure to take corrective action. Taking a position at variance with that of the AFSCME and ANA courts, the Supreme Court held that 'once there is knowledge of discrimination, there is an obligation to correct it' (Dowd, 1986, p. 862). In addition, the Court made it clear that the courts themselves were obliged to assess the job-evaluation evidence.

Furthermore, the Bazemore decision provides another category of discrimination:

> the perpetuation of historic discriminatory practices as analyzed under pattern and practice theory, suggesting that the phenomenon of wage discrimination is sufficiently complex that it cannot be encompassed by a single discrimination theory or general category of causation (Dowd, 1986, p. 862).

This would suggest that the pursuit of comparable-worth objectives by means of Title VII litigation does still have a future. It might yet prove possible to find formulae that the courts will recognise as analagous to established proofs in other Title VII cases (England, forthcoming, chap. 5).

On a more pessimistic note, it seems likely that Reagan's conservative appointments to the federal courts will impede rather than facilitate the development of comparable worth theory (ibid). The political complexion of the Supreme Court has also shifted in a conservative direction under Reagan, causing comparable-worth advocates to hesitate before raising new issues, fearing that their rejection by an unsympathetic court would prematurely foreclose the development of case law.

These fears were confirmed in the summer of 1989, when the Supreme Court gave judgement in another race-discrimination case, *Wards Cove Packing Co.* v. *Atonio* (104 L. Ed. 2nd 733 [1989]). The ruling in this case undermined the concept of disparate impact as established in Griggs (see above p. 35) by substantially increasing the burden of proof carried by the plaintiffs. Not only do the plaintiffs have to identify the specific employment practices which they believe to be reasonable for the disparate impact, they also have to show that these practices are not necessary. Rather than the employer being required to justify the practices, the plaintiffs have acquired a negative burden. The Court has further reduced the burden carried by the employers by redefining the concept of 'business necessity' as 'a reasonable business practice'.[12]

Alternative strategies for promoting comparable worth

Since the courts cannot be persuaded to 'read in' comparable worth to the existing law, some advocates have sought to devise new legislation containing an explicit commitment to the concept. This has been opposed by some comparable-worth advocates who insist that unequal pay for work of equal value is 'garden variety sex discrimination' (Newman, 1986) and by opponents of comparable worth. In the meantime, there has been a tremendous upsurge in comparable-worth activity at the state level, as public service unions and feminists put pressure on legislatures to undertake job evaluation of the state workforce, allocate funds for the reduction of sex-based differences in pay and the eventual implementation of comparable worth (Cook, 1984; NCPE, 1988).

DEVELOPMENTS IN BRITAIN

Using the British Equal Pay Act

In Britain, the relationship between the two major pieces of legislation concerned with sex equality is in some ways reminiscent of the relationship between the American Equal Pay Act and Title VII, even though the two laws were not linked by a Bennett-style amendment. Indeed, the Home Office guide to the legislation insisted that 'there is no overlap between the individual's rights under the Equal Pay Act and those under the Sex Discrimination Act' (Home Office, 1975, para. 3.17). The former deals exclusively with the contractual terms and conditions of employment, including pay. The latter is concerned with the equal treatment of men and women in a variety of activities in the public arena, including employment, but matters relating to pay are specifically excluded. The employment provisions of the Sex Discrimination Act cover the non-contractual aspects of employment, such as recruitment and promotion; they also cover contractual matters (other than pay) for workers complaining of discrimination but unable to satisfy the 'like work' requirements of the Equal Pay Act.

In practice, this sharp separation between the two jurisdictions was not always possible. Both laws came into force on the same date in 1975 (the Equal Pay Act is reproduced as Schedule I to the Sex Discrimination Act) and the same enforcement procedures were established for both. Some cases were filed under both laws; after a number of setbacks, lawyers involved in equal-pay cases were able to persuade the judges to treat the two laws as a 'harmonious code' for certain purposes and so overcome some of the more obvious limitations of the equal-pay legislation. A decisive factor behind this development was Britain's membership of the European Economic Community. If the judges were uncertain as to the relationship between the two domestic laws, they did recognise the need to take account of the requirements of EEC law which prohibited sex discrimination in employment. With so many claims failing to meet the narrow standards set by the Equal Pay Act, claimants and their advisers turned increasingly to Europe for an alternative ruling.

Initially, it was not the judges who faced the problem of how to interpret the sex equality laws, but the people who sat on industrial tribunals. Although the county courts (or sheriff courts in Scotland) were given jurisdiction under the Sex Discrimination Act in matters other than employment, industrial tribunals were chosen as the appropriate forum for handling all equal-pay claims and those sex-discrimination claims relating to employment.[13]

From the very beginning, a potential source of conflict existed. Tribunal members were encouraged to reach commonsense decisions grounded in practical experience, and yet the equality laws are complex and innovative, challenging many commonly-held assumptions and established employment practices. At first, most tribunals responded timidly and unimaginatively to the challenge of equal pay, refusing to accept that the woman's work was the 'same or broadly similar' to that of the man chosen for comparison or that any differences were 'not of practical importance'. Even if the like-work standard was met, most employers had no difficulty in persuading the tribunal that the variation in pay was 'genuinely due to a material difference (other than the difference of sex)'. A number of applicants appealed against these early decisions and the Employment Appeal Tribunal (EAT) adopted a more enlightened view of the new law; consequently, a useful, although limited, body of case law developed under the Equal Pay Act. The EAT was able to block some of the more obvious escape routes by which employers tried to evade their legal obligations, but it was unable to overcome the shortcomings of the legislation itself.

Common Market law to the rescue

If the British law was a maze of restrictions, exemptions and loopholes, the equivalent laws emanating from the EEC seemed by comparison straightforward and broader in conception. In 1970 when the British Equal Pay Act was drafted and again in 1973 when Britain signed the Treaty of Rome to join the Common Market, the only pronouncement in this area was Article 119 of the Treaty. Taken by itself, the Article did not seem particularly promising, as it recognised only the principle of 'equal pay for equal work'. In February 1975 however, ten months before the Sex Discrimination and Equal Pay Acts became law, the Equal Pay Directive was adopted by the Council of Ministers. Directives are issued with the intention that the various member-states pass national laws and so 'harmonise' provisions across the Community (Article 100 of the Treaty of Rome). The Directive expanded on Article 119 in a number of ways: it introduced the concept of 'work of equal value'; it specifically included conditions of work as well as pay, and it emphasised that job-classification schemes must be non-discriminatory.

In 1978, the Equal Opportunities Commission took the unusual step of appearing as an *amicus curiae* (see note 10) in a case before the Court of Appeal. The employer had defended the practice of paying male counterhands in a chain of betting shops at a higher rate than female counterhands because they performed a protective security function, although they received no special training for this additional duty. Giving judgement in favour of the women, the Court of Appeal emphasised that supremacy should be given to Community Law and that this rule applied as much in the tribunals as in the higher courts.[14]

Three months later, the Appeal Court heard a case in which

an employer defended an inequality in pay between a man and a woman on the basis of the need to attract the man from his previous employment. Rejecting this defence, the Court held that such extrinsic factors should be ignored, an interpretation of the Equal Pay Act which it found to be in accordance with Article 119. Lord Denning, presiding at the Court of Appeal, held that:

> The employer cannot avoid his obligations under the Act by saying: 'I paid him more because he asked for more' . . . if any such excuse were permitted, the Act would be a dead letter . . . Nor can the employer avoid his obligations by giving the reasons why he submitted to the extrinsic forces. . . . If any such reasons were permitted as an excuse, the door would be wide open. Every employer who wished to avoid the statute would walk straight through it (*Fletcher* v. *Clay Cross (Quarry Services)* [1978] IRLR 361).[15]

In two subsequent cases, the Court of Appeal was less confident of the correct interpretation of Community Law and so turned to the European Court of Justice (ECJ) for assistance.[16] The first case concerned a woman who claimed equal pay with a man who had held the same job before her. The second, a test case on behalf of some 14 000 women, raised the question of whether an employer's contribution to a retirement benefit scheme constituted 'pay' within the meaning of Article 119. The Court would have dismissed both these cases under the Equal Pay Act, but as a result of the ECJ's response to their questions, both claims were upheld under European law.

A reluctant government enacts the Equal Value Regulations

Informal discussions between the European Commissioners and the British government concerning the adequacy of the British equal-pay law had reached an impasse. The Commissioners brought infringement proceedings before the ECJ and in July 1982 the Court held that by failing to make provision for employees to claim equal pay for work of equal value where no job classification existed, the British government had failed to fulfil its treaty obligations. Whatever the practical difficulties, including opposition from employers, member-states were required to establish procedures which would enable the courts to assess the respective value of different jobs, 'if necessary in the context of adversary proceedings' (*Commission of the European Communities* v. *United Kingdom of Great Britain and Northern Ireland* [1982] IRLR 333 at 334).

The government had dragged its feet on this issue because it preferred wages to find their own level in the market-place with the minimum of legislative interference. This same philosophy is reflected in the wording of the Equal Value (Amendment) Regulations 1983, which came into effect at the beginning of 1984. Although the government had no option but to comply with the European ruling, the regulations are very much an exercise in damage limitation, designed to concede as little as possible.

The obsession with market forces is very much in evidence. Employers are given the opportunity at the beginning of the tribunal hearing to argue that the variation in pay between the man and woman is 'genuinely due to a material factor which is not the difference of sex'. The case may be dismissed at this point; if, however, it proceeds to a full hearing, the employer may raise the same defence later on, after the tribunal has received a job evaluation report on the work of the complainant and her comparators, conducted by an independent expert.[17] In practical terms, it is difficult to think of a defence that would fail to impress the tribunal at the outset of the proceedings but then prove ultimately convincing. This way of drafting the regulations did, however, provide a potential escape route for employers. Introducing the new regulations to the House of Commons, the Under-Secretary of State for Employment explained the 'material factor' provisions in the following terms:

> What we have in mind are circumstances where the difference in pay is not due to personal factors between the man and the woman, but rather to skill shortages or other market forces. If a man is paid more than a woman for work of equal value because his skills are in short supply, this is not sexually discriminatory, provided the reason is genuine and the employer can show this (Parliamentary Debates, House of Commons, vol. 46, col. 486).

Justifying market forces

The new provision had been carefully drafted in order to distinguish it from the Court of Appeal's ruling on 'extrinsic forces' in the Clay Cross Quarry case. In the event, this proved to be unnecessary as the Clay Cross ruling was overturned by a European Court decision in a case referred to it by a German Court (*Bilka-Kaufhaus* v. *Weber von Hartz* [1986] IRLR 317). In this judgement, the ECJ severed the link between indirect discrimination and intention by insisting that in cases of indirect discrimination the employer's defence must be 'objectively justifiable'. At the same time, however, the judgement called into question Lord Denning's total exclusion of 'extrinsic factors' by permitting the employer's 'objective' justification to be couched in economic terms.

In Britain, the Bilka decision had a mixed reception from the supporters of discrimination law: on the one hand, it was generally welcomed for its imposition on employers of stricter standards of review in the general area of indirect discrimination law;[18] on the other hand, its endorsement of the market-forces defence was greeted with some trepidation. These anxieties proved to be well-founded when the House of Lords gave judgement in favour of the employer in a case involving a woman prosthetist (artificial-limb fitter) recruited directly into the National Health Service and paid less than a man employed on like work but recruited from the private sector. The case was brought under the Equal Pay Act in its original form, as no one disputed that the men and women prosthetists were doing the same work; hence the relevance of the Clay Cross decision. The House of Lords however, following the Bilka ruling, dismissed the case on the grounds that there were 'objectively justified reasons' for paying the man more, in order to attract him and his colleagues (all of whom were men) from the private sector (*Rainey* v. *Greater Glasgow Health Board* [1986] 3 WLR 1017).

The House of Lords intervenes

The new regulations were widely criticised, both inside and outside Parliament. The House of Lords was so concerned that it passed an amendment, expressing the belief that the regulations failed to meet Britain's obligations under European Community Law (Parliamentary Debates, House of Lords, vol. 445, col. 886). It was not only the way in which the 'material-factor defence' was designed so as to give employers 'two bites of the cherry' (Lord McCarthy, ibid, col. 887) that gave cause for concern, but also the extreme complexity of the new provisions. In the House of Lords debate Lord Denning said:

> Ordinary people . . . ought to be able to read and understand the regulations. Not one of them would be able to do so. No ordinary lawyer would be able to understand them. The industrial tribunals would have the greatest difficulty and the Court of Appeal would probably be divided in opinion (ibid, col. 901–2).[19]

Despite these difficulties, the number of claims, which had been declining steadily over the years, rose sharply with the passing of the new law. A backlog of claims rapidly accumulated as the tribunals struggled to understand and implement the new measures. Some claims were settled through negotiation; others proceeded slowly through the legal labyrinth. As case law evolved, some of the complexities were ironed out; when in doubt, the Appeal Courts have opted for an interpretation of the regulations which coincides with the requirements of EEC law.

The case of *Pickstone and others* v. *Freemans* offers a clear example of this approach. The employers argued that the women were employed on 'like work' with a man and so were precluded from claiming equal value with another group of male workers. The tribunal and the EAT both accepted this argument thereby creating a major loophole, enabling employers to block a claim by employing one man alongside women workers. The House of Lords overturned the decision on the grounds that such an interpretation of the regulations would conflict with Article 119 (*Pickstone* v. *Freemans* [1988] IRLR 357).

Another case considered by the House of Lords had been dismissed by the courts below on the grounds that the woman (a nursery nurse) and her male comparators (clerical staff) were not 'in the same employment'. They all worked for the same employer and their terms and conditions were governed by the same collective agreement, but they worked at different establishments and their hours and holiday entitlements differed. The House of Lords overturned the decision regarding the 'same employment' finding (*Leverton* v. *Clwyd County Council* [1989] IRLR 28). Although the case was lost on other grounds, it set an important precedent. For example, it enabled a supermarket assistant to compare her job with that of a warehouseman employed at the company's distribution depot several miles away (*O'Sullivan* v. *J. Sainsbury*, Case No. 9831/87) and the outcome of this case was a successfully negotiated settlement between the shopworkers' trade union (USDAW) and the supermarket chain Sainsbury's, involving substantial pay rises for large numbers of women workers.

The material-factor defence

The material-factor defence is proving to be a major stumbling-block thwarting equal-value claims. Historical reasons which have ceased to operate in the present have been rejected by the Court of Appeal as an acceptable defence (*Benveniste* v. *University of Southampton* [1989] EOR No. 24 p. 40); otherwise, a bewildering array of factors has been accepted by the tribunals as a legitimate defence for pay inequalities, including holiday entitlements, shift work, training and experience and separate bargaining structures. In two important cases, the tribunals accepted the 'separate bargaining structures' defence without carefully considering the discriminatory impact of the different structures and without requiring the employers to justify them. In a third case, the tribunal adopted a more rigorous approach and found that the bargaining procedures were 'tainted by direct sex discrimination'.[20]

A recent European case originating in Denmark should help to clarify the confusion surrounding this area of the law by imposing stricter standards of review. The case involved an employer who made additional payments to individual workers within particular grades on the basis of a number of criteria which were not transparent and therefore not open to challenge. A trade union made a claim for equal pay on behalf of its women members on the basis of a statistical survey which showed that the average pay of the female workers was lower than that of the male workers in the same grades. The European Court held that the burden is on the employer to show that the pay criteria are objectively justifiable and not discriminatory. 'Quality of work' is unacceptable as a justification for pay differences as 'it is inconceivable that the work carried out by female workers would be generally of a lower quality'. Seniority is, however, an acceptable criterion; other criteria such as flexibility and vocational training have to be objectively justified (*Handelsog Kontorfunktionaerernes Forbund i Danmark* v. *Dansk Arbejdsgiverforening* (acting for Danfoss) [1990] EOR No. 29 p. 41). It is clear from this decision that in making use of the material-factor defence simple assertions on the part of the employer are unacceptable. Where the criteria used for pay increments have an adverse impact on women, the employer carries the burden of explaining and justifying their use.

The limits of individual litigation

The first equal-value case to be referred to an independent expert was that of Julie Hayward, a cook working for Cammell Laird and claiming equal value with three male craftsmen. Ms Hayward won her claim but was forced to return to the tribunal when the company refused to pay her on the grounds that her terms and conditions of employment, considered as a total package (including holiday and sick-pay entitlement and meal breaks) were no less favourable than those of her male comparators, so that there was no money due to her.

Although the law refers to 'any terms of the woman's contract' being no less favourable than the man's, the tribunal, the EAT and the Court of Appeal all accepted the employer's argument. The EAT members were particularly concerned about the dangers of 'leap-frogging', as different groups of workers each in turn demanded equality of benefits with other groups; they had adopted a 'pragmatic' approach, designed to avoid 'widespread chaos in industry'. The House of Lords, however, took the view that the claimant was entitled to equality with the male comparators in respect of each and every term in her contract. Almost four years after the original tribunal found in Julie Hayward's favour, the House of Lords reinstated the claim.

If the decision has thrown existing pay structures and collective agreements into disarray, at least it seems likely to precipitate a re-examination of out-dated and irrational variations in compensation systems. It also obviates the need for the tribunals to become involved in the invidious process of weighting individual benefits in order to assign an overall value to particu-

lar compensation packages. Above all, the history of this particular case demonstrates the absurdity of relying solely on
individual litigation to resolve equal value claims with such
wide-ranging implications for collective bargaining and employment practices in general.

If the government had wished to provide collective mechanisms, it had at its disposal an already existing body ideally
suited to the task. The Central Arbitration Committee (CAC),
created as a standing national arbitration body in the field of
industrial relations, had been given a limited role in relation to
discriminatory collective agreements under section 3 of the
Equal Pay Act. Instead of expanding the CAC's role to enable it
to handle equal value, its jurisdiction in this field was termi-
nated with the repeal of s.3 (see Sex Discrimination Act 1986).

Article 4 of the EEC Equal Pay Directive requires that:

> Member-states shall take the necessary measures to ensure
> that provisions appearing in collective agreements, wage
> scales, wage agreements or individual contracts of employ-
> ment which are contrary to the principle of equal pay shall
> be, or may be declared, null and void or may be amended.

The Sex Discrimination Act 1986 does include a form of words
designed to meet this requirement, but it is once again a
minimalist response: discriminatory collective agreements are
declared illegal, but no machinery for enforcing this measure is
provided. In practice, the only route currently available for
challenging an indirectly discriminatory pay term in a collective
agreement is the individual litigation route despite the wider
implications of individual cases.

The European Court has confronted this issue in a case
referred by the Hamburg Labour Court. Maria Kowalska made
use of Article 119 to challenge a collective agreement which
excluded part-time employees from a severance payment due
on retirement. The ECJ gave a clear ruling on both the collective and individual dimensions of this case. In view of its disparate impact on women, the collective agreement was held to
contravene Article 119 unless the employer could justify it by
objective factors unrelated to sex discrimination. If the employer failed to do this, individual members of the disadvantaged group would then be treated in the same way as other
workers and receive benefits in proportion to their hours of

work (*Kowalska* v. *Freie und Hansestadt Hamburg* [1990] IRLR 447).

In the context of UK law this case raises two important issues: first, the European Court did not simply declare the collective agreement null and void and send the parties away to redraft its terms, but imposed a solution based on proportionality; second, the decision is effectively a method of smuggling class action in by the back door. If an employee successfully challenges a collective agreement, this decision makes it impossible to deny a remedy to the other workers affected by the same agreement. A type of 'front door' class action is to be found in the EOC's recommendations for strengthening the equal-pay legislation. The Commission proposes that all employees working for the same employer and doing the same or broadly similar work as a successful claimant should be entitled to the same award.[21]

Job evaluation and the role of the unions

In drafting the equal-value regulations, the government had been anxious to protect existing job-evaluation schemes and had therefore excluded all but the most explicitly discriminatory schemes from challenge. The EOC had taken exception to this proposal and in the final version of the regulations, the conditions under which such schemes could be challenged were widened. Despite this revision, a number of early cases under this section were dismissed with little more than a cursory glance at the job-evaluation scheme in question.

The first of these was the much-publicised case of the sewing-machinists at Ford. The case has a long history, as this group of workers had played their part in the passing of the original Equal Pay Act, following an 'equal pay' strike in 1968. Ironically, the legislation proved useless, as job segregation at Ford ensured that there were no men employed on 'like work' with the sewing-machinists. Sixteen years later, the women brought an equal-value claim under the new regulations, only to be told by the tribunal that there were no reasonable grounds for determining that the 1968 evaluation scheme was discriminatory (*Neil and others* v. *Ford Motor Co.* [1984] IRLR 339). After another strike and a period of negotiation, the claim was settled without further litigation; the management and the trade union agreed to refer the dispute to an independent arbitration panel, which found that the women's work had been considerably undervalued and upgraded it accordingly.

This case highlights the need to scrutinise job-evaluation schemes with considerable care, even if on first sight they appear untainted by sex bias. Once again, it was the Court of Appeal and not the industrial-relations experts who sit on the tribunals who recognised this need and established the necessary guidelines. In the case of *Bromley* v. *Quick*, the tribunal and the EAT had dismissed the women's claims on the basis that the existing job-evaluation scheme was non-discriminatory, but the Court of Appeal reversed this and directed that the claims be referred to an independent expert. The Equal Pay Act specifies that the jobs of applicants and comparators covered by an evaluation study must have been valued in terms of the demands made on the workers under various headings, such as effort, skill and decision-making. According to the Court of Appeal, it is not sufficient that selected 'benchmark' jobs have been evaluated analytically in this way, with the remaining jobs slotted into the scheme on a 'whole job' or 'felt fair' basis. The job-evaluation scheme had been designed by a firm of management consultants, but was challenged by female clerical workers with the support of their trade union, the Transport and General Workers' Union (*Bromley and others* v. *H. & J. Quick* [1988] 1 IRLR 249).

An increasing number of employers have shown an interest in job evaluation as a way of pre-empting equal value claims. As a result of this decision, many will have to look at their schemes again; the practical difficulties will be greatest for large-scale schemes, which tend to make extensive use of representative job descriptions. Presumably it was practical considerations of this kind which caused the people who sit on industrial tribunals to shy away from the legislative interpretation adopted by the Court of Appeal; and yet the new guidelines from the Court are evidently needed in order to flush out the direct and indirect discrimination which remains so deeply embedded in many job-evaluation schemes. Clearly, the trade unions have a crucial role to play both in challenging existing schemes and in ensuring that new ones are genuinely non-discriminatory (Gregory and Stoddart, 1987).

CONCLUSION

This account of the major achievements and setbacks in the legal struggles to implement comparable worth in America and equal value in Britain has identified a number of obstacles which impede further progress on this issue. On both sides of the Atlantic, it proved necessary to build bridges between two separate pieces of legislation; one narrowly conceived and relating specifically to equal pay, the other providing a framework for a much more comprehensive attack on discrimination. The American courts have allowed cases to be brought under the wider statute only to a limited extent, allowing comparisons between jobs that are not 'substantially equal' but requiring a high standard of proof, including evidence of intentional discrimination by the employer. Largely as a result of its membership of the European Community, Britain has moved ahead of the USA as regards the development of both statute and case law. Not only has the Equal Pay Act been amended to incorporate the concept of equal value, but cases can be heard on the basis of unintentional indirect discrimination on the part of the employer.[22] Unfortunately, the 'business necessity' test derived from the Griggs case and providing the starting-point for British law on indirect discrimination, has been replaced by the weaker test of 'objectively justified reasons', which enables employers with frequent success to use the market-forces justification for continuing sex-based wage discrimination. Ironically, the Griggs test has been fatally weakened in its country of origin too, as a result of the recent Supreme Court ruling in Atonio (see above p. 44 and note 12).

Where employers have taken advantage of women's weaker position in the market-place in order to pay them at a lower rate than men for identical work, the judiciary in both countries has taken a firm stand against such exploitation. (Compare the judgements against the American company Corning Glass, quoted on p. 37 and against the British company Clay Cross Quarries, quoted on p. 48). Where, however, the comparison is between different jobs to which comparable-worth/equal-value standards have been applied, the judges are much more likely to permit employers to take advantage of labour-market inequalities and also to absolve them from any individual blame for these inequalities. These decisions are out of step with general developments in discrimination case law (with the exception of Atonio), where there is a growing understanding of the historical and structural bases of discrimination and a recognition that employers must begin to take greater responsibility for corrective action.

At first glance, it might seem that the British system of industrial tribunals offers a procedural advantage over the American court structure, by providing a speedy, fair and cheap method of adjudication which explicitly recognises the importance of job evaluation. In practice however, the tribunals have failed to live up to this promise. Their performance in relation to discrimination cases in general has been severely criticised (see, for example, Kumar, 1986; Gregory, 1987 and 1989, and Leonard, 1987). With regard to equal-value claims in particular, the problems are compounded by the complexity of the regulations, so that cases are resolved only after years of litigation and considerable financial outlay by both parties. In this context, the absence of any collective mechanisms for implementing equal value, including the absence of any provision for bringing a class action, becomes an overriding weakness in British law. In the USA, the majority of civil-rights cases, including comparable-worth claims, are fought as class actions; they are brought on behalf of a number of plaintiffs, so that the financial and emotional burden of bringing the case is shared and if the action is successful, all class members benefit. In Britain, unless the employer agrees to regard a particular claim as a test case, each applicant has to file a separate claim.

These procedural difficulties have had a stultifying effect on the development of pay-equity campaigns in Britain. There is nothing in Britain on the scale of the American National Committee on Pay Equity (NCPE), although moves are currently underway to establish networks and launch a campaign; the British Women's Legal Defence Fund was launched as recently as April 1989, whereas its sister organisation in the USA has been active for a number of years. Almost by default, the Equal Opportunities Commission has assumed a major role in pushing back the frontiers of case law in this area. To its credit, it has proved more resistant to political pressures than its American counterpart and has persistently criticised the government for dragging its feet on the issue of equal pay and for failing to respond adequately to the requirements of European law; the government has reacted by curtailing the Commission's activities through budgetary controls (*Equal Opportunities Review*, no. 25, May/June 1989).

In the USA, the campaigns to combat sex-based and race-based wage discrimination are inextricably interrelated. The NCPE publishes information and advice on both issues (see, for example, NCPE, February 1987). In Britain, the equal-pay and equal-value legislation is solely concerned with pay inequalities between men and women. Two separate agencies, the Equal Opportunities Commission and the Commission for Racial Equality, exist to deal with the two issues of sex and race discrimination and the EEC has maintained a complete silence on the question of racial discrimination in the labour market.[23] However, the Race Relations Act 1976 makes it illegal to segregate people on the basis of race (section 1(2) and also to discriminate on racial grounds in 'the terms of employment' afforded to employees (section 4(2)(a)). The potential for using these provisions remains relatively unexplored.

In both the USA and Britain, there is still a great deal of ground to cover before the goal of comparable worth/equal value is attained. In terms of legal strategy, considerable scope remains, both in formulating more effective laws and also in pushing forward the development of case law under existing statutes. There is, however, an inescapable irony in seeking a solution to collective problems by focusing on individual remedies, particularly in Britain where there are no class actions. If test-case strategies are to be successful, it is essential that they be viewed as part of a broadly-based, coordinated campaign in which the centre of activity is the workplace and the central activists are the workers themselves.

Notes

1. *Schultz* v. *Wheaton Glass Co.*, 421 F.2d 259 (3rd Cir.), cert. denied, 398 US 905 (1970). In using the phrase 'substantially equal', the Schultz court had evidently intended to widen the scope of the Equal Pay Act and so reconcile it with the broader provisions of Title VII of the Civil Rights Act. In subsequent cases however, the phrase was used more restrictively (see Barnett, 1982).

2. This measure became the Race Relations Act 1976. Two earlier Race Relations Acts, passed in 1965 and 1968, had proved ineffective. The Sex Discrimination Act was used as the model for the third race discrimination law, so that women as well as racial minorities benefited from the experiences derived from these earlier, more limited laws on race (see Gregory, 1987).

3. It is interesting to compare American and British case law on these particular issues. Like the American courts, the British courts have recognised the need to ensure that the custom of 'red circling' (i.e. protecting the wages of individual employees transferred from a higher to a lower paid post) is not abused. However, the English Court of Appeal has shown a marked reluctance to interfere with the subjective element in employers' grading schemes and has reprimanded the Employment Appeal Tribunal for its reference to 'the heavy burden of proof' that employers must shoulder in equal-pay cases (see *National Vulcan Engineering Group* v. *Wade* 1978 IRLR 225). The case law on market forces is also less clear-cut (see below).

4. Cases involving federal laws are heard initially in federal district courts, with the right of appeal by either party to the Circuit Court of Appeals. The USA is divided into twelve geographical circuits, each with its own appellate court. Decisions made by a circuit court are binding on the district courts within that circuit. Only Supreme Court decisions are binding on the Courts of Appeals, although these courts do take notice of each other's judgements.

5. *Plemer* v. *Parsons-Gilbane,* 713 F.2d. 1127 (5th Cir. 1983). This case is discussed in BNA, 1984, as are the cases referenced in notes 6 and 7.

6. *Power* v. *Barry County,* 539 F. Supp. 712 (W. D. Mich. 1982). Courts in the USA refer constantly to the comments made by legislators when draft laws are under discussion (known as the legislative history). By contrast, British courts usually astutely avoid looking at the relevant parliamentary debates for enlightenment when interpreting statutes.

7. See in particular *Lemons* v. *City and County of Denver,* 620 F.2d 228 (10th Cir. 1980); *Briggs* v. *City of Madison,* 536 F. Supp. 435 (W. D. Wis. 1982); *Spaulding* v. *University of Washington,* 740 F.2d 686 (9th Circ. 1984).

8. In the course of her perceptive analysis of the AFSCME and ANA decisions, Nancy Dowd (1986) gives examples of Title VII cases in which the Supreme Court was prepared to infer discriminatory intent from the circumstantial evidence. These include *International Brotherhood of Teamsters* v. *United States,* 431 US 324 (1977); *Furno Construction Co.* v. *Waters,* 438 US 567 (1978); *United States Board of Governors* v. *Aikens,* 460 US 711 (1983).

9. The EEOC was established by the Civil Rights Act 1964 as the administrative agency with responsibility for investigating and conciliating individual claims under Title VII. Initially, only the Attorney General could initiate civil action where conciliation failed or where there was 'reasonable cause' to believe there existed a 'pattern and practice' of discrimination. These powers were transferred to the EEOC by the Equal Employment Opportunities Act 1972.

10. Organisations who are not parties to the case but who have an interest in the issues it raises may be permitted to participate in the proceedings as an *amicus curiae* (friend of the court) and so present relevant evidence and argument to the court. *Amicus curiae* briefs are a common occurrence in the USA; they are much less frequent in Britain.

11. The criticisms are contained in a report entitled *Pay Equity: EEOC's Handling of Sex-Based Wage Discrimination,* issued in May 1984 by the House Government Operations Committee's subcommittee on manpower and housing. The rejection of comparable worth is made in EEOC Decision No. 85–8, 53 USLW 2633 (25 June 1985).

12. Introducing the concept of 'the reasonable employer' is precisely the strategy used by the House of Lords to dilute the concept of indirect discrimination in British law (see below p. 00) The US Civil Rights Bill 1990 is an attempt to reinstate the Griggs decision by reintroducing the concept of 'business necessity' and restoring the burden of proof as elaborated in Griggs. However, the Bill has some powerful opponents and seems unlikely to become law.

13. There is no equivalent in the USA to the British tribunal system. Part of a wider network of administrative tribunals, industrial tribunals were created in the mid-1960s and began to play a major role in the rapidly expanding field of industrial relations law. As the tribunals were designed to dispense justice informally, cheaply and rapidly, legal representation was considered unnecessary and legal aid was not made available for tribunal hearings. Each tribunal is chaired by a lawyer who sits with two lay members drawn from 'the two sides of industry'. It is only at the appeals stage that a judge puts in an appearance. Either party can appeal against the tribunal decision on a point of law to the Employment Appeal Tribunal (EAT) and at this stage applications for legal aid are permitted. The composition of the Appeal Tribunal mirrors that of the industrial tribunals: a High Court judge sits with two 'wing' members, selected on the basis of industrial experience. On reaching the lofty heights of the Court of Appeal and the House of Lords the representatives of management and unions disappear.

14. *Coomes (Holdings)* v. *Shields* [1978] IRLR 263. This case is also notable for Lord Denning's references to American statute and case law on equal pay. He admits that unlike Community law, American law is not directly applicable but he finds it 'instructive', as the English legislation in this field is based 'a good deal' on American experience (ibid, p. 265).

15. Once again, Lord Denning cited American case law, including the Corning Glass and Schultz cases (see above, p. 37, and note 1). Significantly, he also referred to the Griggs case, a Title VII case (see above p. 35), in order to argue that a variation in pay must be job-related and that motive is irrelevant.

16. The role of the European Court is not to decide particular cases, but rather to interpret Community law by answering questions put to it by national courts, who then apply the interpretation to the specific case.

17. Unless the tribunal is satisfied that 'there are no reasonable grounds' for considering that the work is of equal value, it is required to commis-

sion a report from an 'independent expert', drawn from a panel of people nominated by the Advisory, Conciliation and Arbitration Service. This procedure applies only in equal-value cases, in recognition of the complexity of the job-evaluation task. The experts have been criticised for their tardiness and lack of consistency and various suggestions have been made for streamlining and standardising the procedures (see Justice, 1987; Trade Union Research Unit, 1988; EOC, 1989 and 1990).

18. In indirect-discrimination cases, employers are given the chance to justify the discriminatory practice, a provision initially interpreted by the EAT in accordance with the 'business necessity' standard established in American case law. This standard was progressively weakened by the Court of Appeal and the House of Lords in a series of race-discrimination cases (see Gregory, 1987, chap. 2). As the Sex Discrimination Act and the Race Relations Act contain identical provisions in relation to indirect discrimination, the case law under the two statutes is inextricably linked. In a roundabout fashion then, EEC law can have an impact on race-discrimination law, although Community law is silent on this issue.

19. Lord Denning had by this time retired from the Court of Appeal (his opinion in the Clay Cross Quarry case is given above on p. 48) and had taken a seat in the House of Lords. The House of Lords is the Upper House of Parliament and is composed of hereditary peers; life peers appointed by the Queen; Archbishops and Bishops, and the Law Lords. It can introduce laws and amend laws sent to it from the House of Commons, but it is the latter, as the elected chamber, that makes the final decision on all legislation. When sitting as an appellate court, the House of Lords consists exclusively of the Law Lords. Apart from this brief account of the House of Lords' debate on the equal-value regulations, references in this chapter to the House of Lords are references to the appellate court.

20. In *Reed Packaging Ltd* v. *Boozer and Everhurst* ([1988] EOR No. 21 p. 24) it was the EAT, overturning a tribunal decision, that accepted the 'separate bargaining structures' defence. Although the EAT claimed that this use of the 'objectively justified administrative reason' as a material factor defence was as defined in the Bilka case (see above p. 50)' the Appeal Tribunal did not ask any of the searching questions relating to the potentially discriminatory effects of the separate pay structures nor the business justification for them, as required by the European Court in that case. Similarly, in the case of the speech therapists employed by the National Health Service and claiming equal pay with their NHS colleagues working as clinical psychologists and pharmacists, historical differences in bargaining structures were accepted as a material factor defence without any of the crucial questions being addressed. (*Clark* v. *Bexley Health Authority and Secretary of State for Health* [1989] EOR No. 24 p. 42) In the third case, the tribunal accepted the independent expert's finding that the work of secretaries, a typist and a clerk-typist were of equal value to that of a male messenger and rejected the employer's defence (see 'Lloyds Bank to Appeal' in EOR No. 28 [1989] p. 2).

21. See EOC 1990 p. 14. Similarly, the Northern Ireland EOC recommends that: 'where the individual applicant is successful, the class of employees to which she belongs should be entitled to the same remedy provided they notify the Tribunal within a specified period' (EOC for N. Ireland, 1990).

22. In the early days of the EEC legislation the European Court was much more tentative than it is now in relation both to the interpretation of European law and its direct application in member-states. Presumably the Court wanted to give member-states time to harmonise their laws, but with the passing years has decided to take a firmer line. It is worth comparing two cases concerned with the issue of indirect discrimination against women who work part-time, one originating in the UK in the early 1980s and the other in Germany at the end of the 1980s. In the first case, an exasperated English judge, faced with an unhelpful ruling from the ECJ, decided that domestic legislation conferred rights on part-time women workers superior to those provided by Europe (*Jenkins* v. *Kingsgate*, No. 2 [1981] IRLR 388). In the second case, the ECJ decided unequivocally that German sick-pay legislation which excluded part-time workers was illegal unless it could be justified by objective factors unrelated to sex discrimination. (*Rinner-Kuhn* v. *FWW Spezial-Gebaudereinigung GmbH & Co.* [1989] EOR No. 28 p. 39) The European Court is now leading the way for national courts in a way reminiscent of the role played by the US Supreme Court in the 1970s.

23. The European Parliament has produced a Declaration against Racism and Xenophobia and has also commissioned a report on this subject. However, the power to take decisions resides not with the European Parliament but with the Council of Ministers and they are overwhelmingly preoccupied with the strengthening of external border controls against drug-traffickers, terrorists, criminals and immigrants in the context of the dismantling of internal borders with the advent of the single European market in 1992. The racist implications of these developments are cogently presented by Michael Spencer (1990).

References

Barnett, E. (1982) 'Comparable Worth and the Equal Pay Act – Proving Sex-based Wage Discrimination Claims after *County of Washington* v. *Gunther*', *Wayne Law Review*, 28, pp. 1669–1700.

Bureau of National Affairs (1984) Pay Equity and Comparable Worth: A BNA Special Report (Washington: BNA).

Cook, A. (1984) 'Developments in Selected States', in H. Remick (ed.) 1984.

Dowd, N. (1986) 'The Metamorphosis of Comparable Worth', *Suffolk University Law Review*, XX, pp. 833–65.

England, P. (forthcoming) *Comparable Worth: Theories and Evidence* (New York: Aldine).

Equal Opportunities Commission (1989) *Equal Pay . . . Making it Work* (Manchester: EOC).

Equal Opportunities Commission (1990) *Equal Pay for Men and Women: Strengthening the Acts* (Manchester: EOC).

Equal Opportunities Commission for Northern Ireland (1990) *The Equal Pay Legislation: Recommendations for Change* (Belfast: EOC [N.I.]).

Gregory, J. (1987) *Sex, Race and the Law: Legislating for Equality* (London: Sage).

Gregory, J. (1989), *Trial by Ordeal: a study of people who lost Equal Pay and Sex Discrimination cases in the Industrial Tribunals during 1985 and 1986* (London: HMSO).

Gregory, J. and Stoddart, J. (1987) *Equal Pay: Out of the Ghetto?* (International Labour Reports No. 23 Sept/Oct).

Heen, M. (1984) 'A Review of Federal Court Decisions under Title VII of the Civil Rights Act of 1964', in H. Remick (ed.) 1984.

Justice (1987) *Industrial Tribunals* (London: Justice).

Kumar, V. (1986) *Industrial Tribunal Applicants under the Race Relations Act 1976* (London: Commission for Racial Equality).

Leonard, A. M. (1987) *Judging Inequality: The Effectiveness of the Tribunal System in Sex Discrimination and Equal Pay Cases* (London: Cobden Trust).

Meehan, E. M. (1985) *Women's Rights at Work* (London: Macmillan).

National Committee on Pay Equity (1987) *Pay Equity: An Issue of Race, Ethnicity And Sex* (Washington, DC: NCPE Feb.).

National Committee on Pay Equity (1988) *Survey of State-Government Level Pay Equity Activity* (Washington: DC: NCPE).

Newman, W. (6–7 June 1986) Statement of Winn Newman, Newman and Associates Washington, DC in *Comparable Worth: Issue for the 80's'*, A Consultation of the US Commission on Civil Rights Vol 2 Proceedings p 86.

Remick, H. (ed.) (1984) *Comparable Worth and Wage Discrimination: Technical Possibilities and Political Realities* (Philadelphia: Temple University Press).

Steinberg, R. J. (1984) "'A Want of Harmony'": Perspectives on Wage Discrimination and Comparable Worth', in H. Remick (ed.) 1984.

Spencer, M. (1990) *1992 and All That: Civil Liberties in the Balance* (London: The Civil Liberties Trust).

Trade Union Research Unit (1988) *Independent Experts and their Reports* (Oxford: TURU, Ruskin College).

US Commission on Civil Rights (1984) *Comparable Worth: Issue for the 80s*.

3 Job Assessment, Job Evaluation and Equal Value
Fiona Neathey

Unequal assessment of the job content of 'male' and 'female' jobs is clearly a barrier to equal pay for women. However, this chapter suggests that it is not the only barrier. In addition, while it is relatively easy to identify the problem of unfair evaluation of the relative worth of work done by men and women, finding a solution is more difficult. In the USA much comparable-worth activity is based upon the premise that job content can be assessed on a gender-neutral basis. In Britain, an employer can defeat an equal-value claim at the preliminary stage of the proceedings if the employer can prove the use of an 'analytical' job-evaluation scheme in determining pay, unless such schemes can be shown to be discriminatory. None of the major schemes marketed by consultants in Britain has yet been subject to such a test. However, concerns are developing about their use and their possible bias against certain occupational groups.

Whatever the assumptions implicit in UK equal-pay legislation, it may be the case that it is actually not possible to have a neutral job-assessment system. Those concerned to attribute greater value to work commonly undertaken by women should, therefore, be working for systems of job evaluation that favour 'female' over 'male' skills. This chapter highlights the factors which limit the usefulness of job evaluation as a tool for obtaining equal pay for women and men, before moving on to explore the possibility of 'women-friendly' job-evaluation schemes. It draws on research on the use of job evaluation in the United Kingdom, in particular work undertaken for the independent research organisation Industrial Relations Services (IRS), to suggest directions for such schemes.[1]

UNEQUAL PAY – A RESULT OF UNFAIR ASSESSMENT?

The concentration of women in particular occupations and industries has been well-documented. For example, the Department of Employment Gazette for July 1990 indicates that while in December 1989 women constituted around 48 per cent of the population in employment, 82 per cent of working women were employed in service industries. Similarly, they predominate in certain occupations, such as clerical and secretarial work where around 72 per cent of the jobs are done by women and sales occupations where women are over 60 per cent of the workforce. On the other hand women are underrepresented in certain higher-status occupational groups such as managers and administrators (27 per cent) and professionals (33 per cent). This segregation raises important questions as to the source of pay inequality. Is such inequality the result of pay rates which are low because of the poor performance of the firms or industries involved? To what extent does it result from an undervaluing of the work into which women are segregated? And are women actually over-represented in occupations which have objectively lower levels of skill?

These issues have been addressed by Horrell, Rubery and Burchell as part of their research for the Economic and Social Research Council's (ESRC) Social Change and Economic Life initiative. This research aimed to expand on findings of previous research in the area of equal pay which is largely based on case studies and which has tended to a show a consistent under-evaluation of women's as compared with men's work in individual organisations (Armstrong, 1982; Coyle, 1982; Crompton and Jones, 1984; Craig et al., 1985).

Across the British economy women's average hourly earnings are only 76 per cent of those of men (New Earnings Survey, 1989). It is not clear whether men's jobs attract higher pay because they objectively involve higher skills or simply because women's real skills are unrecognised. As Horrell et al. point out, the extent to which jobs come to be recognised as requiring skills or responsibilities and the status given to such attributes are a socially rather than technically determined process (Horrell et al., 1990). The researchers set out to construct an index of skill against which to measure work done by men and women and as an alternative to conventional forms of occupational classification, which are often seen as undervaluing work commonly done by women. Their assessments of job content are based on the evaluation of the skill components of their own jobs by around 600 men and women in paid employment in the Northampton area in the summer of 1986.

Horrell *et al.* found that male full-time jobs tend on average to be more skilled than female full-time jobs. However, even when differences in job content/skill were taken into account, men still earned more than women. This effect is even stronger when hourly rates of female part-timers are compared with those of male full-timers. The researchers also attempted to measure whether unequal skill distribution or unequal pay at specific levels of skill was more disadvantageous to women. They found that changing the skill distribution to make women's jobs equal to those of men potentially improves pay for women by 26 per cent. However, providing equal pay for the same level of job content would reduce the gap between male and female earnings by 71 per cent. (Horrell *et al.*, 1989).

It is unfortunately not possible to identify from this research the extent to which differences in pay rates for jobs with the same level of skill may be accounted for by the location of women in firms or industries, which, due to their market position, are low-paying. Clearly to address this source of inequality it will be necessary to deal with the obstacles to women's employment in more prosperous sectors of the economy. However where unequal pay is the result of the comparative undervaluing of the job content of female-dominated as compared to male-dominated work within organisations, the research seems to confirm that the undervaluation of women's work is widespread and costly to women. Horrell *et al.* conclude that priority should be put on the 'developing of imaginative and diverse systems of measuring skill which aim to do more than reproduce the current grading and status of jobs if there is to be any real progress towards the aim of equal pay for work of equal value' (Horrell *et al.*, 1990, p. 214) The extent to which such fairer systems of job assessment can achieve equal pay for work of equal value within organisations is addressed below.

HOW PREVALENT IS THE USE OF JOB EVALUATION?

Formalised systems of job assessment are usually known as job-evaluation schemes. The British Equal Opportunities Commission describes job evaluation as 'a system of comparing different jobs to provide a basis for a grading and pay structure' (EOC, 1985, p. 1). Within these parameters the range of job-evaluation schemes available is considerable. However, they can broadly be categorised into 'analytical' and non-analytical or 'whole job' schemes. Analytical schemes break jobs down into job factors and evaluate them in terms of each factor in order to provide a rank order of jobs. Non-analytical schemes rank jobs on an assessment of the whole job. Following the case of *Bromley and others* v. *H. & L. Quick, Ltd* (1988 IRLR 249) schemes which do not evaluate jobs in terms of their 'constituent demand factors' do not offer employers protection under the terms of the amended Equal Pay Act.

Calculations as to the incidence of job evaluation in the United Kingdom vary. The Workplace Industrial Relations Survey (WIRS) conducted in 1984, found that 21 per cent of establishments had job-evaluation schemes covering at least some of the workforce. This proportion had not changed since 1980 when the previous WIRS was conducted. However there had been a substantial increase, from 22 per cent to 34 per cent in the number of these establishments which operate more than one scheme, suggesting an increase in the coverage of job evaluation within organisations. The static figure for the number of establishments with job evaluation also hid a decline in private manufacturing and an increase in private services. However, although in 1984 only 24 per cent of private manufacturing establishments had any formal job-evaluation scheme, some 48 per cent of employees in manufacturing were employed in workplaces where job evaluation was used, showing that job evaluation is much more common in larger manufacturing establishments in the United Kingdom (Millward and Stevens, 1986).

More recent research conducted by the Advisory Conciliation and Arbitration Service (ACAS) on the use of formalised job assessment finds a higher incidence of the use of job evaluation. The ACAS survey, which was based on interviews conducted by advisory staff as part of their usual programmes of visits to employers in 1988, found that 39 per cent of establishments use job evaluation to determine payments for some or all of their employees. ACAS also found that job evaluation was more common in manufacturing (40 per cent of establishments) than service organisations (35 per cent), and in larger establishments (75 per cent of those employing more than 1500 people using job evaluation) (ACAS, 1990).

The higher incidence of job-evaluation use reported by ACAS as compared with WIRS, can in part be explained by the way the research was conducted. The nature of their work means that advisory staff generally visit organisations where changes are being made or are planned while WIRS is based on a cross-section of all kinds of establishment. Whether there has been an overall increase of the dimension suggested by the ACAS study in the use of job evaluation should become clearer in 1991 when the current WIRS is published. However, it is probable that changes in equal-pay legislation alongside other developments in the organisation of work may have prompted an increase in the use of job evaluation in certain sectors.

1989 and 1990 saw a considerable increase in job evaluation in two important employment sectors for women: finance and retailing. In the former case predominantly female clerical, secretarial and typing staff were traditionally paid considerably lower rates of pay than 'technical and services' or messenger employees who are overwhelmingly male. The two groups were not generally covered by the same job-evaluation system, so employers could not argue that the pay of the men and women was the result of assessment under the same evaluation process. A successful equal pay for work of equal value case against one of the major clearing banks – Lloyds (*Longman and others* v. *Lloyds Bank plc 20.7.89 COIT 08056/86*), changes in collective bargaining arrangements and major commercial and technological changes are all factors behind the transformation in the way in which the work of employees of all the big banks is evaluated (IRS, January 1990).

In the retailing sector, comparison has been made between the work of checkout operators, who are usually women, and warehouse workers who are more often male. Again the fear of vulnerability under the equal-pay legislation heightened by the start of a series of tribunal cases against a major employer in the sector – Sainsbury's – seems to have prompted the introduction of new job-evaluated pay structures in various retailing organisations. In Sainsbury's itself the new job-evaluated pay structure combined with the outcome of the annual pay review produced pay increases worth some 16 per cent for check-out operators (IRS, May 1990)

TO WHAT EXTENT DOES JOB EVALUATION DETERMINE PAY LEVELS?

The way jobs are assessed is not the only determinant of the pay levels for those jobs. Even where formalised systems of job evaluation are used to determine basic pay other factors may also influence the total earnings of individuals and groups. Amongst manual workers different groups may, for example, have access to different levels of additional payments such as production bonuses or may have differing opportunities to work overtime or to undertake shift work. Systems of merit assessment – increasingly common as means of progression amongst certain groups of non-manual workers though also present in some manual pay systems – link pay levels to supposed measures of individual performance. In the UK public sector, in particular, certain occupations may attract supplements which are linked to shortage of potential applicants in the market-place rather than the nature of the work itself.

A study, which followed the implementation of a new job-evaluation scheme for local authority manual workers, found that as a result of 'fairer' evaluation traditionally female 'caring' jobs, notably those of home-helps, moved up the job hierarchy at the expense of (predominantly male) refuse-collectors. However, there were no other significant changes in the pecking order. The research found that while most of the 'male' jobs attracted considerable overtime and bonus payments this was not true of 'female jobs'. The effect in one of the boroughs was to put the average earnings of refuse-drivers who were five places below home helps in the basic pay league, at £216 a week while home helps themselves earned only £123 a week. UK case law is only just beginning to address that the implication of potential sources of pay inequality such as these (LEVEL, 1987).

Research by the independent research organisation the Policy Studies Institute (PSI) conducted in 1982, shortly before the introduction of the equal-value amendment to British equal-pay law, examined the implications of the use of job evaluation for the development of pay structures free of sex bias. This research also found that any equitable impact of a job-evaluation system may be reduced or undermined where other sources of payment are also used (Ghobadian and White, 1986).

It seems clear that job-assessment arrangements which give greater credit to traditionally female skills will not alone bring equal pay for women, although they may help to reduce inequality. However, given the current structure of equal-pay legislation in the UK, it is likely that job evaluation will be used by managements as a way of protecting their pay structures against claims of equal pay for work of equal value and may be pushed by unions as a means of improving the pay position of their women members. For these reasons the forms which such evaluation systems take are likely to be central to developments in the area of equal pay.

TRADE UNIONS AND JOB EVALUATION – A TOOL FOR CHANGE OR FOR PROTECTING THE STATUS QUO?

A number of British trade unions which have a sizeable female membership have taken the equal-value amendment as a basis for improving the pay of their women members within and outside the courts through case law and through negotiation. The guidance offered to members and negotiators by unions commonly stresses the central position of job evaluation within the legislation. A strategy of lining-up equal-pay cases whilst pressing management for changed job-evaluation systems which provide a more favourable evaluation of the work of women members has been used in a number of cases. It was employed, for example, by the local government manual-worker unions when negotiating a new job-evaluation scheme for their members and has been used by the Union of Shop Distributive and Allied Workers (USDAW) in the more recent negotiations with retailing employers (Labour Research Department, June 1990). In some cases this strategy has resulted in considerable improvements in the pay position of women workers, though dramatic changes in the pay hierarchy seem less common. The impact of new job-evaluation schemes on the pay position of women employees, which are subject to the limitations already outlined, are also likely to be affected by management commitment of resources to equal pay, by the nature of the scheme selected by management, by unions' power to ensure that such schemes give proper value to work done by women and by the commitment of the unions and their members to a change in the *status quo*.

When negotiating new job-evaluation arrangements union representatives face the dilemma of which scheme to support in their discussions with management. The common consideration in negotiations is whether the off-the-peg schemes offered by a number of management consultants can be used in a way which will achieve the aim of improving the pay levels of their women members. If not, should the union involve itself in the development of an in-house scheme? In this debate unions can be hindered by a lack of experience and information on the subject, particularly when faced with the slick presentations of management consultants. However, over the last five years, certain unions have developed considerable expertise in the area while others more often call upon the services of their own outside expert to counterpoise the consultants' arguments. Additionally the extent to which unions feel that that they can actually determine the job-evaluation scheme which is to be used varies considerably. In the service sector, where union organisation is often considerably weaker than in manufacturing industries, unions have tended to take the approach of using such influence as they have to amend the arrangements proposed by management, rather than seeking a totally different job-evaluation scheme.

One of the leaders in the pay consultancy market is Hay Management Consultants. Their scheme is offered to managements on the implied basis that it satisfies the equal-value legislation and they have drawn up a manual which gives guidance on good equal opportunities practice in the operation of their job-evaluation system. The Hay package also offers organisations access to the consultants' data bank of comparative salary rates as a benchmark for pay determination, which makes it particularly attractive to many employers. A union which generally cooperated with the use of Hay evaluation systems is the Banking Insurance and Finance Union (BIFU) in the finance sector. BIFU guidelines warn of potential disadvantages of the scheme but argue that with union involvement many of the worst aspects can be overcome. Similarly USDAW agreed to the introduction of a Hay-evaluated payment structure at the retailers, Sainsbury's.

Other unions are more resistant to the use of consultants' schemes, expressing the view that factors used in such schemes are biased towards managerial jobs to the disadvantage of both clerical and manual positions; the schemes reinforce the *status quo*, are too complex and are loaded in management's favour. Some union representatives have argued that these weaknesses are inherent to such schemes and cannot be overcome (IRS, September 1989). It appears that some unions, believing that the weaknesses of certain of the schemes marketed by consultants make them discriminatory against women, aim to test this assertion in the courts (IRS, January 1990)

In some cases, unions themselves may have an interest in the *status quo* and this will itself effect the impact of any new evaluation scheme on women's pay. Where, for example, the group which stands to gain from a more equitable evaluation is weaker in terms of number or industrial muscle than those which will lose out, in relative terms, unions may not wish to see the existing pay hierarchy changed too much. Similarly the PSI found that both management and unions tend to look for a new pay structure which is 'felt fair' by the workforce. In some cases the most 'felt-fair' outcomes will be those which reinforce the *status quo*. This may be one reason why in the PSI research job-evaluation schemes were found to be accepted more readily when they were non-analytical than when they were analytical (Ghobadian and White, 1986).

Finally, as IRS found, union representatives involved in designing and/or implementing job-evaluation schemes may develop a strong sense of identification with the scheme. In all three of the IRS case studies they quickly became bound-up in and committed to, the job-evaluation schemes which they were implementing. The outcome of the Save the Children Fund (SCF) scheme was considerable change in the pay structure. However, at UB (Ross Youngs), while women received substantial pay rises, their position in the pay hierarchy remained the same, and the groups which benefited most from the Clarks Shoes exercise were predominantly male-dominated. Whatever the relative merits of the schemes in these three cases, it is common for union representatives who may have spent months involved in the process of job evaluation to be largely uncritical of its outcome, whether or not it has improved the pay position of women members.

TO WHAT EXTENT ARE EQUITABLE JOB-EVALUATION SCHEMES ACHIEVABLE?

As the IRS article explains, many long-standing job-evaluation schemes, including the one which previously applied to local authority manual workers and the one which is in the process of being replaced for non-manual workers, can be criticised for discriminating against jobs commonly undertaken by women on a number of counts. For example, they have become dated and they cannot deal with the range of work undertaken by workers in the 1990s; they are biased towards jobs with professional status and managerial responsibilities and position – features of predominantly male posts – and against skills typical of female jobs such as caring for people; they are too mechanistic in their approach to the education and experience required by a job, emphasising formal qualifications and years of training over valuable experience of other kinds; they emphasise quantity – for example, number of people supervised – over quality; and they emphasise certain forms of physical effort such as that resulting from heavy lifting rather than strain which results from repetition – a common feature of jobs which women do (IRS, January 1990).

The Equal Opportunities Commission, the TUC and individual unions are just some of the organisations to offer advice on job evaluation and equal value. However, despite the implications behind advice provided by the Equal Opportunities Commission and others, it is questionable whether it is possible to have a job-evaluation scheme which does not value the attributes of jobs done by one sex more than those done by another. Discrimination lawyer, Michael Rubenstein, has pointed out that redressing an imbalance towards one set of skills necessarily involves making decisions in favour of another (Rubenstein, 1984). This is the process which took place in two of the case studies described in the IRS research, and which resulted in a substantial improvement in the pay position of women workers; therefore it is probably not possible to have a non-discriminatory job-evaluation system. Changes to job-evaluation schemes which provide a better assessment of the jobs done by women will necessarily be made at the expense of work in which men predominate. So, given continuing job segregation, in order to improve the pay position of women by using job evaluation, it is necessary to look for schemes which are biased less strongly towards 'male' skills and more strongly in favour of the content of jobs typically done by women.

In considering ways of producing job evaluation schemes which give greater value to 'female' skills and attributes, IRS research suggests that it is necessary to distinguish between the design of job evaluation schemes and the process of implementing them, since even where a scheme has been designed with the aim of ascribing the proper worth to jobs done by women, this aim may be undermined when values are given to individual jobs, or when new payment structures are introduced. The following is a summary of the major considerations addressed by the organisations involved in the IRS research when they were designing and implementing job evaluation schemes which attempted to eliminate sex bias (IRS, September 1989).

Designing a scheme

Age of scheme
The EOC advises that any scheme which has been in use for several years should be examined for discriminatory effects with a view to review or overhaul (EOC, 1985). Changes in workforce composition, in technology and in legal context have all been found to undermine the value of job-evaluation systems over a period of time. These reasons have been cited as contributing to the introduction of new job evaluation schemes in the finance sector (IRS January 1990).

Simplicity of the system
In all three of the case studies discussed in by IRS, unions and management stressed that one of the reasons why they chose to design their own schemes was because they wanted systems which were simple, open and easy to understand and which would therefore be more acceptable to the workforce as a

whole. The Hay system was rejected at SCF and Clark's Shoes partly because it did not meet these conditions.

Selecting the factors

Analytical job-evaluation schemes assess job content against a list of 'factors' which may include mental and physical skills and effort; level of responsibility; experience and/or qualifications; and working conditions. Factor choice is inherently selective and it is at this stage that unfair bias against jobs usually done by women commonly creeps in. Commentators such as the EOC stress the importance of ensuring that elements which feature in the jobs done by women are not omitted and that those in 'male' jobs are not given too much prominence (EOC, 1985).

Many job-evaluation systems have been criticised as taking an excessively mechanistic view of job requirements so that prominence is given to paper qualifications while broader experience and skill are undervalued or ignored. This can indirectly discriminate against women who may have had less opportunity to obtain paper qualifications but who will use other valuable skills and experience in their work such as the 'people-centred' skills gained from caring for children or old people.

In each of the IRS case studies, consideration was given to avoiding a perceived bias in previous systems against the jobs done by women. However, since the work undertaken in the three organisations is very different, the means used to redress the balance varied. For example, in one case – the food company UB (Ross Youngs) – the concern was to boost the position of workers on the production line who were largely female. This was done by introducing 'stamina' and 'paced work' subfactors into the scheme. At the children's charity, SCF, the position of women working with pre-school age children was of particular concern so the range and depth of human relationships was one factor to be introduced, and an 'essential skills' factor replaced a previous emphasis on formal qualifications.

Defining 'levels'

Once factors have been selected 'levels' are drawn up under each factor heading representing increasing levels of demand for that factor. To ensure that a job-evaluation scheme is able to compare all the jobs to be covered, levels need to be defined in such a way as to allow proper differentiation between jobs with different levels of demand. A problem with many traditional job-evaluation schemes is that excessively large steps between levels forces work commonly done by women into lower scoring levels which do not recognise the full responsibilities and demands of the job.

Weighting factors
This involves making value judgements concerning the relative importance of factors. The EOC points out that 'it is extremely easy for sex discrimination to appear in a job-evaluation procedure as a result of discriminatory weightings' (EOC, 1985, p. 10); indeed it is questionable whether it is ever possible to apply weightings fairly. Weightings will undermine the effect of carefully chosen factors when they give low values to factors which predominate in 'female' jobs and high to typically 'male' elements.

Implementing the scheme

Composition of committees
It is generally agreed that all committees involved in the design or implementation of job-evaluation schemes should involve equal numbers of men and women, should include workforce representation and should be representative of the range of jobs being evaluated. This is because, however carefully designed, job evaluation is in the end a subjective process which relies on the ability of those applying a scheme to assess the value of the jobs involved. If, for example, women are excluded from decision-making then the danger that old biases against typically female work will remain, is increased, as is the risk that the self-interest of certain groups may lead them to underestimate or understate the the worth of particular jobs.

Training committee members
The EOC stresses the importance of training all those involved in the design and implementation of schemes so that they are aware of pitfalls which may lead to bias against work commonly done by women (EOC, 1985).

The issue of who should conduct this training is a critical, although difficult, one. Some of the consultant's schemes, notably Hay's, are highly complex, and those involved in the evaluation process require considerable technical knowledge of the way the scheme operates and is being implemented in the particular organisation concerned. For this reason it is common practice for both unions and management to receive training from Hay employees. Yet this can be seen to reinforce the likelihood that union representatives will find it difficult to distance themselves sufficiently from the evaluation process to ensure that it is treating women fairly. So there is a strong argument for providing training in the pitfalls of job evaluation which is independent of management and, if relevant, of the consultants implementing the scheme.

Choosing benchmark jobs
In the IRS case studies, all the jobs to be covered by the job-evaluation system were assessed. However, according to the EOC, most schemes involve the selection of benchmark jobs seen as representative of others in the organisation as the basis of the final job-evaluation exercise. This may open the door to an equal-value claim if any woman can show that the benchmark jobs along side which she has been 'slotted' is not fully representative of the work she does as assessed in terms of its 'demand factors'.

Writing job descriptions
Since job evaluation is carried out using written job descriptions, the quality and consistency of those descriptions is very important to the fairness of the outcome. The EOC recommends that a standard format should be used and that guidance notes should be provided to those completing the job description. They also advise that the jobholder, their superior and an independently trained job analyst should be involved in the process (EOC, 1985).

None of the IRS case-study organisations employed a job analyst, although at UB (Ross Youngs) two outside specialists, one appointed by the union and one by management, did have a role. At Clarks Shoes all employees were given two hours training in the completion of job descriptions, which was then carried out by the individuals concerned and their supervisor. Both unions and management report that the quality of job descriptions was dependent on the level of commitment of the supervisor concerned. Union representatives at SCF have expressed concern in retrospect at the lack of independent support to individual members of staff in completing their job questionnaires. Despite detailed guidance notes it is felt that women tended to undersell or ignore important parts of their job.

Designing the payment structure
The EOC warn that even when discrimination has been avoided this far, it may occur when grades or rates of pay are fixed. They advise that grade boundaries should be drawn at the position on the job hierarchy where there is a gap between scores and should be 'objectively based on the evidence provided by the evaluation, irrespective of the sex of the jobholders' (EOC, 1985, p. 13).

Since this is the process which determines the final cost of a job-evaluation scheme to an employer and the relative benefit of the restructuring to different groups of workers, it is hardly surprising that the negotiations involved in setting pay rates can dilute the potential impact of even the most radical job-evaluation arrangements, especially where it is decided, as in the case of local authority manual workers, that significant elements of the payment package are not determined by job evaluation.

CONCLUDING COMMENTS

Job evaluation cannot deal with the effects of job segregation where this results in women being employed in work which is actually less skilled or has fewer responsibilities than that done by men – fairer job-evaluation schemes can simply help to highlight the value of previously ignored job attributes. Whether they do this and whether the eventual payment structure actually reflects these values is a political rather than a technical process and it would be a mistake to put too much reliance on job evaluation as a way of dealing with the weaker position in which women often find themselves in the labour market. Where the social, market and industrial-relations pressures on pay rates are strongest in respect of 'male' jobs, employers will probably resist the introduction of a new job-evaluation scheme which would commit them to pay structure which cannot respond to those pressures.

However, certain developments could tilt the balance in favour of women workers. First, the Labour Force Survey has shown that the number of young people entering the labour market is likely to decline from 2.5 million in 1989 to 2 million in 1994. As this 'demographic time bomb' takes effect, employers are in some instances being forced to look for other sources of labour to undertake work traditionally done full-time by men. Second, as organisations in certain parts of the country, particularly the south-east of England, find labour less readily available in skilled 'female' occupations such as secretarial work they may be forced to acknowledge the value of such work through their payment systems. Additionally, major unions have in recent years introduced campaigns to recruit more female members and to negotiate on issues which are of particular interest to women. These campaigns include the GMB's 'Winning a fair deal for women' and the TGWU's 'Link Up' campaign which aimed to address the interests of part-time workers – a predominantly female group. Finally the major proprietary job-evaluation schemes used in the UK – these include systems offered by Hay, PE Inbucon, Wyatt and other consultants as well as the Institute of Administrative Management system which is used for large numbers of office workers – have yet to be tested in the British courts. Should such a scheme be found to discriminate against women, employers would need to take a fresh look at their job-evaluation arrangements to ensure that they acknowledge the value of work done by their women employees.

Note

1. A key part of the IRS research focuses on case studies of three organisations: Clarks-Shoes Ltd, in the footwear industry; food manufacturer UB (Ross Youngs) and the charity Save the Children Fund. In each case unions and management collaborated in an attempt to design and introduce job-evaluation schemes free of sex bias, although equal-value considerations were only one of the factors behind the decision to go through this exercise.

References

ACAS (1990) *Developments in Payment Systems: the 1988 ACAS survey.* Equal Opportunities Commission (1985) *Job Evaluation Schemes Free of Sex Bias.*

Armstrong, P. (1982) 'If It's Only Women's Work It Doesn't Matter So Much' in West, J (ed.) *Work, Women and the Labour Market* (London: Routledge & Kegan Paul).

Coyle, A. (1982) 'Sex and Deskilling in the Organisation of the Clothing Industry' in West, J. (ed.) *Work, Women and the Labour Market* (London: Routledge & Kegan Paul).

Craig, C., Gannsey, E. and Rubery, J. (1985) *Payment Structures in Small Firms Women's Employment in Segmented Labour Markets* (London: Department of Employment Research Paper 48).

Crompton, R. and Jones, G. (1984) *Deskilling and Gender in Clerical Work* (London: Macmillan).

Department of Employment (1989) *New Earnings Survey* (London: Department of Employment).

Equal Opportunities Commission (1985) *Job Evaluation Schemes Free of Sex Bias* (Manchester: EOC).

Ghobadian, A. and White, M. (1986) *Job Evaluation and Equal Pay* Policy Studies Institute (Department of Employment Research Paper no 58).

Horrell, S., Rubery, J. and Burchell, B. (1989) 'Unequal Jobs or Unequal Pay?' *Industrial Relations Journal*, vol. 20, no 3, pp. 176–91.

Horrell, S., Rubery, J. and Burchell, B. (1990) 'Gender and Skills', *Work, Employment and Society*, vol. 4, no. 2 pp. 189–216.

Industrial Relations Services (1989) 'Job Evaluation: The Road to Equality?' *Industrial Relations Review and Report 448*, pp. 5–10.

Industrial Relations Services (January 1990) 'Job Evaluation and Equal Value: Recent Developments', *Industrial Relations Review and Report 455* pp. 11–14.

Industrial Relations Services (May 1990) 'Conflicting pressure evident in retail pay awards' *Pay and Benefits Bulletin 255* pp. 5–9.

Labour Research Department (June 1990) 'Equal Pay Claims on the Move', *Bargaining Report*, pp. 12–14.

London Equal Value Steering Group (LEVEL) (1987) 'A Question of Earnings – A Study of the Earnings of Blue-Collar Employees in London Local Authorities'.

Millward, N. and Stevens, M. (1986) *British Workplace Industrial Relations 1980–84* (Aldershot: Gower).

Rubenstein, M. (1984) *Equal Pay for Work of Equal Value* (London: Macmillan).

4 Comparable Worth and its Impact on Black Women
Julianne Malveaux

Comparable worth is an issue that has maintained a high place on the 'women's agenda' for social and economic equity since 1980, when the then EEOC Director, Eleanor Holmes Norton, described it as 'the civil rights issue of the 1980s'. Given its visibility it is amazing that little research has focused on the ramifications of comparable worth in the black community, or on the implications of comparable worth for black women. In fact, there seems to be an assumption that because comparable worth is on the 'women's agenda' it will have uniform impacts on black and white women. Alternatively, the assumption has been that there is no reason to focus on the special needs of black women because comparable worth will 'help us all'.

The failure to analyse differences among women, and to note different ways in which policy can have an impact on women, makes the use of the term 'a women's agenda' more exclusive than inclusive. This exclusion (of women who are 'other') is not restricted to analysis of comparable worth. In fact, when one views the use of the word 'woman' in the social-science literature, one is most frequently struck with disappointment at the intellectual myopia that allows researchers to use the word 'woman' globally, but at the same time to assert indirectly that 'women' have similar labour-force characteristics, regardless of race.

Marianne Ferber, for example, criticises male researchers for the global use of terms, while at the same time writing about women and failing to note that not all of them are white. Cynthia Epstein similarly writes about black women in some of her work, but blatantly ignores them in her book *Women and Law* (Ferber, 1982; Epstein, 1981).

Maybe these women ignore the status of minority women

because they think it is identical to the status of white women. After all, a growing literature on 'convergence' asserts that racial biases among women have been eliminated while gender biases remain. This growing literature ignores or rejects the Darity and Myers argument that wage 'convergence' is (i) not dramatic, given the historical differences between black and white women's labour-force participation, and (ii) the result of two very different phenomena – of white women entering the labour market, and of black women doing different jobs (Smith, 1979; Darity and Myers, 1980).

The convergence argument might retire to the obscure cobwebs of theory were it not for the policy implications of the assertion that black and white women are similar. An assertion of similarity suggests that policies designed to improve the status of white women will also improve the status of black women, in the same amounts and for the same reason. But much of my own work shows that this assertion is not true (Malveaux, 1985a).

This chapter explores ways in which comparable worth affects black women. While detailed data on comparable-worth cases is not presented, this chapter explores my assertion that there are different sets of benefits which black and white women will derive from comparable worth.

COMPARABLE WORTH AND BLACK WOMEN

Can comparable worth improve the economic status of black women? To answer this question it is useful to review the occupational status of black women. Like white women, the majority of black women (more than 60 per cent) work in typically female clerical and service occupations. Proportionately fewer black than white women work in management, sales, and professional jobs, while proportionately more black women work in service, operative (manufacturing), and private household jobs (Malveaux, 1985a).

Within occupational categories, though, there are differences in the status of black and white women. Among clerical workers, black women are more likely to be found as filing clerks, typists, calculating-machine operators, and social welfare clerical assistants. Except for social welfare clerical assistants, all these occupations have wages below the median clerical wage (Malveaux, 1984). Among service workers, black women are heavily represented as chambermaids, nursing aides, and practical nurses. Again, pay was lower in those occupations where black women were heavily represented.

Another key difference between black and white women's employment is the heavy concentration of black women in public-sector employment. In 1981, 16 per cent of all workers were employed by federal, state or local governments. In contrast, 26 per cent of black women held government employment. Proportionately more black women than any other race–sex group were employed by governments – 18 per cent of black men, 17.5 per cent of white women, and 12.9 per cent of white men were so employed. 20 per cent of all clerical workers are employed by governments; but nearly 33 per cent of black female clerical workers (compared with less than 18 per cent of white clerical workers) are so employed (Malveaux, 1984).

Because of differences in the occupational status and employers of black and white women, one can conclude that implementation of comparable-worth pay strategies will have a positive impact on the wage status of black women. Comparable worth's positive impact will come both because black women work in typically female clerical jobs that are underpaid, and because a disproportionate number of black women work for governments, where comparable-worth strategies are most likely to be implemented.

There is an additional reason why black women will gain from comparable worth. Although black women work in clerical jobs similar to the clerical jobs in which white women work, they work in a set of clerical jobs that earn lower pay than the clerical jobs in which white women work. In a book in 1984 I explored the concept of 'black women's crowding', which is defined as distinct from the 'women's crowding' that white women experience (Malveaux, 1984). It is noted that although black women are just 5.4 per cent of the labour force, their representation in some jobs is as high as 35 per cent. In this chapter, I suggest that this form of crowding results in lower wages for black women, and note that, in clerical occupations, black women are overrepresented in some of the lowest-paying clerical jobs. This means that black women in clerical occupations tend to be underpaid relative to their white counterparts.

This overrepresentation among the lowest paying jobs suggests differential effects from the implementation of comparable worth. Table 4.1 shows the results of an exercise that illustrates this point. Pay gaps revealed by Remick in State of Washington data were supplemented by data on the percentage of black women in certain jobs (Malveaux, 1984; Remick, 1981). Where all women were overrepresented, but black women were underrepresented, workers were paid an average of 94 per cent of what they should have been paid based on job evaluation estimates. But in jobs where black women were overrepresented (with their representation in a job category of 15 per cent or more), workers were paid 76 per cent of what they should have been paid. Implementation of comparable worth, in this case, would improve the relative position of black women in 'typically black female' jobs.

COMPARABLE WORTH AND BLACK COMMUNITY GAINS

The black community, as well as black women, will accrue gains when comparable worth is implemented. The first gain is an obvious one – the gain from higher black family wages when black women earn equitable pay. Given the large number of black women heading households, the need for black women to earn equitable pay cannot be overstated. But even where there is another household earner, black women's contribution to black family income frequently makes the difference between black family poverty and black family survival (Wallace, 1980).

Black men will also gain from comparable worth because they are more likely than white men to hold those 'typically female' jobs in which pay would be adjusted. In 1982 I noted differences in the distribution of black and white men and speculated this may be because black men have, in the past, been excluded from the professional, managerial, and craft jobs in which white men have been concentrated. In the same vein, Giddings writes of the Moynihan suggestion that black women's jobs be 'redesigned' for black men as one way to combat high levels of black male unemployment (Malveaux, 1982; Giddings, 1984).

There is another potential gain to the black community from

Black Women

Table 4.1 Black women's pay when they are
overrepresented and underrepresented in occupations

Job title	Actual salary	Predicted salary	Ratio	% female Washington State	% Black female national
Black women are *over*represented as:					
Intermediate clerk	921	1208	76.2	81.0	17.9
Intermediate clerk/ typist	968	1269	76.3	96.7	16.3
Telegraph operator	887	1239	71.6	95.7	15.5
Data entry operator	1017	1239	82.1	96.5	18.1
Licensed practical nurse	1030	1367	75.3	89.5	18.5
Average			76.3	91.9	17.3
Black women are *under*represented as:					
Legal secretary	1269	1401	90.6	98.7	5.0
Word processor	1082	1301	83.2	98.3	5.0
Bookkeeper	1122	1269	88.4	87.0	5.2
Administrative assistant	1334	1472	90.6	95.1	2.6
Intermediate accountant	1585	1585	100.0	60.2	4.4
Lab technician	1208	1401	86.2	84.1	5.2
Retail sales clerk	921	1239	74.3	100.0	4.9
Pharmacist	1980	1666	118.8	60.0	2.7
Librarian	1625	1794	90.6	84.6	5.1
Community programme developer	1932	1750	110.4	60.0	4.7
Administrative services manager	1839	1794	102.5	73.4	2.6
Average			94.1	81.9	4.3

Sources: Remick (1981); unpublished BLS data; Malveaux (1984).

adopting a comparable-worth strategy. Comparable worth relies on the implementation of a 'single, neutral' job-evaluation
process and uncovers systematic gender bias that results in very
different rates of pay for workers whose jobs have a comparable

number of evaluation points. Once flaws in the job-evaluation process are uncovered, an examination of job evaluations begin, it is likely that pay inequities will be revealed in job categories where minority males are heavily concentrated. In San Francisco, job evaluation revealed that janitors, mostly minority males, received 97 evaluation points and $18 000 in pay. Truck drivers, mostly white males, had 98 evaluation points, about $27 000 in pay (Shreiner, 1985). In Alameda County, California, a contrast of the job classifications dominated by minorities and those dominated by non-minorities revealed a 76 per cent pay gap, a smaller gap than revealed when job classifications dominated by women, and those dominated by men are compared. (This gap was 37 per cent) (SEIU, 250, 535, 616; 1985). Thus, because systematic racial bias is as likely to occur as systematic gender bias, the adoption of comparable strategies may have a benefit to the black community that is greater than the gain to black women.

Although there is potential for black people to gain from comparable worth in municipalities, it is critical to note that comparable-worth gains will not accrue to the black community merely because comparable worth is being considered in a community. The process of examining job evaluations merely opens the door for black activists and trade unionists to evaluate racial biases that may exist in job evaluation. Clearly, the subjectivity inherent in job-evaluation processes has affected black people (and other minorities) as much as it has affected women. But because comparable worth has been seen as a 'women's issue', the inclusion of jobs that are 'typically' minority in settlement processes may be one of that requires political coalition building tactics.

Some researchers and activists detail ways to include the crowding of minorities into comparable-worth consideration; others see the inclusion of minorities in comparable-worth strategies as 'muddying the waters' (Comparable Worth Project, 1982; Malveaux, 1985b). Still others, for reasons of political pragmatism, choose not to see the connection between race and sex discrimination. But whenever one acknowledges that job evaluations have allowed the introduction of subjective biases in the way wages are paid, then it is a small step to move from correction of gender biases to correction of racial biases.

LIMITATIONS TO COMPARABLE WORTH STRATEGY

While comparable-worth strategies promise clear gains for black women (and men) who are employed in the public sector, the implementation of comparable worth will not solve all the employment problems of the black community. In fact, some have argued that comparable worth is a strategy limited to solving the problems of workers in low-paying, typically female jobs (Killingsworth, 1985). In any case, no assessment of comparable worth's impact on the black community is complete without a discussion of strategy limitations.

Comparable worth's benefits are limited to public-sector employees

Unless far-reaching national legislation is passed, which is not likely before 1989, comparable worth is likely to be implemented in cities and states, and to apply solely to those workers employed in the public sector. Private-sector employers are not likely, in the absence of legislation, to implement comparable worth.

Even as comparable worth is discussed as a strategy, however, workers who were formerly employed in the public sector have found their jobs subcontracted to private employers. These workers are employed primarily in food and cleaning service occupations, and are mostly minorities (Malveaux, 1984).

When jobs leave the civil service structure, the question of 'comparable pay' for those jobs is irrelevant. Instead, because subcontractors compete for contracts on the basis of a low bid it is likely that the wages and working conditions of workers will decline when their jobs move from the public sector to the private sector. Strategies to ensure fair wages, hours and working conditions for these workers are not likely to include comparable-worth strategies.

While this discussion is not meant to minimise the importance of comparable-worth strategies, it makes it clear that a substantial segment of employed black women (more than 22 per cent of whom hold service jobs) are likely to find comparable worth a strategy inapplicable to their situation. Strategies to limit contracting out are more appropriate strategies for improving the status of these women.

Comparable worth strategies are limited to employed workers

Black female unemployment rates are more than twice white female rates (15.4 per cent and 6.5 per cent respectively, in 1984). Strategies to improve the status of employed women will, of necessity, exclude the unemployed. For these women, affirmative-action strategies are likely to facilitate entry into paid employment, while comparable worth will facilitate the equitable pay process.

Comparable-worth strategies may not include women who participate in 'workfare' programmes

Although the mechanics of employment and pay in workfare programmes are in draft stage (at least in California where legislation was passed in 1985), it is clear that a disproportionate number of black women receive public assistance. If jobs are not available in the private sector, then workfare women will be provided with jobs in the public sector, paid below 'market' wages, and possibly 'make-work' jobs (Workfare is a programme requiring work of welfare recipients. Make-work jobs are jobs that are unnecessary, meaningless, routine. Workfare often involves make-work jobs.) These women may be substitutes for unionised civil service workers who perform the same tasks. Given the low pay rates built into workfare legislation, the issue of comparable pay will also not be an issue for these women.

Comparable-worth strategies will not affect women forced to participate in the underground economy

Women on welfare are likely to participate in underground economy employment because welfare payments are not large enough to provide for the needs of their families. Though there is little solid information on employment sources for these women, anecdotal information suggests that these women work in the service sector, in laundries and as hotel maids, and in related 'typically female' service jobs.

It is important to note that discussion of women's participation in the underground economy while receiving welfare benefits is not an attempt to 'blame the victim' or put further restrictions on such women (many of whom are penalised for college attendance by reduction in welfare payments), but rather an attempt to point out the implicit subsidy offered to those employers who hire these women and pay them minimum or below-minimum wages. Reform in this area should begin with investigation of employers, not employees.

In any case, while the number of women participating in the underground economy while receiving welfare payments cannot be estimated, it is likely that a disproportionate number of them are black (because a disproportionate number of the women on welfare are black). Comparable-worth strategies, no matter what their importance to women employed in the public sector, will not help these women.

Comparable worth will not help women who hold semi-skilled and unskilled jobs

Comparable worth may improve the status of women working in jobs where their skills are undervalued, but those women who work in semi-skilled and unskilled jobs will not benefit from implementation of comparable worth. Unionisation is possibly the most direct way to ensure fair wages, hours, and working conditions for these women.

While comparable worth offers the opportunity for improvement of the wages of some black workers, it is a strategy that will not address the employment situation of many others. It is important to view comparable worth, then, as one of a set of strategies to improve the employment status of black workers. Other strategies include affirmative action, full employment legislation, job creation, encouragement of unionisation, and legislation to limit contracting out.

DISTRIBUTIONAL ASPECTS OF COMPARABLE WORTH

Comparable worth is an activist strategy; it is one that requires activists to agitate and lobby legislators to support revising the way state or local civil service jobs are evaluated. While the thrust of this chapter has been to highlight the benefits accruing to black women as a result of implementation of comparable worth, this section raises questions about activist priorities and ways in which they may change depending on the demographics and fiscal realities in a state or municipality. Again, this discussion is not meant to detract from the real value of comparable-worth strategies, but to suggest ways to evaluate the benefits from comparable worth.

How are black women distributed in a given community?

If more black women are service workers than clerical workers, greater impact may be gained by encouraging unionisation and limiting the contracting-out of service activities. While comparable worth will help clerical workers gain equitable pay, institutional arrangements will determine how service workers are paid.

Where will money to pay comparable-worth pay adjustments come from?

If it will come from educational budgets, from community service budgets, or from other budgets beneficial to the black community, then legislators opposed to comparable worth are likely to make that point. (In San Francisco, the mayor has asked all city departments to take a 5 per cent budget cut, supposedly to pay for a $28 million comparable-worth settlement.) If money will come from budget items particularly helpful to the black community, then careful evaluation of the budget process is in order. While comparable-worth wage adjustments should not take the blame for budget shifts (what cost fairness?), activists should be cognisant of budget battles likely to emerge from comparable-worth settlements, and be prepared to fight these battles with broad-based coalitions of black community activists, trade unionists, and female activists.

Will workers in subcontracted jobs be affected?

This question (and its answer) is related to the previous one, but is raised separately because so many minority women are found in subcontracted service jobs. Are there ways in which the impact of such trade-offs can be reduced? It may be appropriate to consider supporting the rights of workers whose jobs may be subcontracted with a coalition similar to the one described above.

Will there be a tax increase to pay for comparable worth?

If so, what is the tax incidence? Tax increases may provide black taxpayers with a springboard for demanding that issues of racial crowding and bias in job-evaluation processes be considered.

What is the relationship between comparable worth and affirmative action?

Since affirmative action deals with all the terms and conditions of employment, including hiring, recruitment, promotion, transfer, and wages, comparable worth should be considered a subset of an overall affirmative-action strategy. However, comparable worth has too frequently been considered a self-standing strategy, and in some cases a sole strategy instead of one in a series of strategies. Black workers who support comparable worth should not lose sight of broader affirmative-action tactics, and should consider brokering their support of comparable worth for stronger support of affirmative-action efforts.

In general, comparable worth will have a positive impact on black women's wages. But the size of the impact will differ by community, and will depend on the proportion and distribution of black women in the public sector. Additionally, the positive impact of comparable worth on black women will depend on how legislators propose to pay for comparable worth and whether black community services or tax payments are adversely affected by comparable-worth costs.

A key point for the black community to consider is the fact that questions about gender bias in job evaluation lead to related questions about racial bias. Comparable-worth strategies are most likely to raise these questions when black workers are involved in defining those strategies. To the extent that comparable-worth strategies raise these questions, and ultimately change these pay scales, black women and the black community are both beneficiaries.

CONCLUSION

Clearly, many aspects of this chapter are conjectural. But it lays out a framework for an empirical investigation of the impact of comparable worth on the black community. Preliminary investigation suggests that comparable worth is likely to have clear positive effects. A discussion of distributional issues highlights ways in which comparable-worth concepts may be used to strengthen the entire employment position of black workers in municipalities.

When employment policies are considered for the black community, an important factor is the diversity of the black population and their employment status. From this standpoint comparable worth should be viewed as one of a series of strategies to improve the status of black women. While comparable worth will not help black women who are unemployed, who work in the private sector, who participate in underground economies or in workfare programmes, it will have a positive effect on black women (and some black men) in public-sector jobs. As long as comparable-worth strategies are developed in tandem with other strategies to improve the employment status of black women, the black community has nothing to lose and much to gain by supporting comparable worth.

References

Comparable Worth Project (1982) *First Steps to Identify Sex- and Race-based Pay Inequities in a Workplace* (Oakland: Comparable Worth Project).

Darity, William and Myers, Sam (1980) 'Changes in Black–White Income Inequality, 1968–1978: A Decade of Progress?', *Review of Black Political Economy*, 10 (Summer 1980) pp. 354–79.

Epstein, Cynthia Fuchs (1981) *Women in Law* (New York: Basic Books).

Ferber, Marianne (1982) 'Women and Work: Issues of the 1980s', *Signs: Journal of Women in Culture and Society*, 8(2) (Winter 1982) pp. 273–95.

Giddings, Paula (1984) *When and Where I Enter: The Impact of Black Women on Race and Sex in America* (New York: William Morrow).

Killingsworth, Mark (1985) 'The Economics of Comparable Worth: Analytical, Empirical, and Policy Questions' in Heidi Hartmann (ed.) *Comparable Worth: New Directions for Research* (Washington, DC: National Academy Press).

Malveaux, Julianne (1982) 'Recent Trends in Occupational Segregation by Race and Sex', paper presented to the Committee on Women's Employment and Related Social Issues, National Academy of Sciences.

Malveaux, Julianne (1984) 'Low Wage Black Women: Occupational Descriptions, Strategies for Change', unpublished paper, NAACP Legal Defense and Education Fund.

Malveaux, Julianne (1985a) 'The Economic Interests of Black and White Women: Are they Similar?', *Review of Black Political Economy*, 14(1) (Summer 1985).

Malveaux, Julianne (1985b) 'An Activist's Guide to Comparable Worth', *North Star*, 1(1) (May 1985) pp. 22–31.

Remick, Helen (1981) 'The Comparable Worth Controversy', *IMPA Public Personnel Management Journal*, 10(4) (December 1981).

Shreiner, Tim (1985) 'How Comparable Worth Plan Works', *San Francisco Chronicle* (13 February 1985).

Service Employees International Union 250, 535, 616 (1985) *Wage Gap and Job Classification Data. Exhibits B and G* (Alameda County: SEIU).

Smith, James P. (1979) 'The Convergence to Racial Equality in Women's Wages' in Cynthia Lloyd *et al.* (eds), *Women in the Labor Market* (New York: Columbia University Press).

Wallace, Phyllis (1980) *Black Women in the Labor Force* (Cambridge: MIT Press).

5 Gender and Class in Comparable Worth
Linda M. Blum

> Of all the charges leveled against feminism . . . probably
> nothing rankles more than the well-worn accusation that it is
> 'just a middle class movement'. I used to have a half-dozen
> rebuttals ready at hand . . . But I have begun to think that it
> does matter.
>
> Ehrenreich, *Ms. Magazine*, 1987, p. 166.

Comparable worth has been praised as 'potentially the most
important development affecting women workers in American
history' (Freeman and Leonard, 1985, p. 2). And in the USA
much has been written about this potential from a public policy
perspective, discussing such issues as methodologies to measure wage inequities (Beatty and Beatty, 1984; Steinberg and
Haignere, 1987; Treiman, 1979, 1984), costs of implementation
(NCPE, 1984), and legal approaches for fighting through the
courts (Heen 1984; Dean *et al.*, 1984). However, in addition to
its policy implications, comparable worth can have important
political and ideological effects, transforming working wom-
en's awareness of class and gender inequality. This, in turn, can
have important ramifications for the American women's movement. It will be the purpose of this chapter to focus on this less
directly practical side of comparable worth, to place the issue
within the larger context of feminist politics in the USA. In
particular, the political and ideological effects will be examined
in the two local comparable-worth campaigns which I studied
in California.

As many social movement scholars have noted, the US wom-
en's movement has tended to be an élite movement with a
primary constituency of middle- to upper-class, white, highly
educated women (Carden, 1974, 1978; Eisenstein, 1981; Freeman, 1975). Although it tends to frame its issues as in the
interests of all women, and to express concern consistently for

95

all groups of women, the liberal feminism which predominates in the USA has done little for less affluent women. Nonetheless, overlooking this class limitation, analysts such as sociologist Carol Mueller (1987) and political scientist Joyce Gelb (1987) argue that American feminism should be considered successful because it has raised national awareness of gender issues and created widespread agreement with its central tenets, including 'equal pay for equal work'. Yet, as others point out (Katzenstein, 1987), compared with less-popular European movements, American feminism has gained few of the substantive benefits which working women so desperately need. Moreover, working-class and black women, whose agreement with feminist principles is quite high, tend to have a low sense of inclusion within the movement (Klein, 1987).

I argue that comparable worth has the potential to enlarge the base of the American feminist movement. Although it derives much of its rhetoric from liberal feminism, it also addresses and benefits women in a particular class location – the poorly paid, traditionally female jobs of the pink-collar ghetto. However, real differences of interest persist among women in spite of their shared gender. These differences have characterised the history of the struggle for women's rights. In addition, these conflicts affect the success and the shape of contemporary comparable-worth efforts.

THE HISTORICAL STRUGGLE

In the USA, the history of class divisions behind women's rights issues and conflict over *which* women feminism should represent dates back, at least, to the end of the suffrage era and the winning of the vote for women in 1920. During the struggle for the vote, trade-union women worked with élite suffrage groups like the National Women's Party and played a major role in the campaign to pass the 19th Amendment, the amendment to the Constitution which granted women the right to vote (Foner, 1980, pp. 56–60). (Unfortunately, this alliance did not extend to black women; white suffrage leaders were willing to use racist tactics in the Southern states [Giddings, 1984]). After the passage of the 19th Amendment such coalitions broke down, as unionists and élite groups developed competing approaches to the promotion of women's rights. Winning the passage of an Equal Rights Amendment (ERA), proclaiming the equal citizenship rights of women in all areas, became the major objective of the National Women's Party. However, most advocates of working-class women strongly opposed the ERA, and these two groups were to fight over this issue for the next forty years.

The National Women's Party campaign for the ERA between the 1920s and the 1960s represented 'an élite-sustained stage' of American feminism characterised by a small number of activists who 'pursued [the Amendment] doggedly and single-mindedly' (Taylor, 1986). In fact, the ERA defined women's rights as formal legal rights and property rights. Such a definition was most relevant to élite professional women (Rupp and Taylor, 1987, pp. 50, 200). However, this rights-oriented politics antagonised both black women and trade-union women, more interested in substantive protections such as labour regulation and voting rights. Mary Anderson, a leader of the Women's Trade Union League (WTUL) – an organisation formed in 1903 to further the interests of working-class women (Lehrer, 1987, p. 115) – and first director of the Women's Bureau of the Department of Labor, went so far as to accuse the National Women's Party of embracing 'a kind of hysterical feminism with a slogan for a program' (cited in Hole and Levine, 1971, p. 79). For their part, the union women in the WTUL and Women's Bureau put greater efforts into opposing the pro-ERA feminists than into either organising working women or fighting the exclusionary practices of the American Federation of Labor (Foner, 1980, pp. 138–9, 150; Rupp and Taylor, 1987, pp. 5–6, 144–53).

Trade-union women and their allies opposed the ERA because of their struggles to gain special protective legislation for women workers. Such legislation, restricting the hours and the conditions of women's employment, would have been invalidated by the Equal Rights Amendment – and it did, at least in part, represent some actual protection for working women from exploitative, dangerous, working conditions. However, protective legislation also justified occupational sex-segregation and lower pay, as it implied that women were demonstrably weaker than men, or that as mothers and potential mothers, women had 'special' needs. Because it inscribed gender difference into the law and restricted women's labour-market opportunities, protective legislation was vehemently opposed by the élite, pro-ERA feminists who defined women's interests strictly in terms of equal treatment. Further, many of these women shared a conservative, *laissez-faire* view of the labour market in which legal intervention was undesirable, hindering competition and handicapping women workers.

Although the context was greatly changed, the issue of the ERA v. protective legislation continued to divide and antagonise women's rights advocates even into the 1960s era of resurgent, mass-based feminism. When the National Organization for Women (NOW) initially endorsed the ERA, for example, union women were placed in a difficult position because their organisations still opposed it (Freeman, 1975). On the other hand, many trade-union women viewed protective measures as largely obsolete, if not discriminatory, by that late date. Therefore, by 1970, when Title VII of the Civil Rights Act had formally invalidated such special restrictions through the courts, a new generation of women could at last form a more broadly based movement for the Equal Rights Amendment (Freeman, 1987).[1]

The issue of protective legislation has been much debated by feminist and labour historians. Some argue that the National Women's Party, in promoting strict legal equality, represented the only group with 'a truly feminist standpoint' (Lehrer, 1987, p. 239; also Hole and Levine, 1971. Others argue, in contrast,, that the WTUL members should be considered 'industrial feminists' who pursued special legislation because, within the constraints faced, it was the most effective strategy available to better conditions for working-class women (Kirkby, 1987; also Feldberg, 1980). This debate highlights the complex relation between class and gender interests in the construction of women's issues.[2] But it also exemplifies the conflict between versions of women's interests which accept gender difference and women's 'special' traits and those which emphasise equal treatment and strict gender 'sameness'. This larger issue continues to be a problem for the American feminist movement and underlies some debates about comparable worth. Comparable worth – both because it calls for the recognition of women's distinct skills, and because it acknowledges that equal treatment accomplishes little when most women are not equally situated – is neither a gender-blind policy nor an argument for a gender-neutral labour market. Thus, some arguments made against it

– that it will in the long-run restrict women's opportunities and reinforce occupational segregation – parallel arguments made against protective legislation.

In contrast to women's legal and property rights, equal pay has long been a labour issue promoted by leftists and union women. Equal pay emerged as a demand in some of the earliest organising efforts of women clerical workers. In 1908, for example, the Bookkeepers and Accountants Union Local 1 of New York chose 'equal pay for equal work' as their slogan, implicitly including a comparable-worth standard by arguing that they were paid less than unskilled male hod-carriers (Feldberg, 1980, p. 57). After the Second World War, the Women's Bureau made the issue a priority, and the Equal Pay Act was introduced in every session of congress from 1945 until it was finally passed in 1963. This Act, which, like protective legislation, also serves to protect men from competition with cheaper female labour, originally included a comparable-worth standard of 'equal pay for jobs of equivalent value'. However, after seventeen years of failing to pass the Congress, the Equal Pay Act was finally passed in a narrower version, with an *equal* work standard (Johansen, 1984, pp. 31–3).

Although class divisions on the equal-pay issue were not as overt as those on the ERA and protective legislation, they were present. The pro-ERA National Women's Party remained publicly neutral, but worked against the Equal Pay Act behind the scenes (Freeman, 1987, p. 219). Women's Party members clearly believed the Equal Pay Act was a distraction from the more important objective of the ERA, and resented the leadership of the Women's Bureau, their long-standing antagonist (Rupp and Taylor, 1987, p. 175). For their part, Women's Bureau leaders pushed the Equal Pay Act during the Kennedy administration (1960–3) at least in part to defuse support for the ERA and the Women's Party (Mansbridge, 1986, pp. 9–10). Finally, Women's Bureau leaders later claimed they continued to fight the ERA mainly because the Women's Party had fought them on the Equal Pay Act (Rupp and Taylor, 1987, p. 176).

Interestingly, by the end of the 1970s, a nearly-reversed class and gender configuration had emerged around the ERA – in the context of the resurgent movement pro-ERA forces had finally come to represent a more inclusive alliance of middle- and working-class feminists. However, the moderate Republican women who were traditional supporters of the Amendment had been pushed out of any voice in their party by the rise of the New Right. As a result of such shifting alliances, much of the business community had reversed its historical support of the amendment. The ERA was no longer an anti-regulatory, anti-labour measure, but part of a liberal interventionist agenda (Freeman, 1987, pp. 220–1; Mansbridge, 1986, pp. 8–16). Yet, even in the 1970s, the campaign for the ERA continued to alienate black, union and working-class women from the women's movement (Giddings, 1984, pp. 340–8; Rupp and Taylor, 1987, p. 192). Feminist consensus in favour of the ERA did not mean that class divisions between women were now wholly unimportant. Differing class interests continued to affect feminist politics and the construction of policies.

COMPARABLE WORTH

After being dropped from the Equal Pay Act in 1963, comparable worth re-emerged as a distinct issue during the 1970s, primarily among women state and municipal workers. Public-sector unions with large female memberships have played a leadership role; the American Federation of State, County and Municipal Employees (AFSCME) in particular, has been at the forefront of the issue, and was involved in both the local cases which I studied.

In the private sector, with so few unionised women, there has been much less activity. But within the unionised pockets, some activity occurred in the 1970s, for example, among electrical and communications workers. The International Union of Electrical Workers continued efforts dating back to the Second World War to gain wage equity for women in the electrical industry; and the Communication Workers of America began to address the wage disparity issue in contract negotiations with AT&T, and continue to do so within the 'Baby Bells', the regional communications companies formed after the legally mandated break-up of AT&T (Grune, 1980).

Comparable worth did not really gain national prominence, however, until Eleanor Holmes Norton chaired the Equal Employment Opportunity Commission during the Carter Administration. She identified comparable worth as a priority issue, calling it the employment, civil rights *and* women's issue of the 1980s. During her tenure, national hearings were conducted on occupational segregation and wage disparities, the National Academy of Sciences produced an influential report on the topic, and the door was opened for litigation by the Supreme Court's decision in the Gunther case. This case stopped short of endorsing comparable worth, but it did allow claims of sex-based wage discrimination to be brought without meeting the strict equal-work requirement.

It was within this climate of growing national attention that the San Jose, California, case came to prominence. This case was one of the first successful cases of comparable-worth implementation, it was the first to involve a strike, and local activists used the timing of important national developments to attract extensive media coverage.

In the early 1980s San Jose, the fourth-largest city in California, employed only some 900 women and 3000 men. About 50 per cent of the women employees were clerical workers; another 20 per cent were semi-professionals employed in library and recreation jobs. After efforts to extend the benefits of the city's affirmative action policies throughout the 1970s, women employees led by their AFSCME bargaining agent prevailed upon the City to conduct a job-evaluation study like the Washington State study.[3] The study confirmed the existence of large sex-based wage inequities, ranging from 15 to 30 per cent, but the City resisted implementation of comparable-worth adjustments and negotiations dragged on over the next year with little progress. When the Supreme Court's favourable decision in the Gunther case was announced in June 1981, the San Jose union immediately filed an EEOC complaint and two weeks later called a strike. The strike lasted nine days, and because of the national focus on comparable worth, it garnered a great deal of media attention. The mayor of the city and the AFSCME bargaining agent, for example, were both flown to New York in the midst of the strike to be on 'Good Morning America', the nationwide network news programme.[4] The strike concluded when the union settled for $1.5 million in comparable-worth adjustments, covering about 700 women workers. The settlement stipulated that comparable-worth adjustments would be in addition to the general cost-of-living increase, rather than reducing the general increase, as the city had insisted. This settlement did not create full parity between equally evaluated male and female jobs. But the adjustments were substantial (as much as 15 per cent over two years), contract language was changed, and the precedent of the increases allowed for future progress (Flammang, 1986, 1987).

Originally in San Jose women had not been union-identified, but had organised and articulated their grievances as women and as predominantly female occupational groups. In efforts which were distinct from the union and from any class-based alliance with unionised male employees, both library and clerical employees formed their own groups and pressed for women's mobility, largely within the terms set by existing affirmative-action policies.[5] Although some women were trade-union members, few were active, and many did not see the local union as the appropriate vehicle for raising their concerns. This changed only as the limits of affirmative action became apparent and comparable worth was made a priority issue at the end of the decade. The involvement of a female AFSCME bargaining agent also contributed to this shift. However, until the late 1970s the union was led by and seen as primarily appropriate for blue-collar men. A fairly typical attitude was expressed by one woman:

> I was a member of the union for less than a year. I joined when I first came to the city. But I quit because the technicians got such a big raise that year, more of a raise than us. So I wanted to keep the dues for myself.

That women clerical workers were initially identified as feminists is demonstrated by the fact that they began meeting in a group called the 'City Women for Advancement' and engaging in what several described as consciousness-raising activity. One woman described herself, for example, by stating: 'I'm a real woman's libber!' This group began comparing wages of male and female jobs on their own, several years before the notion of comparable worth was introduced. The women's comparisons revealed, as one put it: 'we earned less than men who washed cars for the city!' However, another woman explained that comparing the men and women was not seen in any larger context at that time; and it was not seen as a union or bargaining issue:

We did that study years and years ago. And at that point it wasn't called comparable worth. And it wasn't a widespread thing. At that time, it wasn't related to the union at all. And we didn't really push for it. We always kind of talked about the inequities, whenever a group of women would get together, but we didn't begin to really push for changes to be made until we started talking about the Hay [job-evaluation] study.

Instead of 'pushing for changes to be made', the clerical women's group concentrated on making recommendations to top officials and the City Council. For example, in 1977 they presented a report to the council in which the unfair basis of women's wages was listed along with some twenty other points on which they hoped officials would act. Because of this consensual or 'ladylike' lobbying approach and lack of union affiliation, the City Women's group was later criticised by some as being all talk and no action, or for being primarily a social club.[6] But with the comparable-worth issue, many of these same women realised the need to have a voice, or power, in contract negotiations, and to some degree, became more sympathetic to a union identification.

Library workers also had their own organisation to improve their standing as members of a low-paid female-typed profession. One woman's comments exemplify this identification:

I don't want to leave librarianship to make an adequate salary in some field that pays more money. Why is that other field more financially rewarding? The only explanation I could come up with was because library work is run by women, and that's why it's not valued.

Comparable worth was embraced readily by librarians when introduced by AFSCME, although like the clerical workers, librarians had previously seen their efforts as distinct from and inappropriate to a union approach. The same woman explained the appeal of comparable worth:

I started in the library ten years ago, and when we'd say we wanted to raise our salaries and they'd say 'okay, sure fine. What are librarians in other jurisdictions getting?' Well, of course, we were all getting coolie wages because there was no sense comparing me to another coolie in another jurisdiction.

One of the reasons women employees in this case directed their efforts towards top officials rather than towards union activity was that San Jose had a relatively large number of women in top positions. The area had a high level of organised feminist activity, and women were very successful in gaining access to elected office (Flammang, 1985, 1986, 1987). In fact in 1974, with the election of a woman from the San Jose district to the State Assembly, and the election of a former council-member, Janet Gray Hayes, as San Jose mayor, Hayes and others began touting the city as 'the feminist capital of the nation'. By 1981, the year of the comparable-worth strike, women held a majority of seats on the city council, Mayor Hayes had been re-elected, the deputy city manager was a woman, and the city had inflated its slogan from 'the feminist capital of the nation' to the 'feminist capital of the world'. This climate led many of the low-paid women to expect some degree of support, and certainly less resistance from the City administration than they in fact encountered. And the antagonism toward female officials which developed among low-paid women during the comparable-worth effort was captured by one slogan on the picket line: 'If I hear the Mayor say this is the feminist capital of the world just once more, I'll puke!'

The female officials in San Jose were undoubtedly sincere in their feminist convictions, even as they opposed the union's actions, resisted the implementation of comparable worth, and threatened the jobs of those who participated in the strike. The Mayor in particular was embarrassed politically by the comparable-worth strike, and stated repeatedly to the press that she sympathised with those on strike, only disagreeing with their impatience (Tong, 1981). She also implied that city officials deserved principal credit for advancing the issue, calling the union's actions 'a giant step backwards for women's rights' (Keppel, 1981). Similarly, the woman assistant city manager told me that she felt comparable worth was a legitimate issue, but that San Jose could not get too far ahead of other employers. Low-paid women, in her view, should take a long-term perspective. However, for those whose pay-cheques were at stake, it was difficult to agree with this interpretation of progress on women's rights. A union woman explained her attitude toward women at the top this way:

It's funny because there were women with the power at that time. The opposition to comparable worth wasn't a real male trip. There wasn't a lot of badmouthing of the issue, and nobody ever came out and said: 'hey, that's all you should get paid!' I guess I just expected plain old empathy, from the mayor and from the city manager. A lot of the older gals on the picket line were saying: 'And where in the hell did she come from?' I mean, was she born with some silver spoon in her mouth?

The other local case which I studied, Contra Costa County, was influenced both by national events and by the San Jose effort. After the successful San Jose strike, a Contra Costa County comparable-worth coalition, representing some 2300 of the 3600 women employees of the County, was formed. The labour coalition included the large clerical union – like San Jose, an AFSCME local – along with the smaller social workers' union and nurses' association. After initial success in gaining endorsement for the principle of comparable worth, the Contra Costa coalition however, had more trouble gaining implementation than in San Jose. There were a number of reasons for this: the more hostile national climate created by the Reagan administration, the strained County budget, and the more conservative local gender politics. Efforts to gain a formal job-evaluation study documenting the extent of pay discrepancies repeatedly failed. Women activists, however, demonstrated impressive organising and negotiating abilities over a lengthy period, and conducted their own preliminary studies. Incremental adjustments were negotiated in three successive contracts, amounting to approximately 9 per cent in total increases. Because of this progress, the National Committee on Pay Equity had cited the Contra Costa case as a demonstration that the issue can be advanced, even within the context of 'fiscal stress' (NCPE, 1984, pp. 40–9).

In Contra Costa County, although social workers and nurses were more like women professionals in San Jose, the large clerical women's union was a more class-identified group and approached comparable worth with a different emphasis. Unlike San Jose women, they felt little initial tie to feminism. They referred to themselves not as women suffering discrimination, but as the 'working poor' (Vogt, 1972) and as poor 'breadwinning mothers' (*Contra Costa Times*, 1972; *Martinez Morning News-Gazette* 1972).

Clerical women in Contra Costa had organised on their own, unaffiliated with any national union, in a group called the United Clerical Employees in 1970, and conducted a successful strike in 1972. Because of the intensity of the strike experience, which lasted about a month, and the much-needed support they received from unions in the area, the clerical workers then affiliated with AFSCME and joined the regional labour council, identifying themselves as part of the larger labour movement. This labour identification was evidenced in their response to the County's justification for their low pay – the low pay of clerical workers in other localities. Rather than responding as the librarian in San Jose had to such arguments, that is, by seeing the problem as one of gender, they responded instead by identifying the need for unions. As one woman put it: 'There weren't any clericals *organized* in this whole state, so what did it prove if we all had the same wages?'

Other evidence that this group saw themselves first and foremost as *working-class* women can be found in press statements made during their strike in 1972. Their sentiments at that time anticipate comparable worth in many respects. One statement read:

> Ours is a truly oppressed class, penalized for being women and paid as if we were a bunch of kids fresh out of high school and still living at home with Daddy. Our ranks include highly skilled technicians who earn a top salary that is hundreds of dollars less than most unskilled labor earns. We approached management with a modest proposal this year and got kicked in the teeth for our efforts . . . and we intend to kick back! (*Martinez Morning News-Gazette*, 1972).

As I said earlier, the Contra Costa clerical workers' union only formally took up the comparable-worth issue after the San Jose strike. As one woman explained:

> In the early years of the United Clericals we did make some comparisons of job skills, test requirements and so forth, for clerks with janitors and laborers and so on. Some laborers made three or four times as much as us. And their only test was to fill out the application. Comparable worth is really just

a continuation of all our efforts. But nobody had a real good handle on it until the study was done in San Jose.

Other women commented on their lack of identification with the feminist movement. A more sympathetic clerical activist stated: 'I never considered myself a feminist, until I discovered I was one.' Another made her class antagonism more explicit:

> Say if you belong to NOW, you don't even need comparable worth. They're all upper-middle class, and mostly single. They don't have much to do with the day-to-day things of life, like whether you have any health insurance, or what to do if your husband leaves you with three kids.

Finally, another simply remarked: 'I'm not a women's libber, but I do believe that you have to have some education to be a clerical worker!'

One reason for low-paid women in Contra Costa to be less identified with feminism than San Jose women was that there were fewer local examples of its success. There were far fewer women in top positions, and many of the male officials were seen as very traditional in their views of women. Contra Costa would not be considered a feminist capital by any criteria. On the other hand, low-paid women did work closely with several women in middle management and with one in a top elective office, County Supervisor Sunne McPeak, in the comparable-worth efforts. And certainly, much was gained politically from this cooperation. However, beneath the appearance of solidarity between élite women and the women's labour coalition, there were tensions. One of the coalition leaders brought up this issue and discussed it at length in our interview. She pointed out, for example, that in alliances with élite women, the 'ownership' of the issue can become a problem. She explained it this way:

> Unions are the ones doing comparable worth; they're the ones who actually have to bargain wages and comparable worth at the table. On the other hand, there's a lot of sense of ownership of the issue among women. But women in management and political leadership feel they're special, and don't accept collective action. They don't want to be contaminated with a labor association. I think some women

in politics see their own political futures in comparable worth. Certainly this is a good issue if you're a Democrat and female and you want to distinguish yourself. But Sunne McPeak [county supervisor] has gone around the Country claiming *her* success on this issue, when by the County's own figures there's still a 33 per cent wage gap! We've been willing to let Sunne take a lot of the credit, she deserves it. But, if you want to make history, you have to *do* something. You can't just talk about it!

Later in the interview she explained further the problems of working with management women. In a joint labour/management task force on comparable worth, the management women had balked at making actual comparisons between men's and women's jobs when the County manager opposed this step. This led to a breakdown in the process, and union women were frustrated and disappointed.

I have this friend, a woman manager who was on the Task Force. After one of our big confrontations, I was really angry. And we had lunch. And I said: 'Listen, are you a *woman* – or are you *management?*' And she said: 'Is that a choice?' And I said 'Well, it may be!'

In San Jose, then, gender was the more salient category, and it was as women that clerical and library employees originally organised. Their efforts were initially directed at top officials, many of whom were women. But frustration with this approach, and the realisation that in spite of shared gender, women did not all share the same interest in comparable worth, led to low-paid women becoming more union-identified and working with unionised men. (In fact, participation in the 1981 strike was estimated as half men and half women.) In Contra Costa County, on the other hand, comparable worth was approached from a stronger class identification, evident in the autonomous organising of clericals. Unlike women employees in the 'feminist capital', low-paid women in Contra Costa had little sense of initial identification with feminism, but this developed with involvement in the comparable-worth issue. In the end, both cases illustrate that the political process surrounding comparable worth can lead to a degree of convergence, revealing both class and gender interests of low-paid women. For it was San

Jose's initially feminist-identified activists who stated that the major lesson from their experience was showing that unions are valid for women. And it was Contra Costa's initially class-identified activists who marched in pink with the slogan 'Smash the pink-collar ghetto!'

Both cases also illustrate, however, that the problem of class differences in the construction of feminism persists. The 'ownership' problem described by the Contra Costa activist underlies feminist agreement in principle with comparable worth. Although women managers and politicians may be better placed to get the issue onto political agendas, once there, they may differ with union women, as they did in both these cases, on what actually ought to be done. In my view, the real danger for low-paid women is that too much will be given up, compromised, or put aside so that élite women can claim an easy success. Women officials, in spite of sincere desires to assist low-paid women, face a different set of institutional constraints, which influence the policy they are likely to pursue. Both the San Jose and the Contra Costa cases indicate that with the difficult realities of implementation, alliances between women can become strained and 'ownership' contested. Ultimately, the question again is, which women's interests will be best represented in the name of feminist progress.

CONCLUSION

Historically, the construction of feminist or women's rights issues has at times been contested on a class basis, although certainly there have been issues which created cross-class alliances. However, the feminist movement itself, because it grew out of efforts to extend liberal democratic rights to women, has tended to be defined by the activity of middle-class and élite women. Such a restricted definition can lead to misinterpretations. For example, Jane Mansbridge points out that some historians have failed to recognise the conflict between the ERA and protective legislation as a dispute *among* feminists (Mansbridge, 1986, p. 220, n.3). To overlook the contested ownership of comparable worth in a similar manner, I argue, can also be problematic.

On the other hand, comparable worth is interesting because

it has emerged and become a popular demand at a time when awareness of the economic problems of women has increased, particularly within the feminist movement.[7] One critic has even commented that: 'the Women's Movement has become obsessively preoccupied with how much money women earn' (Roback, 1986, p. 2). Because of the broad agreement with the principle of just wages for women, comparable worth has the potential to bring low-paid and middle- and upper-class women together politically to strengthen the feminist movement and move it beyond its legacy of élitism, as well as to strengthen coalitions between labour and feminism.

The cost of conflict among women or among 'feminisms' in the earlier era, expressed in the fight between protective legislation and the ERA, was perhaps largely the diversion of activists from their main objectives into fighting one another. And as both unionists and pro-ERA activists became too entrenched in their antagonistic positions, viable cross-class alliances became impossible. This seems less the danger today than that of denial; that is, the danger that the privileged women, who are still the core of the women's movement, feel they act on behalf of *all* women and attempt to build support by denying the significance of class and race differences among women. This danger is exacerbated by the fact that the major branch of the movement has favoured top–down approaches and has lacked efforts to mobilise at the grassroots (Gelb and Palley, 1987). In several large State cases, comparable worth has followed such a trajectory; it has become redefined largely as an administrative reform to be handled from above by élite women, losing much of the radical potential I observed in grassroots cases (Acker, 1989; Evans and Nelson, 1989; Steinberg, 1987a).

However, comparable worth, even in the grassroots cases I examined, is certainly no panacea. As a policy approach to the problems of wage discrimination and job segregation, as well as an approach to feminist organising, it has several important limitations. Some of these include the possibilities of: reinforcing the existing gender division of labour, creating labour divisiveness between men and women, and reifying job hierarchies, particularly those based upon educational credentials (Brenner, 1987). In addition, comparable worth is likely to provide concrete benefits to only a portion of low-paid women. To date, it has primarily been a public-sector approach, and as an immediately practical strategy, it is unlikely to increase wages of women in non-unionised, competitive sectors of the economy. In my view, the principle of comparable worth goes further on the political and ideological levels to combat the market devaluation of women's work and transform the awareness of low-paid women, than on the strictly practical level as an immediately viable policy approach (Steinberg, 1987b). But, while attacking the norm of the male breadwinner, comparable worth will ultimately be most successful if treated as an issue for a conscious cross-class feminist alliance rather than if left to the present denial or the damaging conflict among 'feminisms' of the past.

Notes

1. Obviously, this did not lead to ratification of the Amendment however. For an analysis of why the ERA failed, see Mansbridge (1986).
2. Admittedly, as Lehrer documents (1987), the class and gender lines were not as simple as my brief discussion might suggest. There were some groups of women workers opposed to protective legislation; primarily these were printers and streetcar operators who were displaced as a result of night-work restrictions. Also, some members of the Women's Trade Union League struggling for protections were middle-class reformers who identified as allies of labour. Nonetheless, the largest groups opposed to protective legislation were employers and élite women using *laissez-faire*, anti-labour arguments. And the largest groups working for the protections were the trade unions led by the WTUL and Women's Bureau, which reasoned that although a number of women were displaced by men, this was very small compared with the many thousands in the 'women-employing' industries who would be protected (Foner, 1980, pp. 148–50).
3. Washington State was the first to use job-evaluation techniques to examine sex-based wage inequities. In 1973 AFSCME, along with the state's Commission on the Status of Women, requested a job-evaluation study. Such studies assign points and rank jobs according to such 'universally compensable factors' as skills, effort, accountability and working conditions. The study found that women's jobs were paid only 75–80 per cent as much as salaries for the equivalent men's jobs, with virtually no overlap between men and women in any given point range (Remick, 1984).
4. Ironically, the San Jose strike segment featured in the East Coast broadcast, was pre-empted in the Western time zones by coverage of the nomination of Sandra Day O'Connor to the Supreme Court. One piece of feminist news pre-empted the other.

5. That affirmative action contributes significantly to these efforts, shaping expectations and consciousness of women, is a theme I have expanded upon elsewhere (Blum, 1991), but leave aside in this chapter.
6. Feldberg discusses how the pressure which clerical women experienced to win job improvements in an appropriate, ladylike fashion, and not to act militantly or wield power directly – like men – hampered efforts at unionisation in earlier historical periods (Feldberg, 1980, pp. 60–2). Lynch suggests that the traditional gender identity of many clerical women continues to inhibit militancy today (Lynch, 1986).
7. Unfortunately, however, some black and working-class women were alienated by the mid-1980s 'feminisation of poverty' rhetoric. They argued that the feminist movement only became concerned with poverty when formerly middle-class, white women became affected (Burnham, 1985; Malveaux, 1985a; Sparr, 1984).

References

Acker, Joan (1989) *Doing Comparable Worth: Gender, Class and Pay Equity* (Philadelphia: Temple University Press).

Beatty, Richard W. and Beatty, James R (1984) 'Some Problems with Contemporary Job Evaluation Systems' in Remick, Helen (ed.) *Comparable Worth and Wage Discrimination: Technical Possibilities and Political Realities*, (Philadelphia: Temple University Press).

Blum, Linda M. (1987) 'Possibilities and Limits of the Comparable Worth Movement', *Gender and Society*, vol. 1, no 4, December.

Blum, Linda M. (1991) *Between Feminism and Labor: The Significance of the Comparable Worth Movement* (Berkeley: University of California Press).

Brenner, Johanna (1987) 'Feminist Political Discourses: Radical versus Liberal Approaches to the Feminization of Poverty and Comparable Worth', *Gender and Society*, vol. 1, no 4, December.

Bureau of National Affairs (1981) *The Comparable Worth Issue: A BNA Special Report* (Washington DC).

Burnham, Linda (1985) 'Has Poverty Been Feminized in Black America?', *The Black Scholar*, March/April.

Carden, Maren Lockwood (1974) *The New Feminist Movement* (New York: Russell Sage).

Carden, Maren Lockwood (1978) 'The Proliferation of a Social Movement: Ideology and Individual Incentives in the Contemporary Feminist Movement', *Research in Social Movements, Conflict and Change*, vol. 1.

Contra Costa Times (1972) 'CCC Clerical Employees Ponder Strike Over Wage, Benefit Offer', 20 June, p. 1.

Dean Virginia, Roberts, Patti, Boone, Carroll (1984), 'Comparable Worth under Federal and State Laws' in Remick, Helen (ed) *Comparable Worth and Wage Discrimination: Technical Possibilities and Political Realities* (Philadelphia: Temple University Press).

Ehrenreich, Barbara (1987) 'The Next Wave', *Ms Magazine*, no. 1–2, July–August.

Eisenstein, Zillah R. (1981) *The Radical Future of Liberal Feminism* (New York: Longman).

Evans, Sara M. and Nelson, Barbara J. (1989) *Wage Justice: Comparable Worth and the Paradox of Technocratic Reform* (Chicago: University of Chicago Press).

Feldberg, Roslyn L. (1980) 'Union Fever': Organizing Among Clerical Workers, 1900–1930', *Radical America*, vol. 14, no 3 (May–June).

Flammang, Janet (1985) 'Female Officials in the Feminist Capital: The Case of Santa Clara County', *Western Political Quarterly*, vol. 38, no 1, March, pp. 94–118.

Flammang, Janet (1986) 'Effective Implementation: The Case of Comparable Worth in San Jose', *Policy Studies Review*, vol. 5, no 4, May, pp. 815–37.

Flammang, Janet (1987) 'Women Made a Difference: Comparable Worth in San Jose', in M. F. Katzenstein and C. M. Mueller (eds) *The Women's Movements of the United States and Western Europe* (Philadelphia: Temple University Press), pp. 290–312.

Flexner, Eleanor (1975) *Century of Struggle: The Women's Rights Movement in the United States* (Cambridge: Harvard University Press).

Foner, Philip S. (1980) *Women and the American Labor Movement: From World War I to the Present* (New York: Free Press).

Freeman, Jo (1975) *The Politics of Women's Liberation* (New York: Longman).

Freeman, Jo (1987) 'Whom You Know versus Whom You Represent: Feminist Influence in the Democratic and Republican Parties', in M. F. Katzenstein and C. M. Mueller (eds) *The Women's Movements of the United States and Western Europe* (Philadelphia: Temple University Press), pp. 215–44.

Freeman, Richard B. and Leonard, Jonathan S. (1985) 'Union Maids: Unions and the Female Workforce', National Bureau of Economic Research, Working Paper no 1652 (Cambridge, Massachusetts) June.

Gelb, Joyce (1987) 'Social Movement "Success": A Comparative Analysis of Feminism in the United States and the United Kingdom', in M. F. Katzenstein and C. M. Mueller (eds) *The Women's Movements of the United States and Western Europe* (Philadelphia: Temple University Press).

Gelb, Joyce and Palley, Marian Lief (1987) *Women and Public Policies* (New Jersey: Princeton University Press).

Giddings, Paula (1984) *When and Where I Enter: The Impact of Black Women on Race and Sex in America* (New York: William Morrow).

Grune, Joy Ann (1980) *Manual on Pay Equity: Raising Wages for Women's Work* (Washington DC: Committee on Pay Equity, Conference on Alternative State and Local Policies).

Heen, M. (1984) 'A Review of Federal Court Decisions under Title VII of the Civil Rights Act of 1964' in Remick, Helen (ed.) *Comparable Worth and Wage Discrimination* (Philadelphia: Temple University Press).

Hole, Judith and Levine, Ellen (1971) *Rebirth of Feminism* (New York: Quadrangle/New York Times).

Johansen, Elaine (1984) *Comparable Worth: the Myth and the Movement* (Boulder, Colorado: Westview Press).

Katzenstein, Mary F. (1987) 'Comparing the Feminist Movements of the United States and Western Europe: An Overview', In M. F. Katzenstein and C. M. Mueller (eds) *The Women's Movements of the United States and Western Europe* (Philadelphia: Temple University Press).

Keppel, Bruce (1981) 'San Jose on New Ground in Women's Wage Debate', *Los Angeles Times*, 30 June.

Kirkby, Diane (1987) 'The Wage Earning Woman and the State: the National Women's Trade Union League and Protective Legislation, 1903–1923', *Labor History*, vol. 28, no 1.

Klein, Ethel (1987) 'The Diffusion of Consciousness in the United States and Western Europe', in M. F. Katzenstein and C. M. Mueller (eds) *The Women's Movements of the United States and Western Europe* (Philadelphia: Temple University Press).

Lehrer, Susan (1987) *Origins of Protective Legislation for Women: 1905–1925* (Albany, NY: SUNY Press).

Lynch, Roberta (1986) 'Organizing Clericals: Problems and Prospects', *Labor Research Review*, 8 (Spring), pp. 91–101.

Malveaux, Julianne (1985a) 'The Economic Interests of Black and White Women: Are They Similar?' *Review of Black Political Economy*, vol. 14, no 1, pp. 5–27.

Malveaux, Julianne (1985/1986) 'Comparable Worth and It's Impact on Black Women' *Review of Black Political Economy*, vol. 14, no 2–3, pp. 47–62.

Mansbridge, Jane J. (1986) *Why We Lost the ERA* (Chicago: University of Chicago Press).

Martinez Morning News-Gazette (1972) 'CC Clerical Employees Vote Strike: County, Union Still Continue Negotiations', 20 June, p. 1.

Moore, Richard and Marsis, Elizabeth (1983) 'What's a Woman's Work Worth?' *The Progressive*, vol. 47, no 12, pp. 20–3.

Mueller, Carol M. (1987) 'Collective Consciousness, Identity Transformation, and the Rise of Women in Public Office in the United States', in M. F. Katzenstein and C. M. Mueller (eds) *The Women's Movements of the United States and Western Europe* (Philadelphia: Temple University Press).

National Committee on Pay Equity (1984) *The Cost of Pay Equity in Public and Private Employment* (Washington DC: NCPE) December.

Remick, Helen (1984) 'Major Issues in *a priori* Applications', in H. Remick (ed.) *Comparable Worth and Wage Discrimination* (Philadelphia: Temple University Press).

Roback, Jennifer (1986) *A Matter of Choice: A Critique of Comparable Worth by a Skeptical Feminist* (New York: Priority Press) A Twentieth Century Fund Paper.

Rupp, Leila J. and Taylor Verta (1987) *Survival in the Doldrums: The American Women's Rights Movement, 1945 to the 1960s* (New York: Oxford University Press).

San Francisco Examiner (1986) 'Pay Equity Breakthrough', 2 February.

Sparr, Pamela (1984) 'Re-evaluating Feminist Economics: "Feminization of Poverty" Ignores Key Issues', *Dollars and Sense*, no 99, September.

Steinberg, Ronnie J. (1987a) 'From Radical Vision to Minimalist Reform: Pay Equity in New York State, the Limits of Insider Reform Initiatives', paper presented at the Department of Sociology, Pennsylvania State University, 10 April.

Steinberg, Ronnie J. (1987b) 'Radical Challenges in a Liberal World: The Mixed Success of Comparable Worth', *Gender and Society*, vol. 1, no 4, December.

Steinberg, R. and Haignere, L. (1987) 'Equitable Compensation: Methodological Criteria for Comparable Worth' in Bose, C. and Spitze, G (eds), *Ingredients for Women's Employment Policy* (Albany, NY: State University of New York Press).

Taylor, Verta (1986) 'The Continuity of the American Women's Movement: An Elite-Sustained Stage', presented to the Annual Meeting of the American Sociological Association, New York, September.

Tong, David (1981) 'San Jose Mayor, Union Chief to Address Issues on TV'. *Oakland Tribune*, 7 July.

Treiman D. R. (1979) *Job Evaluation: An Analytic Review: An Interim Report to the EEOC*, (Washington, DC: National Academy of Sciences).

Treiman, Donald J. and Hartmann, Heidi I. (1981) *Women, Work and Wages: Equal Pay for Jobs of Equal Value* (Washington DC: National Academy Press).

Vogt, Rick (1972) 'Decision Due Monday; CC Employees' Talks at Impasse', *Contra Costa Times*, 22 June, p. 1.

Part II

Case Studies of Equal Value/Comparable Worth Campaigns, Litigation and Implementation in the Public and Private Sectors

6 Equal Value in British Banking: The Midland Bank Case

Alan Arthurs

INTRODUCTION

The British banking industry employs over 200 000 women, mostly in lower paid work, and hence the 1983 Equal Value (Amendment) Regulations brought the threat of a major increase in labour cost. In this chapter we examine the response of the English Clearing Banks,[1] and, in particular, discuss the way in which the Midland Bank avoided the potential threat of legal action by introducing an integrated job-evaluation system which it believed to be free of sex discrimination in its construction and implementation. These recent changes will be considered in the context of the history of women in British banking, trade unions in banking, previous equality initiatives, and the Midland Bank's perception of its commercial interests.

The banks appeared to be vulnerable to equal-value claims under the new legislation, but the Midland Bank disagreed with the Federation of London Clearing Bank Employers about how to deal with the potentially large rise in labour costs that could result. The Midland Bank, conscious of its competitive situation, wanted to be free to negotiate its own solution, devised as a result of studies carried out during the enactment of the new legislation. Even though the banking unions had been putting some pressure on the banks, the agreement reached on equal value in the Midland Bank was largely management-initiated and its implementation remained at all times under the control of the bank.

119

WOMEN'S WORK IN BRITISH BANKING

Six out of every ten employees in British banks are women. It was not always so: in the late nineteenth and early twentieth centuries few women, perhaps only 1 per cent of the staff, were employed in banking. During the First World War (1914–18) women were recruited by banks into clerical work in large numbers, joining the few women already working mainly as typists, telephone operators and accounting-machine operators. Some took up clerical work which had previously been carried out only by men. A few were allowed to work as cashiers, despite resistance from male staff and customers. After the war many of these women left or were dismissed in order to make way for the men returning from military service, but some were able to stay on and they maintained their foothold in clerical work. They constituted around 20 per cent of bank staff and were mainly single women.

A similar surge of female recruitment took place during the Second World War (1939–45) and by 1942 over 40 per cent of bank staffs were women, compared with only 22 per cent three years earlier (Blackburn, 1967, pp. 121 and 157). Although women's employment in banking declined in the immediate aftermath of the war, an increasing number were now in jobs, such as cashiers, which had been reserved for men in the previous generation. With the expansion of banking and an increasingly tight labour market for white-collar male staff in the 1950s and 1960s the absolute and relative numbers of women employed by the clearing banks grew. By 1959 40 per cent of the staff in the clearing banks were women and this increased to 48 per cent by 1965 and 53 per cent by 1970 (Morris, 1986, p. 91). Although some women were promoted through the clerical ranks into management positions the overwhelming majority remained in the more routine and lower-paid work. Male entrants to banking had a one-in-three chance of becoming a manager, but in 1965 only two out of more than 8000 branch managers were women (Lockwood, 1958, p. 65; Blackburn, 1967, p. 71)

The position of women in banking at this time has been explained in terms of an implicit, and often explicit, dual career structure (Crompton, 1989). Whilst men were recruited with a view to a progressive career, women were not. They were seen by the banks, and saw themselves, as having only a limited time in bank employment – four years was the norm. Girls recruited into banking generally had lower academic qualifications than the boys, since most of them were not expected to stay long enough to progress to the more responsible jobs. Few of them sought banking qualifications or promotion and such expectations were not normally encouraged. Women usually carried out routine work and left by their mid-twenties. They were given a lump sum of money when they married, since it was assumed that they would be leaving the bank.

By the end of the 1960s these attitudes were beginning to be challenged on the grounds both of social justice and of business rationality. It was argued that the banks needed to take steps to encourage the recruitment and retention of women employees in career posts. During the 1980s banking employers acknowledged this by taking a number of equality initiatives, as outlined later.

WOMEN IN BANKING UNIONS

Trade unionism in British banking is characterised by a dual structure. The Banking, Insurance and Finance Union (BIFU), a TUC-affiliated union, is recognised by all the English Clearing Banks. Most of the clearing banks also recognise their own internal staff unions, which have consistently recruited more members than BIFU.[2] An exception is the Midland Bank, where the Association of Scientific, Technical and Managerial Staffs (ASTMS)[3] took over the staff association in the early 1970s and maintained a bargaining foothold alongside the much larger membership of BIFU until 1989, when the bank withdrew from the relationship.

BIFU has had a presence in banking for over seventy years and gained bargaining rights with all the clearing banks in 1968. It is a moderate union, but is prepared to take industrial action if necessary. The different staff unions for the separate banks go back almost as far, yet only in the 1960s did they develop a real financial independence from the banks. They have evolved to the point where during the 1980s they were prepared to take sanctions against their employers. The staff unions have maintained a cooperative stand towards the banks, an approach which appears to have had the approval of the majority of bank employees. Although BIFU has fewer members in the clearing banks than its rivals, it has maintained a strong presence. Attempts to merge the staff unions with BIFU have foundered on ideological and personal antagonisms (Morris, 1986b).

BIFU and its predecessors has always had women members, but some of the staff unions have not.[4] As late as 1935 an approach by women to join the Staff Association of the National Provincial Bank was turned down (Blackburn, 1967, p. 153). Women formed 9 per cent of the membership of BIFU in 1922. In 1939 they were still only 12 per cent of the membership (Blackburn, 1967, pp. 121 and 277). The rise in the proportion of women employed in banking has been reflected in their growing membership of BIFU and the staff unions. The percentage of women members in BIFU rose from 26 per cent in 1952, to 35 per cent in 1962 and today is approximately 50 per cent.

Women have always been underrepresented in proportion to their total numbers employed in banking, in both BIFU and the staff unions, partly because of their relatively high turnover compared with male staff. Since the mid-1970s their presence has been increasingly felt in the counsels of the unions, although 'men predominate to a very considerable extent in all "official" positions' (Egan, 1982, p. 29).

BIFU formed an equality working party in 1975, which became the Equal Opportunities Committee in 1980, reporting directly to the Executive Committee of the union. Such activity has helped to put women's issues on the agenda for both BIFU and the staff unions and has been instrumental in putting pressure on the bank employers to improve the position of their female employees.

EQUAL OPPORTUNITY INITIATIVES IN BANKING

Spurred on by external and internal reports and the belief of some managers that they are not making the best use of all their female staff, most of the banks have, over the past fifteen years, taken a series of initiatives to improve the opportunities for women in banking. Consultants, researchers and the Equal

Opportunities Commission have sought to raise awareness of equal opportunity issues and have put forward proposals for change. BIFU, ASTMS and some of the staff unions have also pressed for better opportunities for women. As a result many of the banks have taken actions such as issuing policy statements on equal opportunities; carrying out equal-opportunity audits or reviews; and designating a manager or managers as responsible for equal opportunities. Other developments, such as re-entry arrangements, have been introduced to help women to combine careers and domestic responsibilities; recruitment and selection policies and practices have been critically reviewed; the content and methods of training have in some cases been revised to include equal-opportunity issues; and a few women-only courses have been run (*Equal Opportunities Review*, No. 28, 1989).

These developments have not been universal. It is too early to judge whether fundamental and lasting changes have occurred in opportunities for women. The increasing recruitment of women as management trainees will certainly mean that the number of women in managerial posts will continue its current expansion.[5] There is evidence of more women being promoted into the higher-graded clerical jobs and into the 'appointed' categories above those. Whether the overwhelming concentration of women in the lower clerical grades and secretarial and typing work will substantially alter must be an open question.

EQUAL PAY IN BANKING

Until 1972, women in banking, like those working in most other sectors of the British economy, were paid on different salary scales from their male counterparts. Their pay was age-related until the age of 31. The different age-scales for men widened after the mid-1920s in favour of the males, on the assumption that the men would by then be progressing onto more responsible and complex work (Morris, 1986a, p. 90). One consequence of this policy was that it was possible for a man doing the same clerical work as a woman to be paid three or four times as much (Povall, 1986, p. 29).

By the late 1960s the banks were experiencing labour-market

and political pressures which led them to review their pay systems for clerical staff (Morris, 1986a, pp. 46–9) A report in 1969 from a government agency, the National Board for Prices and Incomes, recommended that the banks introduce productivity reforms in the shape of a pay structure which would be related to the work performed rather than the age of the job-holder. At the same time the banks had labour turnover problems, particularly amongst women. Also some discontent, exacerbated by the passage of the Equal Pay Act 1970, had grown where women, carrying out the same work as men, were paid substantially less.

The introduction of a national clerical job-evaluation system across all the clearing banks in 1972 attempted to tackle these issues by building a pay structure based more on task than age and more on achievement than seniority. It provided, for the first time, a clear career progression through at least four grades for both male and female clerical staff and equal pay for women, where they were carrying out work rated as equivalent under the job-evaluation scheme.

EQUAL PAY FOR WORK OF EQUAL VALUE

In a study conducted in 1985 in the British finance sector, over a year after the introduction of the new law giving the right to equal pay for work of equal value, less than a third of the organisations said that they had either reviewed or revised their payment systems (Povall, 1986, p. 36) For some the lack of response was due to a belief that their pay practices were consistent with the new law. Others were less confident, but the ambiguities in the law did not encourage action which might prove to be premature.

ASTMS and BIFU were reported in this same study as 'actively investigating the possibilities of the use of the equal-value provisions to bring equal-value cases' (Povall, 1986, p. 37) but not until 1986, nearly two and a half years after the introduction of the new law, did the issue of equal value become a live one in British banks. In March 1986 eleven female print-finishers, supported by their union, BIFU, brought an equal-value case against Lloyds Bank. The women, who worked at a factory in Sidcup, Kent, which made cheque books, claimed that their work was equal in value to that of higher-graded male printer. In January 1988 an industrial tribunal found in favour of the women.

In April 1986 seven women working as typists, secretaries and a clerk/typist brought another case against Lloyds Bank. The women, who were supported by their small staff union, the Lloyds Bank Group Staff Union, worked in different parts of England in branches of the bank. They claimed that their work was equal in value to that of five male messengers. The messenger jobs chosen for comparison ranged from a basic-grade messenger to a senior deputy head messenger and the men worked in different locations in London and South East England. The women won their case in 1989, but the bank appealed to a higher court.

In June 1986 the Midland Bank unveiled its proposals for a new integrated job-evaluation scheme which would eventually cover all its staff and take into account equal-value considerations. The development, negotiation, implementation and results of this integrated job-evaluation system are described and discussed in the remainder of this chapter.

IMPACT OF THE 1984 LAW ON THE MIDLAND BANK

The Midland Bank responded to the publication of the draft Equal Pay (Amendment) Regulations in 1983 by reviewing its pay and benefits policies and practices in order to assess areas where it might be vulnerable under the forthcoming legislation. Four groups of employees, all in separate predominantly male bargaining units, were a cause for some concern, since they had over the previous fifteen years won salaries which had increased their differentials over equivalent clerical staff. Electronic data processing (EDP) staff's salary scales partially reflected the labour market of the early 1970s where the fast growth in demand for such work and the culture of mobility had created severe difficulties for the bank in recruiting and retaining computer staff. Typists and secretaries had benefited from high demand in the mid-1970s that had produced greater-than-average salary increases.

By contrast engineers and messengers had used their industrial muscle in strategic areas of banking in order to push up their salaries. The engineers had taken industrial action in the bank's computer centres in 1978 and 1979 to enhance their pay. The messengers took industrial action in 1980 in the National Westminster Bank, believing that their pay differentials over the clerical staff had been eroded. By withdrawing their labour from the clearing department of the National Westminster Bank and picketing the other major clearing banks they stopped the processing of cheques. Severe damage was quickly inflicted on the banks, who capitulated within days and conceded pay rises of well over 30 per cent. The relative pay advantages gained by these four groups had not been eroded significantly in subsequent years, and some had even increased their differentials over the clerical staff.

In addition to overall salary comparisons other sources of possible discrimination were identified:

1. Junior clerical staff were paid on age-related scales, rather than the rate for the job identified by job evaluation.
2. A time promotion system, providing automatic grade progression once training standards were achieved, was applied to only some of the EDP staff.
3. The use of separate job-evaluation systems for different groups of staff, the factor weightings used in these systems and the choice of breakpoints between grades might be interpreted as having a potentially discriminatory impact.

VULNERABILITY TO EQUAL-VALUE CLAIMS

The bank's personnel department also carried out a comprehensive risk analysis of possible equal-value claims. Jobs held predominantly by women were compared with a variety of jobs held predominantly by men. Since they all had job descriptions and most had been job-evaluated it was possible to do cross-evaluations from one pay structure to another, using the accumulated experience and expertise of the bank's job-evaluation specialists. For example, the job of the branch cashier was evaluated using the messengers' evaluation system; the messengers' job was evaluated with the clerical system; and both were evaluated by the Hay system.

Using this information the bank was able to identify those predominantly female jobs, choosing appropriate comparators, which might lead to successful claims under the legislation. Nine jobs were particularly vulnerable to being found by an expert to be undervalued in relation to a male comparator.

Further analysis assessed the risk of equal-value claims being made by job-holders. It was assumed that the greater the pay difference between the woman's job and that of the comparator the more likely was she to make a claim. Since a claim would be unlikely to succeed unless legal and moral support was available, it was calculated that cases would be most likely to be pursued where the employees concerned were densely unionised. An assessment was made of the probability of union support for any particular group. In addition a judgement was made as to whether a case would attract the support of the Equal Opportunities Commission.

The next stage was to assess the cost to the bank of a successful individual claim. For ten different jobs it was estimated that a tribunal victory for one woman would cost in excess of £1000 a year. Although the bank would be legally bound to increase the pay of only those individual women who had won a case it would be unlikely to be able to contain the situation, since the union would inevitably use the case as a bargaining counter in negotiations or would support similar multiple actions through the legal system. In addition the bank would face considerable unfavourable publicity if it were seen to be continuing to maintain a pay-system which had been found by an industrial tribunal to be discriminatory. Therefore estimates were made of the potential knock-on effects of the women's pay-increase on other eligible staff. For each of three jobs this was found to be in excess of £1 million a year. In these cases the comparison which made the bank so vulnerable was that between a predominantly female job and a messenger's job.

However, it was possible that the bank could justify the pay difference. The proposed legislation allowed an employer to argue that the difference in pay was not due to sex discrimination but to a 'material factor'. It was not made clear in the legislation to what extent or whether such factors as market forces, skill shortages or bargaining strength would be accepted as justifying pay differences. Whilst some commentators and advisors were confident that employers would be able to call upon a wide range of reasons to justify their pay structures, others believed that the legal interpretation would severely constrain such defences.

Such uncertainty meant that the Midland bank had to look very critically at major and expensive changes to its pay structures, since they might be found, in the light of subsequent legal judgements, to have been premature or unnecessary.

A range of possible changes to reduce the bank's vulnerability were analysed with a view to action where costs were relatively low or in order to prepare contingency plans to avoid future claims, if these came to appear more probable in the light of legal judgements and bargaining developments elsewhere. One option was to adopt a single job-evaluation system for all staff, which would assess the value of all jobs using a method free of sex bias. The considerable cost implications meant that, in view of the uncertainties in the legislation, such a wholesale change was not seen to be justified at that time, particularly since the bank was facing increased competition and severe pressures on profitability.

However, it was agreed to avoid making changes to the pay and conditions of predominantly male categories of employee which would improve their relative position. Where possible the bank would reduce the differentials in order to make itself slightly less vulnerable to equal-value claims and to lower the cost of any future job-evaluated realignment of pay between male-dominated and other categories of staff. A further way in which future costs of adapting to equal value could be reduced was by continuing, as far as possible, the reduction in the numbers of messengers employed. This would lower the ultimate cost of buying-out certain benefits in their remuneration package.

Other actions planned in order to conform more closely with equal-value principles were:

- to remove the age-related pay for junior clerical staff;
- review the time promotion system used for some EDP staff;
- to carry out evaluations to remove limited anomalies, particularly at grade boundaries and at the cross-over between different evaluation systems.

RE-ASSESSING THE LEGAL POSITION

In the two years following the enactment of the new equal pay legislation it attracted little public attention. Those cases which had been brought to tribunals took longer than had been expected and therefore few significant judgements were given. However, by late 1985 several cases, in particular that of *Hayward* v. *Cammell Laird,* raised awareness of the legislation and also suggested that it could be used successfully by applicants. Commentators pointed to banking as an area of employment where equal-value cases might successfully be brought. A continuing series of studies and articles drew attention to the issue of equal opportunities for women in banking.

These developments stimulated further discussions in the Midland Bank about the need to be prepared to take action to reduce its vulnerability to equal-value claims. It was argued that such claims, if successful, would raise staff costs substantially during a period when they needed to be tightly controlled. Careful choice of comparators might allow groups of female staff to use the legislation to achieve very large increases in pay. A more manageable and more rational response would be to move towards a situation where a common basis of terms and conditions would apply to all levels of employee; where work was found by job evaluation to be of equal value to the bank it would be rewarded in the same way.

LEAVING THE FEDERATION

During this time active discussions were held with the other Clearing Banks which were members of the Federation of London Clearing Bank Employers. All faced similar issues as a result of the equal-value legislation and were exploring strategies on how to respond. Employment structures in the other banks were not dissimilar from those in the Midland Bank. All the members of the Federation had clerical staff and Technical and Services Staff messengers in separate bargaining units and in different pay structures. A common Clerical Job Evaluation system had applied to all the banks since 1971, although local implementation meant that differences existed. Technical and

Services Staff, an overwhelming male group, were subject to coordinated policies, but each bank had a different approach – only the Midland had applied job evaluation to these staff.

Attempts to get agreement within the Clearing Bank employers to the development of a single job-evaluation system, which would cover Clerical and Technical and Services Staff in all the banks and be used as a basis for integrated pay scales that could be extended to other groups, were not successful. The Midland Bank, unlike some of the other banks, did not want to modify and adapt the existing job-evaluation scheme but to extend the Hay system which was already used for the bank's managerial staff.

Lack of agreement over the response to equal value was only one of the strains being experienced by the Federation in 1985. Differences existed over the degree of autonomy individual banks should be allowed in formulating and operating their salary systems. For example, some banks wanted to keep only common minimum salaries for a grade, but with discretion for each bank over the rate of salary advancement and the maximum salary for the grade. Other problems derived from the desire of some banks to vary the job-evaluation system which they used, albeit using common benchmark jobs and common grade structures with the other banks. Other differences centred on the pace of change towards a common job-evaluation system.

Even if these differences could have been resolved the Midland Bank would still have been significantly constrained by the policies of the Federation and the need to preserve common features of their pay systems. Additionally the bank was dissatisfied with the arrangements at the Federation, where two competing unions, the Banking and Finance Union (BIFU) and the Clearing Banks Union (CBU), negotiated with the bank employers. The CBU did not represent staff in the Midland Bank, but a third union, the Association of Scientific, Technical and Managerial Staffs, did so. The desire to develop more flexible payment structures and systems and a new job-evaluation structure to cover the wider range of jobs developing in banking, coupled with a wish to negotiate in-house with only BIFU and ASTMS led to the Midland Bank withdrawing from the Federation in December 1985. It stated that 'The highly competitive market conditions in which Midland operates now make it essential for the Bank to be free to determine with its staff unions pay and conditions more closely aligned to its changing business objectives and organisational structure.'

PLANNING THE INTRODUCTION OF THE REVISED PAY STRUCTURE

In 1986 the Midland Bank's staff were separated into seven main groups: senior and executive management; managers and appointed officers; clerical staff; technical and services staff; typists and secretaries; electronic-data-processing staff and engineers.

The job-evaluation or job-ranking schemes had been introduced and operated with union involvement, except for jobs in senior and executive management. Any change to these systems and the associated grade structures and salary scales would need to be negotiated with the two unions concerned. Preparatory analysis of job-evaluation systems capable of spanning a wide range of different jobs had already been carried out before the bank decided to go it alone. The bank favoured the Hay system, which was tested and judged to be sufficiently flexible and discerning to accommodate evaluations of clerical, typing, secretarial and technical and services work.

In the run-up to the pay negotiations in mid-1986 the bank developed proposals that would help to ease the introduction and minimise the cost of the planned integrated pay structure. A major aim was to reduce pay differentials between those groups of staff for which the job-evaluation testing exercise had shown a need for pay convergence. Another aim was to reach a settlement which would reassure staff and their unions that withdrawal from the Federation was not simply a device for lowering the pay of Midland Bank staff relative to those in other clearing banks.

In the event, the negotiations achieved both objectives. The settlement in June 1986 gave all clerical and typing staff a flat-rate increase in salary, which favoured the lower-paid staff. The overall salary increase for this predominantly female group compared favourably with that for the predominantly male technical and services staff. Another change which was made in order to ease the introduction of an integrated pay system and deal with equal-value considerations was the replacement of age-related salary scales for junior clerical and typing staff by performance-related scales; no changes were made to the age scales of technical and services staff. This small erosion of differentials between the clerical and technical and services staff served to demonstrate that the bank was prepared to change established relativities. The acceptance by technical and services staff of lump-sum cash payments instead of a higher basic salary increase suggested the feasibility of using this approach in subsequent negotiations to integrate the salary systems.

NEGOTIATING THE INTEGRATED JOB EVALUATION SCHEME

The bank presented its plans for an integrated pay structure to the unions in July 1986. This first meeting excluded consideration of the technical and services, engineering, and electronic-data-processing staff and discussed only the extension of the Hay system to clerical, secretarial and typing staffs. The bank set out a timetable which they hoped would result in agreement on a new grade structure by March 1987.

The first stage of the process consisted of joint management and union testing of the Hay system on 500 job descriptions, using a cross-section of clerical and typing jobs in the bank. This work was carried out by a joint working party which drew from a pool of twenty union representatives who, having being trained in the Hay method, were involved full-time for six weeks in the programme. Each job was assessed by a testing committee consisting of eight management representatives, four BIFU representatives and four ASTMs representatives, chaired by the bank's job-evaluation manager. The Hay consultant was present for the early meetings, but gradually withdrew.

Over the next four months the evaluation results for the benchmark jobs were reviewed by each union and the bank separately. In subsequent negotiations over the number of grades the unions favoured up to eight clerical grades, but the bank argued that this would inhibit flexibility in branches which had an average of only twelve staff and typically contained fourteen staff. Negotiations over the number of grades and the location of the break-points between grades continued for two months before agreement in principle was reached in November 1986 on a five-grade structure.

INCORPORATING THE TECHNICAL AND SERVICES STAFF

The bank had always known that the major obstacle to a new integrated pay structure would be the technical and services staff. Most of these were in the messenger grades and all but about seventy of the 1600 staff were men.

The messengers in all the clearing banks have a distinct culture and, for over a century, had been treated as separate groups with their own pay structures. Although in the same unions as clerical staff, they had maintained their own sections and separate negotiations. BIFU had a technical and services section which covered messengers in all the Clearing Banks and had its own annual conference. Integration of messengers with clerical staff in the Midland Bank would be seen as a threat to messengers in all the banks.

Emphasis was given by the bank to the job-security advantages of an integrated pay structure in which messengers would be able to take on and be trained for new responsibilities outside the confines of the traditional messenger role. Job security was a key issue for messengers since their numbers had reduced from 2300 to 1600 in the previous three years, due to the bank's policy of non-replacement of messengers who left or retired.

To persuade the BIFU technical and services representatives to join the negotiations the bank decided to communicate directly with the messengers. The messengers reacted vehemently to the prospect of their representatives not being involved in integration discussions with the bank and BIFU representatives soon agreed to participate jointly with ASTMS in conducting a testing programme, which led to an agreement in April 1987.

THE AGREEMENT

Most staff moved as a result of the job re-evaluation to a similar salary in the integrated structure. The exceptions were:

1. nearly 5500 mainly female clerical staff who were upgraded;
2. a significant number of the messengers who came out at a lower equivalent grade;
3. some senior secretaries (appointed officers) whose new salary scales were below their existing ones.

The new structure produced a more even distribution of clerical staff across the new grades, in contrast to the previous position where the majority had been in the lowest two grades. For secretaries the results were more mixed, since their new salaries were related to the intrinsic nature of the work they performed rather than, as previously, being primarily a function of the status of their boss.

The technical and services staff, despite in many cases being evaluated at a lower grade than previously, did not come out as badly as many of them had initially feared. The positioning of the basic-grade branch messenger in the same S3 grade as the cashier job was particularly helpful in gaining their acceptance. Other arrangements that sweetened the pill of the new grade-structure were the agreement to give full salary protection to all existing staff, not only in terms of their current salary, but in terms of their future salary expectations; and compensation of up to £1250 in a lump sum and consolidation into their salary for loss of benefits, such as uniforms and for the replacement of service awards by merit-based salary progression.

CONCLUSION

The Midland Bank has provided a model for other British employers who seek to respond to the 1984 legislation on equal pay for work of equal value. At least two of the other large banks have discussed similar changes.

By taking the initiative the bank was able to plan, negotiate and implement change at its own pace and with due considera-

tion for the potential implications of introducing a new grading
and pay structure. The alternative policy would have been to
wait longer and see whether the new law was making an impact.
Only when the case in which Lloyds Bank secretaries and typists
are claiming equal pay with messengers is finally decided will it
be possible to judge whether the Midland Bank might have
fought off the challenge of equal value. Yet even if this had
been possible the cost in the goodwill of female staff and customers might have been high. The approach taken by Midland
Bank has not been without considerable cost, since it is estimated to have added 1 per cent to total pay-costs for the staff
grades. However, the potential costs, including the knock-on
effects of losing a legal battle over equal pay for female clerical
staff could have been at least ten times the cost of bargained
change. Yet comparison with competitors showed overall salary
increases in 1987 not dissimilar from the Midland Bank.

From the point of view of the female staff it could argued
that, since they might have gained a great deal more by pursuing an equal-value case through the courts, the collective-bargaining process has failed to achieve a just settlement. Yet given
the competitive pressures and the profitability of the Midland
Bank it is far from certain that a legal victory would have led to
pay increases on the scale which, in theory, the law might have
given them. The threat of job losses might have acted as a major
deterrent to the pursuit of their legal rights.

It is probably unrealistic at the present time to expect radical
change in the overall position of female employees in British
banking. Given the history of female employment in banking it
is not surprising that improvements in their position are likely
to come only slowly, and then only if they continue to press for
them. Demographic changes will reduce the supply of school-
leavers over the next ten years; the potential shortage of appro-
priately qualified entrants to banking employment will provide
a fertile environment in which female employees will be able to
claim greater recognition for their contributions. Banks will
need to adapt more to the needs of women with family responsibilities if they are to attract and retain qualified womanpower.
The 1990s may therefore see a series of incremental changes
which will improve women's positions in the banking labour
market; but they are unlikely to alter radically the current
sexual division of labour and valuation of women's work.

Notes

1. The London Clearing Banks are a small group of major retail banks, with branches all over Britain, who use the London Bankers' Clearing House for the exchange and settlement of cheques drawn on each other (Perry, 1984, p. 69).
2. Unions affiliated to the TUC are independent unions which normally negotiate with more than one employer. 'Staff Unions' are internal to one employer with whom they negotiate. Although many were originally company-sponsored or supported, some have subsequently achieved a credible degree of independence and remain attractive to employees.
3. ASTMS changed its name to the Managerial, Scientific and Finance union (MSF) in 1988.
4. In the letter on the formation of the Midland Bank Staff Association in 1919 the Bank Chairman stated that 'It is not proposed to invite the Ladies' Staff to become members of the Association' (Blackburn, 1967, p. 143).
5. In some banks the growth in the number of female managers has been rapid. For example, in Lloyds Bank, in the three years up to March 1989, the number of female managers increased from 75 to 223; and assistant managers from 228 to 614. Even after this expansion only 5 per cent of managers and 15 per cent of assistant managers were women.

References

Blackburn, R. M. (1967) *Union Character and Social Class* (London: Batsford).
Crompton, R. (1989) 'Women in Banking: Continuity and Change since the Second World War', *Work, Employment and Society*, 3, pp. 141–56.
Egan, A. (1982) 'Women in Banking: A Study in Inequality', *Industrial Relations Journal*, 13, pp. 20–31.
Equal Opportunities Review (1989) 'Attracting and Retaining Women Workers in the Finance Sector' *Equal Opportunities Review*, 28, Nov/Dec 1989, pp. 10–20.
Lockwood, D. (1958) *The Blackcoated Worker* (London: George Allen & Unwin, 1958)
Morris, T. (1986) *Innovations in Banking* (London: Croom Helm).
Morris, T. (1986b) 'Trade Union Mergers and Competition in British banking', *Industrial Relations Journal*, 17, pp. 129–40.
Perry, F. E. (1984) *The Elements of Banking*, 4th edn (London: Methuen).
Povall, M. (1986) 'Equal Opportunities for Women in British Banking', *Equal Opportunities International*, 5(2), 1986, pp. 27–44.

7 'We Can't Eat Prestige': The Yale University Workers' Campaign for Comparable Worth

Kathleen Kautzer

This chapter focuses on landmark collective-bargaining agreements won by unionised clerical and technical workers at Yale University, a prestigious private university in New Haven, Connecticut. These agreements have dramatically upgraded women's and minorities' salaries. The contract victories in 1985 and 1988 were preceded, first, by a union-organising drive beginning in 1982 and, then, once the union was legally established, by an ongoing campaign for union objectives. Comparable worth was an idea central to union activity throughout the period, though neither of the two formal agreements included explicit comparable-worth language and the union's commitment to comparable worth was limited. Yale's clerical and technical workers were successfully organised and subsequently represented by Local 34 of the Federation of University Employees, an affiliate of the Hotel and Restaurant Employees International Union (HERE). Local 34's achievements at Yale represent a milestone in an ongoing social movement to unionise clerical and technical workers.

My interpretation of the Yale case differs from other published accounts (Gilpin, Isaac, Letwin, McKivigan, 1988; Ladd-Taylor, 1985; Hurd, 1986; Cupo, Ladd-Taylor, Lett, Montgomery, 1984). These earlier accounts attribute Local 34's victory primarily to the democratic approach of Local 34's organisers, reflected in their highly effective campaign strategies based upon grassroots organising and community outreach. Consistent with these accounts, my interpretation also credits Local 34 for devising effective bottom-up organising strategies that contrast with the bureaucratic approach of many labour unions. By way of contrast, however, my analysis concludes that Local 34's victories reflected a skilful blending of grassroots organising and strategic innovation by Local 34 staff, coupled with generous financing and expertise from HERE, Local 34's international affiliate composed of locals throughout the USA and Canada.[1] This analysis also sustains a focus on the comparable-worth issue through the 1988 contract, seeing it as integral to the union's complex and effective strategy.

HISTORICAL CONTEXT OF THE YALE CASE

In many respects Yale University proved to be an ideal testing-ground for an attempt to organise relatively low-paid women workers and to attend to the arguments underlying comparable worth. Before they won a union contract in 1985, Yale's clerical and technical employees earned an average salary of only $13 424, an income considerably below the average salaries earned by Connecticut office-workers as a whole and below the salaries earned by predominantly male service and maintenance workers at Yale, such as truck drivers who earned $18 470.[2] The union's bargaining unit covers a variety of clerical and technical occupations, including secretaries, administrative assistants, library workers, telephone operators, computer programmers, research assistants and practical nurses. 82 per cent of Yale's clerical and technical workers are female, a figure which corresponds to the percentage of women in clerical occupations nationally (80.5 per cent; Feldberg and Glenn, 1984). Clerical workers made up the bulk of the bargaining unit.

The negative impact of gender-segregation in the US workforce as a whole is revealed dramatically by clerical occupations. They represent the largest single occupation for women, employing over 33 per cent of all women workers. In addition, clerical work clearly became devalued only after women replaced men as the dominant job occupants (Feldberg and Glenn, 1984). Before 1910 office work was performed almost exclusively by men who enjoyed better salaries, status, and opportunities for advancement than factory workers. As the occupation became increasingly feminised,[3] it suffered a dramatic decline in status, so that by 1970 the average combined male–female clerical wage had slipped below the combined male–

female blue-collar wage. At present, the occupation includes primarily dead-end jobs with highly routinised and fragmented duties imposed on the basis of 'scientific management', but also many jobs involving unrecognised and uncompensated skills (Feldberg and Glenn, 1984; Davies, 1974; Braverman, 1974; Karen Brodkin Sacks, 1988). Universities frequently exploit the pool of highly educated and under-employed women in college communities by recruiting women with skills in foreign languages, research, composition and copy-editing to fill clerical positions.

Despite their low pay, however, clerical workers have been ill-equipped to recognise and advance their right to comparable pay because most lack any form of union or collective representation. Male-dominated unions have traditionally regarded clerical workers as a difficult segment of the labour force to organise because of their docility, vicarious identification with their bosses, lack of a collectivist work ethic, and weak labour-force attachment because of present or future family roles. Only 10 per cent of women workers are unionised in the private sector, in comparison with 33 per cent of women workers in the public sector.[4]

Prospects for successful clerical organising at Yale, in the private sector, were boosted by a nationwide movement, partly catalysed by the Women's Movement, to organise clerical workers. From 1975 on, campaigns to organise office workers developed both within and outside the confines of existing labour unions. Initially, many feminists who led these campaigns were reluctant to affiliate with existing unions because of both the sexist reputations of the organisations and the patronising treatment by union officers. Many organising campaigns among clericals applied feminist strategies such as 'speak-outs' and 'consciousness-raising groups' in their attempts to form employee committees in various work-places. Grassroots feminist organisations of clerical workers sprang up in many major cities; ten of these groups affiliated with the Boston-based Nine-to-Five Organization, which later inspired a movie and television series with the same time. (The film and television series dramatised feminist themes in situation comedies featuring assertive, competent secretaries collaborating to avoid the foibles and sexual advances of buffoonish male bosses.) These organisations engaged in public education, pursued class action suits against employers whose policies violated the Civil Rights Act of 1964, and formed work-place employee committees to press for change and lay the groundwork for union campaigns.

Since 1975 clerical workers have found public and private universities fertile ground for organising, because they generally provide at least the trappings of a liberal, open atmosphere, consistent with their claims to be 'free market-places of ideas' that preserve academic freedom. So while unions are barred from work sites of business enterprises, they are generally allowed to hold meetings on college campuses, and their campaigns often receive enthusiastic support from left-leaning faculty and staff. In fact, clerical and technical workers are unionised at 25 per cent of the nation's largest private universities, and 50 per cent of the largest public universities (Golden, 1988).

Various characteristics of Yale Universities made it a favourable target for a clerical and technical organising drive in the 1980s. Yale was widely recognised as a wealthy institution that could painlessly finance upgraded salaries for its clerical and technical workers. Its endowment was over $1 billion, and it enjoyed a budget surplus of $35 million in fiscal year 1982–3, the year before Yale began contract negotiations with Local 34 (Gilpin, Isaac, Letwin, and McKivigan, 1988).

The gap between Yale's progressive rhetoric and its character as an élitist and sexist institution also made the university a plausible target for union charges that Yale's administrators were hypocritical and disrespectful of Yale's venerable motto '*Lux et Veritas* (Light and Truth). Yale's progressive reputation probably reached its zenith under Bartlett Giamatti, Yale's President when Local 34 won union recognition and its first contract covering Yale workers. Giamatti prided himself on his progressive stance on many public issues, criticised right-wing spokespersons such as evangelist Jerry Falwell, and promised that the university would subsidise the tuition of students who lost federal loans through their failure to register for the draft (Gilpin, Isaac, Letwin, and McKivigan, 1988).

Yet under Giamatti's tenure Yale retained its character as a prestigious and powerful institution long recognised as a training-ground for the nation's élite. Yale men have consistently held 10 per cent of nation's diplomatic posts. On average, 15 per cent of members of Congress each year are Yale graduates

(Gilpin, Isaac, Letwin, and McKivigan, 1988). Yale's élite and paternalistic character also continued to be reflected in its authoritarian governance structure, which has always been dominated by successful businessmen.[5] Yale lacks any kind of faculty senate, the undergraduates have no college council or student government, and neither students, faculty nor employees have any influence on the composition of Yale's Board of Trustees.

Yale did not even admit women into its undergraduate college until 1969, and currently only 5 per cent of Yale's permanent, tenured faculty positions are held by women. Many female students and faculty at Yale became active supporters of Local 34, claiming that Yale's inequitable personnel policies reflected the same discriminatory attitudes which they had encountered in battles with the Yale administration over such issues as rape and sexual harassment. Even anti-union Yale economist, Jennifer Roback, wrote that women are treated like servants at Yale, 'the most sexist institution I've ever had anything to do with' (Ladd-Taylor, 1985, p. 478).

LOCAL 34'S ORGANISING CAMPAIGN AT YALE, 1982

Local 34's campaign was initiated by Yale employees who were disaffected by the bureaucratic organising tactics of other unions and were impressed by the democratic, militant reputation enjoyed by Local 35 of the Hotel Employees and Restaurant Employees (HERE), which represented Yale's maintenance and service workers (Hurd, 1986). John Wilhelm, business agent (chief administrative officer) for Local 35, responded enthusiastically to request that his union sponsor an organising drive among Yale clerical and technical workers.

Wilhelm's own local was eager to forge an alliance with Yale's clerical and technical employees, who for the most part had failed to honour Local 35's picket lines during its four strikes between 1968 and 1977. Local 35 recognised that its ability to win significant concessions from the Yale administration would be enhanced by pursuing joint negotiating strategies and/or strikes with Yale's clerical and technical workforce.

Wilhelm was also convinced that his own union was well-positioned to launch a successful organising effort because it had the insider contacts and strategic insights missing in the organising drives sponsored by other unions at Yale. Clerical and technical workers had previously rejected unionisation three times between 1967 and 1982; successive campaigns sponsored by District 65 of the Distributive Workers of America (DWA), the Office and Professional Employees International Union (OPEIU), and the United Auto Workers (UAW) all failed. Unlike either OPEIU or UAW, Local 35 had an established reputation on campus as a union that was responsive to members and capable of effectively challenging the Yale administration. Local 35 had the added advantage of being able to recruit the original technical and clerical organising committee from friends and neighbours of its own union-members.

In many respects, Wilhelm's initial recruitment strategy was not substantially different from that of other unions involved in campaigns to organise university office workers. For example two unions which sponsored numerous campaigns among clerical workers, namely District 65, of the Distributive Workers of America (DWA)[6] and Local 925 of the Service Employees International Union, shared Local 34's emphasis on building a grassroots participatory campaign. All three recognised that campaign literature could only supplement their essential recruitment strategy, which required rank-and-file members to serve as the link between union staff and the bulk of potential members, many of whom were at least initially reluctant to attend union meetings or read union literature.

By way of contrast, however, Local 34's campaign was considerably better-financed than many other campaigns to organise university clerical workers. For example, campaigns sponsored by Local 925 and District 65 were shoestring operations relying often on budgets of less than $100 000. Limited financial resources restricted the number of paid organisers for each campaign.

Local 34, however, received generous financial backing from its International, HERE, which just prior to the Yale campaign, had decided to invest heavily in organising to offset a decline in its membership.[7] Although Local 34 officials did not keep records of expenditures during the Yale campaign, they acknowledge costs were 'substantial' and included extensive assistance from HERE. The International provided over $2 million in contributions and a core of trained organisers, including Local 35's business agent, Wilhelm, who proved to be a clever and charismatic strategist. Local 34 also received financial support from Local 35, members of which twice voted to raise their dues to assist the organising drive. As a result of this generous financial support, Local 34 acquired a paid organising staff that numbered twenty by the date of the election and financed glossy professionally printed campaign literature (Gilpin, Isaac, Letwin and McKivigan, 1988).

Hence the Yale victory represented a skilful blending of a grassroots structure that elicited rank-and-file participation, complemented by an extensive core of skilled organisers who provided oversight and direction for a prolonged campaign that encountered intense resistance from the Yale administration. Far from representing a low-cost campaign carried by workers alone, Local 34's participatory campaign probably required more staff than a conventional bureaucratic campaign, since Local 35 helped to create a stable and dedicated rank-and-file organising committee by nurturing recruits with lavish attention and hands-on-training.

The union's organising campaign championed the rights and dignity of clerical workers; this emphasis helped to lay the groundwork for the more explicit introduction of the comparable-worth issue during negotiations for the first contract. The organising committee argued that forming a union was an act of assertion necessary to attain fair wages and professional status for clerical and technical workers, whose jobs reflected the devaluation associated with traditionally female occupations. Yale workers were well aware of their devalued status; they were all too familiar with the indignities of trying to survive on a Yale salary, and many complained openly about personnel policies and lack of recognition for their contributions. However vocal Yale workers were about their grievances, they would vote for union representation only if they became convinced that Local 34 could elicit substantial concessions from the Yale administration. Several Yale workers explained that they had failed to support prior organising drives because the unions involved seemed to be paper tigers, long on militant rhetoric but short on concrete plans for winning a good contract.[8]

Largely because of its carefully orchestrated, well-financed, and intensive organising campaign, Local 34 succeeded in convincing Yale's clerical and technical workers that it could provide effective leadership. It won the union-certification election, however, by the narrowest of margins – winning only 50.9 per cent of the 2505 votes cast. In the year of this victory, unions nationwide won only 10 per cent of union representation elections in bargaining units of over 2000 workers (Kautzer, 1985). The confidence which Yale workers expressed in Local 34 proved justified by the innovative strategy the union devised to win its impressive first contract from Yale.

LOCAL 34 EMBRACES COMPARABLE WORTH IN ITS BATTLE FOR ITS FIRST CONTRACT, 1984–5

In crafting a strategy for Local 34, chief negotiator Wilhelm recognised that the union's strength and even survival would face its most severe test in the battle to attain a good first contract.

Soon after the union victory, the Yale administration signalled its confrontation intentions by hiring the Chicago-based law firm, Seyfarth, Shaw, Fairweather, and Geraldson, regarded by the AFL–CIO as 'one of the most notorious anti-union law firms in the country' (Gilpin, Isaac, Letwin, and McKivigan, 1988, p. 34). This firm represented one of hundreds of 'union-busting' firms that advise American employers how to defeat unions through legal manoeuvring and campaigns of psychological manipulation and misinformation.

For its part, the union hardly approached the bargaining table from a position of strength. On the contrary, support for the union was relatively weak. Moreover, negotiators faced difficulties in their relationship with union supporters. The elation that accompanied the union victory led union supporters to hope that their first contract would produce dramatic and substantial gains. If members were disappointed in the first contract they might very well opt to decertify Local 34 when the contract expired. In addition, members' lack of union experience left them without realistic guidelines for assessing contract proposals or their potential for winning a strike. At the outset of negotiations, union leaders were not certain that their members would be willing to initiate or sustain a strike.

Under these circumstances, Wilhelm recognised that Local 34 could acquire leverage at the bargaining table only by strengthening membership commitment and by surprising Yale administrators and their team of union-busting attorneys with a bold and imaginative strategy. The miscalculations which the Yale administration displayed during the strike probably stemmed from their expectation that Local 34 would pursue a standard union bargaining strategy. In this strategy, unions centre contract demands almost exclusively on economic issues and rely primarily on strike threats to elicit concessions.

Wilhelm realised that conventional union tactics were proving increasingly ineffective, even for established militant unions such as the United Auto Workers (UAW). In 1984 in the USA as a whole, union contracts registered the lowest wage increases in 17 years, and the percentage of union members nationwide had slipped to less than 20 per cent of the labour force (Lacombe and Sleemi, 1988). Manufacturing employers in industries such as the auto industry were positioned to endure lengthy strikes, to demand 'givebacks' or 'concessions' (in which unions forfeit benefits achieved previously), and/or eliminate unions altogether through decertification elections and lockouts; employers' growing strategic advantage was due to increased reliance on automation, their development of production facilities abroad in low-wage economies, and an expanding pool of unemployed workers in the USA (Kautzer, 1985).

Employers' willingness to pursue aggressive anti-union strategies was enhanced by US public opinion's increasing hostility to unions (Keegan, 1987). Since unions for the most part failed to make their case to the American public, employers could justify their hard-line stance by 'crying poor mouth' (pleading lack of funds), and depicting unions as greedy dinosaurs, unable to adapt to the harsh fiscal realities and new management practices of the 1980s.

In a very real sense, then, the negotiating strategy crafted by Local 34 was the counterpoint to the standard union tactics that were spelling defeat and retreat for established labour unions. Far from ignoring public relations, the primary thrust of Local 34's campaign was building support for its demands among the Yale and New Haven community. Local 34 embraced comparable worth as its primary issue precisely because it enabled the union to champion social justice rather than simply demand higher wages. Wilhelm's strategy represented a return to the historic mission of American unions, which originally attracted members and won concessions from management by championing social justice and mobilising community coalitions (Boyer and Morals, 1955).

Local 34's public campaign reached a climax during its ten-week strike, which commenced on 26 September 1984, but began with the onset of negotiations in October 1983. It was highly sophisticated and extensive – it included a range of attention-grabbing demonstrations, petition drives and rallies, as well as attractive, readable and persuasive professional position papers and press releases. In recognition of the academic character of the Yale community, the union also provided documentation for its positions, publishing, for example, the results of its salary survey, which showed that women and black workers, even when they have had longer years of service, earned substantially less than white male workers.[9]

The issue of comparable worth became a key focus of the union's strategy not only because it raised issues of economic justice and questions that clearly applied to the structure of employment at Yale, but also because it was effective in attracting media attention. Local 34 spokespersons convinced the media that the struggle at Yale had national significance because it centred on an intriguing new concept that could potentially become a widespread demand in collective bargaining. The significance of the Yale strike seemed confirmed by the appearance at rallies of famous feminist and labour leaders, including Judy Goldsmith, then President of NOW, the largest feminist advocacy organisation in the USA, and Lane Kirkland, President of the American Federation of Labor–Congress of Industrial Organizations, the US trade union confederation. Consequently, the strike received widespread coverage in local and national newspapers, magazines, and news programmes; it was even discussed on the Phil Donahue show, a popular nationally distributed TV talk-show.

The comparable-worth issue attracted the interest and support of a wide range of faculty and students, particularly feminist groups which were delighted that a battle over this path-breaking concept was being launched in their own backyard. Eager to protect their reputation for progressive leadership, Yale administrators could not simply mimic Reagan officials, who dismissed comparable worth as 'looney'. Instead the tone of their response was defensive and apologetic, as in the oft-quoted statement of Yale Provost, William Brainard:

> I know that one can't live the way one would like to, or the way one's family would like to live, on a Yale clerical and technical salary. That's a national problem, which Yale can't be expected to solve (Gilpin, Isaac, Letwin, and McKivigan, 1988).

Yale administrators apparently found their position so difficult to defend that they avoided the media during the strike.

The support which Local 34 had accumulated became manifest during its ten-week strike, which dramatically disrupted university operations, barely allowing Yale to maintain its educational and research functions. 95 per cent of Yale's service and maintenance workers honoured Local 34's picket signs. Their absence from work resulted in the closing of all but one campus dining hall and the development of unsanitary conditions in dormitories. This show of solidarity on the part of Local 35 was particularly noteworthy in the light of members' bitter memories of Yale clerical and technical workers crossing their picket-lines on three occasions. Moreover, Local 35 might have resented Local 34's comparisons of the low salaries of Yale's clerical and technical workers with the higher salaries of the 'male' occupations represented by Local 35. However, bonds of respect and affection were forged between members of the two locals, as Local 34 members demonstrated verve and stamina on the picket-line and exposed their shockingly low salaries (Gilpin, Isaac, Lewin and McKivigan, 1988). Serving as chief negotiator for both locals, Wilhelm seems to have been able to persuade both groups of their mutual interest in collaborative strategies.

Students and faculty were almost evenly divided into pro- and anti-union factions, but those who were sympathetic to the union walked picket-lines and circulated petitions supporting union demands. Pro-union faculty moved over 400 classes of off-campus locations, and over a hundred pro-union students filed a lawsuit charging Yale with breach of contract for failing to provide necessary services during the strike. A group of alumni circulated a petition among Yale graduates pledging to withhold donations until the strike was settled. Local 34 strikers also received varying forms of support from the city of New Haven, including $100 000 in donations to the strike fund from local unions and a resolution from the New Haven Board of Aldermen, the municipal governing body of elected officers, urging Yale to end the strike through arbitration or compromise.

In addition to facing these pressures, Yale administrators were caught off guard by Wilhelm's innovative and flexible strategy. Again deviating from standard union practice, he viewed a strike as a tactic that would be employed only under conditions favourable to the union. Hence, when Local 34 reached its first strike deadline of 28 March 1984, Wilhelm persuaded union-members to accept a partial contract, which would codify all the concessions the union had negotiated at that point. He recognised that a strike begun in late spring would be poorly timed, since university operations slowed down over the summer. Although union members initially feared a partial contract was a form of cooptation or retreat, it proved to preserve important gains and prevent the university from resorting to a lock-out when the union went on strike on 26 September 1984.

Wilhelm devised a similarly un-conventional and flexible proposal dubbed 'Home for the Holidays' for ending the strike that began in September. On 4 December he perceived that returning to work temporarily would alleviate the economic stress many strikers were experiencing and would relieve the union of carrying a strike during the slow ten-week Christmas break. The plan had the added advantage of presenting Yale with an ultimatum to make acceptable contract offers to both Local 34 and 35 or face a joint strike on 19 January, the date Local 35's contract expired. Despite strong objections by some female strikers who feared they were being asked to 'subordinate their own struggles to the Local 35 guys' (Ladd-Taylor, 1985), Wilhelm persuaded strikers to endorse his proposal by a vote of 800 to 250 (Gilpin, Isaac, Letwin, and McKivigan, 1988).

The strategy seemed to bear fruit when, after an all-night negotiating session on 19 January, Local 34's bleary-eyed negotiating committee triumphantly announced that they had tentatively approved a contract offer. The contract, ratified by the members two days later, included a 20.25 per cent across-the-board pay rise over 3 years and a revision to the salary structure to correct discrimination against long-term employees whose incomes had remained at the bottom of their salary grade. By the close of their contract, Local 34 employees received average pay increases of 32 per cent a figure which reflects both across-the-board increases and rises based on seniority and classification. The elimination of the lowest grade, which included many older black women, increased the wages of some of the lowest paid workers by 80–90 per cent and revalued the contributions of these workers. The contract included a new seniority system, a new dental plan, improved pension benefits and job security. Many new benefits were geared towards the needs of women workers (Ladd-Taylor, 1985). In contrast to the 32 per cent average achieved by Local 34, union wages in the private sector in the USA as a whole rose only 8.7 per cent and clerical wages only 16 per cent between 1984 and 1987 (Lacombe and Sleemi, 1988).[10]

Thus Local 34's strategy for winning its first contract represented the same balance of grassroots participation and adequate financing that had characterised its campaign for union representation. Local 34's high level of membership involvement enabled the union to sustain and suspend their strike at critical points in the negotiations. Financial assistance from HERE also assisted the strike and the intensive public-oriented campaign.[11] Comparable-worth arguments were part of a strategy oriented towards social justice. Discussions over comparable worth also convinced union officers that job-classification issues were critically important to Yale staff and merited attention in the next contract. While the union did not achieve any contract language referring to comparable worth in its first contract, it did lay the groundwork for revising Yale's job-classification system by obtaining a clause establishing a Joint Committee on Job Descriptions and Classifications, composed of four union representatives, four university managers, and a neutral faculty chairperson. This joint Committee later played a critical role in Local 34's drive to win a new job-classification system in its second contract. Finally Local 34's new contract included a number of beneficial provisions for women workers including clauses on affirmative action, sexual harassment and personal work.

LOCAL 34'S BATTLE FOR A NEW JOB CLASSIFICATION SYSTEM AND A SECOND CONTRACT

Local 34's first contract settlement generated the momentum necessary to sustain union supporters as they undertook the task of converting their loosely structured organising committee into a stable, cohesive union. Given the high turnover and dispersed nature of Local 34's bargaining unit, organisers recognised that they would retain a high degree of allegiance among Yale workers only by remaining a visible and persistent advocate for employee interests. After conducting surveys among and informal discussions with union members, union leaders identified Yale's job-classification system as a central grievance to be redressed when the union negotiated its second contract in 1988. Besides faulting the system for discrimination based on race and gender, employees claimed that salary grades were not assigned on the basis of uniform, rational criteria, but rather reflected the clout of the boss or department. Union members approved a package of contract demands that prioritised a new job-classification system.

The union had laid the groundwork for reforming the old system by obtaining a clause in its first contract establishing a Joint Committee on Job Descriptions and Classifications. This Committee was charged with reviewing and recommending reforms in the existing Clerical and Technical Job Classification Structure. Local 34 became the dominant force on this Committee, in large measure because the university administration failed to match the union's intensive and sophisticated efforts to influence Committee recommendations. Yale's Department of Human Resources (DHR) simply defended the system as highly rational and efficient, yet flexible enough to adopt to variable conditions within the university and the labour market as a whole.

The union, on the other hand, worked to document and draw attention to the flaws in the system. The 400 persons who packed the Committee's two public hearings on the classification system were primarily union members, many of whom related their problems. The union also flooded the Joint Committee with requests to review job-audit decisions of the DHR by providing aggrieved employees with official union representatives to guide them through the process. In July 1987, after reviewing the case histories of aggrieved employees, the Joint Committee issued a report challenging the rationale and equity of the system (Report of the Joint Committee on Job Descriptions and classifications, 1 July 1987).

The union then bolstered its argument that Yale's existing classification system was discriminatory by conducting and publicising a highly sophisticated evaluation of the system. It assigned one of its six full-time staff positions to a 'Job Evaluation Specialist'. Consistent with its emphasis upon building a locally-controlled, participatory union, Local 34 hired Janet Rozen, a long-term Yale employee to fill the post; Rozen maintained close links with Ronnie Steinberg of Temple University, a nationally recognised expert on comparable worth who had conducted a pay-equity study in New York State. Rozen began by preparing a questionnaire soliciting a broad range of data from each employee about the nature and range of her qualifications and work. The questionnaire proved to be a powerful organising tool, since it was completed during personal interviews between union officials and both union and non-union workers. The process took an entire year and yielded responses from only 50 per cent of the bargaining unit. In order to use their survey data most effectively, the union hired a Connecticut data-entry firm to code and keypunch survey results and a New-Haven-based consulting firm to analyse survey results by using linear regression techniques.

In order to analyse survey results, each employee's position was scored according to the nine criteria that Yale identified as the basis of its job-classification system. Statistical tests were applied to determine if there was a correlation between the independent variables (i.e. Yale's nine criteria) and the dependent variable (i.e. the actual ranking assigned to each position). The study also tested whether there was a correlation between a number of factors which union members believed influenced classification decisions (such as gender, race, work-setting, contact) and actual job rankings.

The results of the analysis were a devastating indictment of Yale's system and a ringing affirmation of criticisms voiced by employees. According to the study, several of the factors which Yale identified as criteria, namely 'independence,' 'experience,' and 'knowledge and skills,' bore no relationship to actual placement of job-titles in salary grades. In other words, positions which scored highly on these criteria were not assigned correspondingly higher salary grades. The criterion of 'education required' showed the strongest relationship to salary grade.

The study also supported union claims that race, gender, and/or work-setting (department of campus) were influential in job classifications. By comparing salaries of women and men in comparable positions, the survey revealed that the average woman in the bargaining unit was underpaid by approximately $1280 per year. Ethnicity also influenced salary grade; the average non-white worker was underpaid by approximately $700. The factor 'work-setting' also influenced salary grade; certain departments consistently assigned employees higher grades than employees performing comparable work in other departments.

The union released the findings of its pay-equity study in the autumn of 1987, just prior to the beginning of negotiations for its second contract. Its campaign for winning a new job-classification system was to some degree modelled on the strategy that had proved effective during the 1984–5 strike, the strategy of 'beating Yale at its own game'. Yale was a noted research centre, but it was the union that produced a sophisticated evaluation of Yale's classification system and designed an alternative system based on more just and consistent criteria. Yale prided itself on its management expertise, but the recommendations of the Joint Labor/Management Committee essentially endorsed reforms advocated by union representatives. Consequently the union assumed a highly credible and confident posture as it presented its contract demands to the media and the Yale community. The university was once again forced into a defensive, embarrassed position, from which it escaped only by succumbing to union demands.

On the other hand, however, Local 34's success in winning its second contract required a public relations campaign based on tactics decidedly different from those which produced the first settlement. Local 34's ability to attract national media was this time hampered by the fact that its battle with Yale over pay equity was 'old news', and it achieved a second contract without resorting to the dramatic strike that had polarised Yale in 1984–5. Yale's new President, Benno C. Schmidt, Jr., reversed the secretive and evasive media relations of his predecessor by appointing articulate and accessible press spokespersons.

Under these conditions, the union focused on building a solid core of supporters within Yale and the larger New Haven community. Students formed a union support committee with over 80 active organisers. Over 5000 faculty, students, and New Haven residents wrote to the administration urging a peaceful settlement. By opting to engage in joint contract negotiations with Local 35, the two unions were able to present joint demands on some issues, while signalling their intention to strike jointly if either side failed to obtain a satisfactory settlement. The union also featured Presidential candidate, Jesse Jackson, at a packed union rally three days before the union's strike deadline. Jackson emphasised the national significance of the struggle over comparable worth at Yale, concluding, 'We must not demean the people in structured economic violence' (Coyle, 1988).

The union achieved impressive gains in its second contract, including a new job-classification system, salary increases averaging over 26.2 per cent over four years, a fund of $200 000 for job training, and improved dental and mental health benefits. The terms of the contract were so generous that university administrators were forced to defend themselves against charges that they had totally 'caved in' to union demands (Carey, 1988).

The new classification scheme upgraded all but twenty positions, while reserving the most dramatic upgrading for employees in the lowest grades who had been the most obvious victims of discriminatory policies. The overall thrust of the new system was the establishment of a more egalitarian distribution of salaries by reducing the number of salary grades from ten to four, including new factors for evaluating jobs (including stress, safety, risk, effort), and by emphasising work experience more than formal education.

Once again, the union's winning strategy blended grassroots outreach to university and community groups with expert oversight, including experienced negotiators and technical consultants. The peaceful contract settlement bolstered the new President's image as a competent and humane administrator who spared Yale the disruption of another strike. Schmidt's approval of the union's job-classification proposal may have reflected his eagerness to put to rest the comparable-worth controversy, that had consistently evoked awkward and embarrassed reactions from university administrators. The university was apparently so eager to rid itself of the comparable-worth controversy that it allowed the union unilaterally to determine the terms of the new classification system rather than insisting upon the give-and-take that is standard practice in collective bargaining.

IMPLEMENTATION OF THE NEW CLASSIFICATION SYSTEM

Predictably, implementing the new job-classification system mandated in Local 34's contract proved to be a consuming and difficult task for both the Yale Personnel Department, which retained formal authority over the process, and Local 34 staff, who closely monitored every new job description and classification determination affecting members of their bargaining unit. According to Michael Boyle, the Local 34 staff person responsible for overseeing classification issues, the union successfully challenged the Personnel Department's attempts to misclassify certain categories of employees during the implementation phase. Similarly the union expects to win approximately 50 per cent of the grievances employees have filed regarding those cases the union was unable to resolve during the implementation phase.

Not surprisingly the whole classification process has proved to be something of an administrative nightmare for the union because handling so many grievances requires inordinate amounts of staff time. In Boyle's opinion, this process is worthwhile when groups of employees in similar positions fight reclassification decisions collectively, because the struggle teaches workers the value of collective action. However grievances affecting single employees are intensely time-consuming and considerably less valuable as organising tools.

Currently there is no systematic data available for evaluating the impact of Yale's reclassification on previous systematic inequities. A note of caution is clearly sounded, however, by Boyle, who reported that the Personnel Department was fairly responsive to appeals for upgrading highly technical positions (such as computer programmers and copy-editors), but highly resistant to appeals for upgrading positions such as library clerks and secretaries (that did not require highly specialised training or experience). Boyle also notes that the new classification system produced resentment among those workers who were unsuccessful in their appeals to the Personnel Department for upgrading. As a result of these problems, Boyle questions whether the union might possibly have achieved more equitable benefits for all its members through a standard contract granting across-the-board rises, rather than insisting on a messy reclassification process that disappointed many members.

THE SIGNIFICANCE OF THE YALE CASE

Unquestionably Local 34 has made a positive contribution to the campaign for comparable worth by making this issue the cornerstone of its highly-publicised contract battles with Yale. Local 34 enhanced the visibility and credibility of the issue by emerging as an articulate and effective advocate of comparable worth, and by winning public endorsements of its demands from a range of civil rights and union officials, including Lane Kirkland, President of the AFL–CIO, and Ralph Abernathy of the National Association for the Advancement of Colored Persons (NAACP). Remarkably, none of the principal players in the Yale case argued against the logic of the union's demands for pay equity. On the contrary, Yale officials implicitly endorsed comparable worth by arguing that essentially only financial constraints inhibited Yale from seizing the leadership initiative on this important new principle of social justice.

Most important, Local 34's contract victories increase the likelihood that other unions would engage in contract battles over the issue of comparable worth, which proved to be a powerful propaganda device in the Yale case. Admittedly, Local 34's strategy is likely to prove most effective against employers like Yale who cultivate a progressive image. Most notably, there are obvious parallels between the Yale case and Harvard University, where clerical and technical workers voted in favour of union representation with the American Federation of State, County and Municipal Employees (AFSCME) in May 1988. Harvard employees identified 'pay equity and child care' as priority demands for their first contract. In June 1989 they won a contract granting average salary increases of 32 per cent over three years, as well as a low-cost child-care centre.

Needless to say, however, unions cannot expect demands for comparable worth to evoke a uniform reaction from all private sector employers. Profit-making corporations, in particular, frequently profess conservative values, and would probably respond to union demands for pay equity by adopting the 'looney tune' rhetoric of the Reagan Administration. By the same token, even employers who profess liberal values are unlikely to model their own anti-union strategy on the defensive, self-defeating posture evidenced by the Yale administration. In fact Yale Vice President, Peter Vallone, publicly advised Harvard that:

> The first contract at Yale would not be a benchmark for other universities. It probably did go too far. I'd advise Harvard to be very, very conservative (Golden, 1988, p. 44).

In keeping with this advice, Harvard's President Bok initially adopted a pugnacious strategy, attempting to overturn the recent union election by charging the union with unfair labour practices. At first Bok appeared impervious to public criticisms that his anti-union stance contradicted his reputation as a liberal advocate of collective bargaining.[12] By November 1988, however, Bok opted formally to recognise the union after the National Labor Relations Board dismissed Harvard's anti-union charges as 'frivolous'. Bok's about-face can probably be credited to the public pressure mustered by AFSCME, whose officers considered withdrawing support for the trade union programme at Harvard if Bok failed to recognise the union. Once Harvard recognised the union, a spirit of cooperation and mutual respect governed contract negotiations, and a settlement was achieved in six months, a remarkably short period for a first contract. Harvard's conciliatory spirit at the bargaining-table reflects Bok's desire to avoid a disruptive work-stoppage or negative publicity.

The Yale case also suggests that it is possible to mobilise male workers and even predominantly male unions to support contract demands for pay equity. Interestingly, Local 34 even persuaded its 'brother union' Local 35 to negotiate a revised classification system to ensure equity for male and female service and maintenance workers at Yale. The solidarity achieved between Local 34 and Local 35 at Yale was no doubt facilitated by the fact that these Locals were both affiliated with HERE and shared Wilhelm as their chief negotiator. The likelihood of forming similar alliances at other universities or institutions is diminished by the fact that service and maintenance workers are frequently affiliated with different unions from those which represent campus clerical and technical workers. Moreover despite the commonalities shared by Local 34 and Local 35 at Yale, tension occasionally surfaced between the two groups. Nonetheless both unions ultimately became convinced of the benefits of collaboration by the impressive contract gains they achieved following their joint negotiations in 1988.

Despite these achievements, the potential contribution of Local 34 to future battles over comparable worth is diminished by the fact that the union never phrased a single contract demand in comparable-worth terminology, and hence the term 'comparable worth' (or equivalent phrases such as 'pay equity') are not included in their formal contract agreements.[13]

In a very real sense, the Yale case reveals the tensions and contradictions inherent in strategies designed to weld feminist and trade-union objectives. Local 34's failure even to demand contract language on comparable worth indicates that their principal identity and mission was that of a labour union intent on winning tangible gains for all its members. For this reason Local 34 was primarily attracted to the comparable-worth issue for rhetorical rather than ideological reasons, and tended to play down the feminist principles which underlie the concept of comparable worth.

This conclusion is supported by the fact that Local 34 devoted minimal effort to educating its members or the larger public about the meaning or implications entailed in the principle of comparable worth. Consequently union officers concur that few of their members are familiar with the term 'comparable worth' and few would identify themselves as 'feminist'. While workers strongly favored Local 34's demands for a new job-classification system, they were at least as concerned about correcting inequities between and among departments at Yale as they were about eliminating discrimination based on race and gender.

In addition, Local 34 consistently played down the feminist

implications of the comparable-worth issue whenever it threatened to alienate male members of the bargaining unit. For example, some male workers took strong exception to the feminist rhetoric expressed at some union meetings and complained that a settlement based on comparable worth would penalise male workers. Union officers apparently quelled these grievances by insisting that males in predominantly female occupations were victims of discrimination to the same degree as their female colleagues. This argument, however, is contradicted by Local 34's own research, which uncovered 'robust sex and race discriminated' in their study of Yale's job-classification system, and which produced two contract agreements that favoured female and minority employees. For example, Local 34's first contract increased wages for the bargaining unit as a whole by 32 per cent, but wages of black women increased by 36 per cent while those of white men increased by only 28 per cent (*Common Sense*, 6 October 1987).

Local 34 officials also deflected criticisms of male members by arguing that each contract would target different inequities, but eventually all categories of workers would receive consideration. Hence the first contract contained seniority increases most beneficial to long-term workers, while the second contract reserved the highest increases for workers in the lowest grade positions who were misclassified under the old system. Clearly, however, this argument is based on convoluted logic since women workers (at Yale or elsewhere) will never achieve pay equity if every increase they receive is eventually offset by a comparable increase for male workers.

Local 34's equivocal responses to male members reflect its preoccupation with protecting its primary source of strength as a labour union, namely a large and cohesive membership. Perhaps union officials were so convinced of the merits of their strategy that they never recognised the contraditions inherent in basing union demands on feminist rhetoric. For the same reason they apparently had no objections to Wilhelm's role as principal spokesperson for Local 34, despite the fact that the media portrayed him as something of a white knight rescuing the damsels in distress at Yale.[14] In any event, while Local 34 may have played down feminist principles, its achievements were also consistent with a number of feminist objectives.

First, the gains achieved by the union in its first two contracts conferred on Yale's predominantly female work-force the standard union benefits (including higher starting salaries and a seniority system) that until recently were restricted primarily to male workers in industrial occupations. These benefits dramatically increased the average salaries of Yale's clerical and technical workers from a low of $13 424 before unionisation to an impressive $21 200 at the close of the second contract. Future studies by the union and/or other researchers could evaluate the extent to which Local 34's contract gains eliminated the wage gap between Yale's clerical and technical positions and comparable occupations at Yale and elsewhere. Future studies could also evaluate the overall impact of Yale's new job-classification system, which Local 34 designed to ensure an equitable system of classifying jobs within its own bargaining unit.

Second, Local 34 demonstrated that the process of unionisation complements the feminist objective of cultivating leadership and assertiveness skills among women workers. Throughout its seven-year history, Local 34 has provided both formal and informal leadership training to many rank-and-file members and has actively recruited women and minorities to serve the union as staff, officers and members of negotiating committees. Consequently women and minority representation in all union leadership positions corresponds to the representation of these groups within the bargaining unit. Several union activists, including Local 34 President, Lucille Dickess, credit the union with igniting or expanding their allegiance to the women's movement, and frequently pepper their speeches at union rallies or press conferences with feminist rhetoric. Even many union members who reject the 'feminist' label emphasise that participation in the union has enhanced their sense of dignity and self-worth, and taught them to view conflict and controversy as challenging and creative rather than intimidating and distasteful.

Perhaps Local 34's greatest contribution to the women's movement is the fact that its impressive contract gains are likely to inspire future union organising efforts among women workers, particularly the 85 per cent of non-unionised clerical workers. To date the Yale contract has already been utilised in a number of union campaigns, including successful campaigns at

Columbia and Harvard universities. Organisers in these campaigns make frequent reference to the Yale contract to rebut anti-union propaganda emphasising the minimal gains achieved by unionised clerical workers in a number of workplaces.

Organisers have also countered arguments that unionisation will create divisive unpleasant working atmospheres by featuring rank-and-file members of Local 34 at union rallies and informational meetings. These speakers provide compelling personal testimony about how unionisation has enhanced their dignity and respect and improved their overall job satisfaction.

The Yale case also vividly demonstrates the potential leverage which unions can attain by devising flexible, innovative strategies that strike a balance between grassroots participation and expert oversight. One important lesson of the Yale case is that successful organising campaigns among clerical workers probably require the investment of substantial resources as well as participatory organising tactics.

Another important lesson which the Yale case offers the American labour movement is that strikes may not be the most effective method of securing contract gains, since like Local 34, unions are frequently restricted in their ability to command the loyalty of members or disrupt operations at a particular workplace. By involving the New Haven community and national media in their contract battle, Wilhelm revealed that university officials were at least as interested in protecting their public image as they were in maintaining university operations. In the same vein, by presenting its case in a highly articulate, vigorous and imaginative fashion and by reclaiming labour's historic role as the champion of social justice, Local 34 demonstrated the extent to which community support can be mobilised by and on behalf of labour unions.

Finally, by designing a highly pragmatic and flexible strike policy, Local 34 revealed that potential risks of striking can be minimised (by limiting walkouts to high-impact periods and approving partial contracts that prevent lock-outs), while the public relations benefits of strikes can be maximised (by engaging in community outreach on picket lines and staging 'media events' featuring celebrity endorsements).

In conclusion, the Yale case reveals both the potential and limitations of achieving comparable worth through collective bargaining. On the one hand, unions can provide workers with the resources necessary to document and focus public attention on inequitable wage policies, and the leverage to obtain substantial salary increases and reforms in personnel policies. On the other hand, unions will probably remain unwilling to risk membership divisiveness by explicitly asking male members to endorse policies preferential to their female colleagues. In the same vein, unions will probably refrain from educating members about the feminist principles that underlie demands for comparable worth. Finally unions may also shy away from contract demands for new classifications systems because they require expensive administrative oversight and/or educating workers in the purposes and techniques of job evaluation.

As a model of labour relations designed to mediate between employers and employees, the trade-union model necessarily remains an imperfect vehicle for mediating gender-based inequities. By the same token, however, advocates of comparable worth cannot afford to bypass collective bargaining since it represents a primary vehicle whereby male workers have attained their privileged position within the labour market. Perhaps by exploring and utilising collective bargaining to its utmost potential, feminists will gain the insights and alliances necessary to replace it with a more effective, genuinely feminist method of promoting women's interests.

Notes

1. My alternative interpretation draws on an implicit comparison of Local 34's strategy with that of other campaigns to organise clerical workers. It is also consistent with the 'resource mobilisation theory' of collective behaviour which points to resources as a critical factor determining the likelihood of group mobilisation and the ability of groups to promote their own interests. See, for example, Meyer Zald and John McCarthy, *The Dynamics of Social Movements, Resource Mobilisation and Tactics* (Clanham, MD: University Press of America, 1968).

2. Figures on Yale salaries quoted here and throughout the chapters are based on data presented in a variety of leaflets and booklets published by Local 34.

3. After the turn of the century, women were recruited to fill the ever-expanding number of clerical positions required by the large-scale corporate enterprises that came to dominate the economy in the twentieth century. Although employers originally doubted their competence, female clerical workers quickly proved themselves to be reliable, capable workers who were less expensive and more available than male workers (Feldberg and Glenn, 1984).

4. These 1984 figures are cited in Table I of Richard Freeman and Jonathan Leonard, 'Union Maids: Unions and the Female Work Force' in Clair Brown and Joseph Pechman (eds) *Gender in the Workplace* (Washington, DC: Brookings Institution, 1987) p. 191. According to the US Bureau of Labor Statistics, there are no current statistics on percentages of women workers organised in the public and private sectors.

5. For example, at the time of Local 34's strike, the three members of the Yale Corporation who were widely considered to exert the most influence over financial decisions included J. Richardson Dilworth, financial advisor to the Rockefeller family; John D. Madden, managing partner in the Brown Brothers, Harriman and Co. Bank; and Cyrus Vance, former Secretary of State and current member of the boards of US Steel, Manufacturers Hanover Trust, and IBM (Gilpin, Isaac, Letwin, and McKivigan, 1988).

6. District 65 affiliated with the United Auto Workers in 1980. The union continues to sponsor campaigns among clerical workers, and currently represents the clerical and technical staff at Boston University and Columbia University.

7. It is interesting to note that HERE's decision to invest heavily in the Yale campaign reflected the 'old boy network' in that this policy directive was issued by Vincent Sirabella, shortly after he was appointed HERE's Director of Organization, after serving as head of HERE's New Haven Local 217. One can only speculate whether Sirabella's decision to invest heavily in the Yale campaign was influenced by the confidence he displayed in his New Haven colleague John Wilhelm, who directed the Yale campaign. Unlike Wilhelm, the female organisers at Harvard did not receive substantial contributions from AFSCME until they had established an extensive campaign organisation.

8. Generalisation about the opinions of Local 34 members included here and throughout this chapter are based primarily on interviews I conducted with five current and former Local 34 members in July of 1988. My generalisations correspond to the findings of Nina Gregg, who is currently completing a doctoral dissertation based on forty interviews with Local 34 members.

9. Local 34's survey revealed the following salary distribution by race and sex for Local 34's bargaining unit:

Table 7.1   Salary distribution (Local 34)

Group	Average salary	Average years at Yale
White men	$14 324	5.7
White women	$13 408	5.8
Black men	$12 813	5.3
Black women	$12 603	7.1

Source: A Report to the Community from the Members of Local 34, Federation of University Employees, AFL–CIO, September, 1984.

10. These figures tend to overstate the significance of the gains achieved by Local 34. Unions typically attempt to achieve large rises in a first contract in order to bring wages up to union scale. Furthermore, a true comparison of the gains achieved in varying contracts would require figures on base salaries and the dollar amount of average raises. Hence the 20.5 per cent across the board increases in Local 34's first contract would translate into higher raises for Local 35 members (whose salaries average $10 470 in 1985) than for Local 34 members (whose salaries averaged $13 424 prior to unionisation).

11. HERE provided Yale members in Local 34 and Local 35 strike benefits of $50 per week commencing three weeks after the onset of the strike.

12. Harvard's President, Derek Bok, attained his reputation as an advocate of American labour unions by co-authoring *Labor and the American Community*, an acclaimed analysis of the labour relations in the USA.

13. One account (Ladd-Taylor, 1985) states that Local 34 intentionally avoided use of comparable-worth terminology in demands for their first contract since the term is based on technical studies confusing to members, and reinforces hierarchical assumptions about salaries and job classifications. By the second contract, however, Local 34 had engaged in its own very technical studies documenting its recommendations for a new job-classification system. The system crafted by Local 34 was hierarchical in nature (though decidedly less so than the pre-existing system). In any case, by the second contract Local 34 could no longer claim that ideological objections prevented it from including comparable-worth terminology in its contract demands.

14. This 'white knight' theme is particularly evident in two articles on the strike both printed in *The New York Times*: Serrin, William, 'Strike at Yale Is Being Watched by Many' (11 October 1984) and Serrin, William, 'Union's Success at Yale: New Focus on White-Collar Women' (10 April 1984).

References

Acker, Joan (1989) *Comparable Worth: Gender, Class and Pay Equity* (Philadelphia: Temple University Press).

Boyer, Richard O., and Morais, Herbert (1955) *Labor's Untold Story* (New York: Cameron Associates).

Braverman, Harry (1974) *Labor and Monopoly Capital: The Degradation of Work in the Twentieth Century* (New York: Monthly Review Press).

Carey, Mary Agnes (1988) 'Union Negotiators Quietly Crow Over Gains at Yale', *New Haven Register*, 31 January.

Coyle, Paula (1988) 'Yale Unions to Rally with Jackson', *New Haven Register*, 19 January.

Cupo, Aldo; Ladd-Taylor, Molly; Lett, Beverly; and Montgomery, David (1984) 'Beep, Beep, Yale's Cheap: Looking at the Yale Strike', in *Radical America*, vol. 18, no 5, pp. 7–19.

Davies, Margery (1974) 'Women's Place Is at the Typewriter: The Feminization of the Clerical Workforce' in *Radical America*, vol. 3.

Feldberg, Roslyn L. and Glenn, Evelyn Nakano (1984) Clerical Work in Female Occupations' in Freeman, Jo (ed.) *Women: A Feminist Perspective* (Palo Alto, California: Mayfield Publishing Company).

Gilpin, Tony; Isaac, Gary; Letwin, Dan; McKivigan, Jack (1988) *On Strike for Respect: The Yale Strike of 1984–5* (Chicago: Charles H. Kerr).

Golden, Daniel (1988) 'Taking on Harvard', *The Boston Globe Magazine*, 7 August.

Hurd, Rich (1986) 'Bottom-Up Organising: Here in New Haven and Boston' in *Labor Research Review*, 8, Spring.

Kauffman, Matthew and Citron, Roger (1988) 'Yale Unions Say Four-Year Contract Opens a New Era', *The Hartford Courant*, 27 January.

Kautzer, Kathleen (1988) 'Charting a New Course for the American Labor Movement' in Gil, Eva and Gil, David, *Toward Social and Economic Justice* (Cambridge, Massachusetts: Schenkman).

Kautzer, Kathleen (1988) 'University of Hard Knocks, Lessons from the Yale Strike', *Dollars and Sense*, May.

Keegan, Carol (1987) 'How Union Members and Nonmembers View the Role of Unions', *Monthly Labor Review*, August.

Lacombe, John J. and Sleemi, Fehmida R. (1988) 'Wage Adjustments in Contract Negotiations in Private Industry in 1987', *Monthly Labor Review*, May.

Ladd-Taylor, Molly (1985) 'Women Workers and the Yale Strike', *Feminist Studies*, Fall.

Sacks, Karen Brodkin (1988) *Caring by the Hour: Women, Work and Organizing at Duke Medical Center* (Chicago: University of Illinois Press).

Sokoloff, Natalie J. (1988) *Between Love and Money: The Dialectics of Women's Home and Market Work* (New York: Praeger).

8 Fighting for Equal Value: Health Workers in Northern Ireland
Kathy Sutton

INTRODUCTION

On the Falls Road in West Belfast, minutes from the Springfield Barracks, lies the Royal Victoria Hospital. It is here that arguably the most important and significant battle has been fought by women in Northern Ireland against low pay and for equal pay (*McCauley and others* v. *Eastern Health Services Board*). In January 1985, Mary McCauley, Rosaleen Davidson, Margaret Spotswood, Mary Hughes and Sarah Devlin – five part-time domestic assistants at the hospital, all of them night workers – lodged their claim for equal pay for work of equal value to that of porters and ground staff employed at the hospital. Their case has been assisted by their trade union – the National Union of Public Employees (NUPE)[1] – and the Northern Ireland Equal Opportunities Commission.

The struggle of ancillary workers to get equal pay has not been confined to taking a legal test case but has incorporated the concept of equal value into collective-bargaining claims. In doing so, the struggle has been a bold one, challenging both the discriminatory pay structure of the local health board and the national health policies of the United Kingdom (UK) government. The campaigners have used equal value as a tactical weapon in a wider campaign against poverty, low pay and deterioration in the standards of the health service in Northern Ireland. The struggle is also a salutary lesson for those who underestimate the significance of Northern Ireland to the processes of social change in the UK as a whole.

Despite the fact that Northern Ireland has been for so long, and still is, the most deprived area of the UK, poverty has never been central to the parliamentary agenda concerning North-

165

ern Ireland. Northern Ireland politics in the UK have been dominated by one issue – that of the defence or destruction of state power. As Boyle and Hadden (1988, pp. 247–8) point out, 'politicians and students . . . (tend) to regard it (Northern Ireland) as marginal to the mainstream of developments . . . '. But local struggles about issues of national importance, such as the one at the Royal Victoria Hospital can cure this unidimensional view of Northern Ireland in the rest of the UK. In Northern Ireland, equal-pay legislation, with all its current faults, has been used to highlight an alternative agenda concerned with the key socio-economic issue of poverty and its connections with long-term industrial decline.

The next part of this chapter sets out the background against which the Royal Victoria Hospital/NUPE campaign has taken place. The chapter then deals with the way that the issues of equal value came to be articulated as collective bargaining demands and with the legal case, including its lessons. Thereafter, the chapter considers the connections between valuing women's work and maintaining the quality of public services in the face of government policies on privatisation. Again, this is an insight that is important for the UK as a whole as the use made by NUPE (NI) of the undervaluing of women's work as a factor in the decline of quality is unusual, though, in other ways, unions elsewhere have tried to emphasise the common interests of service providers and service consumers (Foster, 1991). The main lessons of this chapter are that the Northern Ireland legal case highlights deficiencies in the UK legislation but that discussion leading to the use of the law and about the legal processes enabled the concept of equal value to be a mobilising factor both among union members and in the wider community.

On the first point, the chapter emphasises the very long delays that result from cumbersome equal-value procedures. As is shown here, equal value claims can be debarred where a non-discriminatory job-evaluation study has been carried out. This possibility was exploited by Mary McCauley's employers to the extent that her case, and that of her colleagues, is (at the time of writing) still not resolved. A successful outcome has the potential for benefiting thousands of women in Northern Ireland at a cost of £5 million a year (Maxwell, 1988) and for paving the way for claims in the National Health Service in the rest of the UK. What is even more important, however, is the second point: the use of equal value to mobilise the grassroots membership and the local community in overall struggles against inequalities, low pay and privatisation. The taking of a test case has made NUPE's lowest-paid women in the most deprived area of the UK visible. As Rosaleen Davidson put it:

> While we're invisible no value is put upon us. We realised that we would have to value ourselves if we wanted other people to do likewise, so we started to get active. The cases aren't just about our take-home pay, but other things too, like recognising that women's jobs shouldn't get stuck at the bottom of the pay scales; and recognising that part-time workers should have the same rights as full-time workers (quoted in McKeown, 1988).

Before moving on to the campaigns themselves, it is necessary to show just how badly-off women are in Northern Ireland.

THE ECONOMIC AND SOCIAL BACKGROUND

The general condition of poverty in Northern Ireland has been reinforced by the industrial crises of recent years which have implications for women's employment as well as that of men. Since the early 1970s, the Northern Irish economy has suffered crisis and decay with industrial employment and output falling. Because of the fragility of its manufacturing sector, Northern Ireland has a higher level of dependence on public expenditure than elsewhere in the UK. Its economic problems have been made worse by the fact that the present UK government is committed to the reduction of public expenditure. As in the rest of the UK, a major shift to service employment has taken place in Northern Ireland and there have been two major slumps in 1974 and 1979–80 bringing a growth in manufacturing to a halt. The public sector plays a major role in the labour market. In 1988, 30.3 per cent of male employees were employed in public administration and other services compared with 21 per cent for the whole of the UK; more than one in two females were employed in this sector (54.6 per cent) compared with 42.3 per cent in the the whole of the UK (CSO, 1989, p. 24).

Poverty in Northern Ireland

> In my first visit to Belfast in 1968 . . . I was struck not only by
> the evident poverty in Catholic and Protestant areas alike,
> but by scenes which seemed to belong more to the 1930s – of
> red-haired boys using scales on a cart drawn by an emaciated
> pony to sell coal by the pound, teenage girls in a second-
> hand clothing shop buying underslips and skirts, and some
> of the smallest 'joints' of meat in butchers' windows that I
> have ever seen. (Townsend, 1979, p. 558).

Northern Ireland is the most deprived region in the UK. This is
reflected in its higher rates of unemployment, lower level of
earnings and lower household expenditure and income.

Unemployment in the province has historically been higher
than in the rest of the UK. In the past ten years, although the
trends have been similar to those in the rest of Britain, the gap
between unemployment figures in the province and elsewhere
has increased as unemployment has risen at a faster rate and
has fallen at a slower rate. In 1988 the annual average rate of
unemployment in Northern Ireland was 16.4 per cent – higher
than any other region in the UK and more than double the UK
average (HMSO, 1989, p. 27). In March 1990 unemployment
for Northern Ireland stood at 14.1 per cent compared with 5.6
per cent for the UK as a whole. The second highest region in
the UK for unemployment was the Northern region with unemployment standing at 8.6 per cent (Department of Employment, 1990).

As unemployment has been higher in Northern Ireland,
earnings levels have been far lower, according to official government data. This is particularly pronounced for manual workers. In 1989 weekly earnings for adult men in Northern Ireland
stood at £225.95 representing 83.8 per cent of adult male weekly
earning in Britain (*New Earnings Survey*, 1989).

In Northern Ireland average household incomes are much
lower than UK averages. In any case, average figures tend to
disguise the fact that households are larger in the province.
Over the year 1986–7 household expenditure in the province
averaged £179 compared with the UK average of £183 (CSO,
1989, p. 27). Expenditure per person was lower than elsewhere
in the UK apart from Wales. A greater proportion of the North-

ern Irish family's income is spent on basic necessities such as fuel, light and power, food and transport. It is estimated that the purchasing power of an average family in Northern Ireland represented only 75 per cent of the UK averages.[2] Northern Ireland has the lowest proportion of the UK population having access to central heating, washing, machines, telephones, televisions and cars. It consumes less meat, cheese, fresh fruit and vegetables than any other region.

Low levels of income and high levels of unemployment are accompanied by poor housing stock. According to the latest figures produced by the Northern Ireland Housing Executive, 8.4 per cent of dwellings were unfit in 1987 and 5.5 per cent of dwellings required at least one or two improvements. 22.5 per cent of dwellings required repairs of over £3000. Only 62.1 per cent of all dwellings did not require urgent repairs.

Northern Ireland households had the lowest percentage of income from investments and annuities and pensions and other sources in the UK in 1986–7 (Department of Employment, 1989, p. 91). They also had the highest percentage of income from social security benefits: 19.3 per cent of gross household income came from social security benefits as compared with 12.5 in the UK as a whole (Department of Employment, 1989, p. 91).

If the government has been content to dismiss the central significance of poverty to Northern Ireland politics, it has also been happy to use the province as a testing ground for some of its more controversial policies concerned with the management and state control of the poor. The Payment Of Debts Act, 1971, introduced during rent strikes, allowed the government to institute measures to recover non-payment of rent from state benefits and earnings. As state control, repression and relative poverty increased in Northern Ireland, trade unions and other organisations have led the way in the UK in creating imaginative and forceful anti-poverty campaigns of which equal value is a concomitant part.

Women and work in Northern Ireland

Women in Northern Ireland, as elsewhere, carry a particular burden in living and managing with poverty. With the decline of manufacturing and industries which traditionally employed women, such as the clothing, tobacco and shoe industries, there has been a shift of women's employment into the public sector. Whereas men have lost relatively more jobs, women have only benefited to the extent that part-time jobs in the services sector have expanded. Between 1971 and 1972 for example, the amount of part-time work increased by 84 per cent. By 1981 38 per cent of women were employed in part-time jobs.

The nature of women's work in Northern Ireland has changed little. The majority of women continue to work in low-paid, low-status jobs and part-time workers continue to face poor and vulnerable working conditions. Approximately 92 per cent of part-time workers are employed in the public-service sector – the highest proportion of anywhere in the UK, which makes the campaign against privatisation, discussed later, particularly important.

The structure of the labour market continues to be highly segregated by sex and women's earnings have reached a barrier of around 77 per cent of male earnings in the province (Equal Opportunities Commission (NI), 1987). Because of the lower level of male earnings in the province, women's earnings are higher in proportion than are comparative figures in Britain. In 1989 women's weekly earnings stood at 77.52 per cent of men's, inclusive of overtime, and 78.6 per cent of men's, exclusive of overtime. But, as Table 8.1 shows, they are much worse off than all workers in Great Britain.

Not only do women in Northern Ireland face the brunt of poverty and have to rely on the lowest level of regional earnings of all workers in the UK but they also face inequalities in equality legislation itself. This arises from the fact that although

Table 8.1 Average weekly wages, inclusive of overtime, of women in Northern Ireland compared with the rest of the UK

Northern Ireland		% of UK women	% of UK men	% of all UK
Manual	116.4	86.3	53.4	57.3
Non-manual	180.3	92.5	55.7	68.1
All	160.2	87.9	59.4	66.8

Source: New Earnings Survey, 1989.

Northern Ireland equality legislation mirrors British legislation, there is often a time-lag in changes being introduced in
Northern Ireland. For example, it took two years for the changes
contained within the Sex Discrimination Act, 1986, to be introduced into Northern Ireland by a comparable Order.

TACKLING DISCRIMINATION IN THE HEALTH SERVICE: INITIATING DEBATE AND FORMULATING COLLECTIVE BARGAINING DEMANDS

In Northern Ireland, the public-sector workers' union representing some of the lowest-paid workers in the country – NUPE
– devised a strategy for combating low pay and poverty among
its membership, which was primarily composed of women. It is
a distinct strategy with a commitment to utilising test cases
along with collective-bargaining tactics. This dual strategy con-
trasted with that of NUPE's national organisation which has,
until recently, laid more emphasis on collective bargaining. In
1986, NUPE emphasised that it regarded national bargaining
as the appropriate method of achieving change. It argued that
many cases would cut across procedures and be potentially
detrimental to the union's bargaining position (Incomes Data
Services, 1986, pp. 5–6).

NUPE in Northern Ireland – a divisional committee of the
main body in the rest of the country – is more strongly representative of women than are most other unions. The Divisional
Officer, Inez McCormack, heads a team in which three out of
the four full-time officers are women. As research from the LSE
shows, women officers are more fully committed to taking up
issues of equal pay than are men (Heery and Kelly, 1988, 1989).
In Northern Ireland, the dual form of the campaign was determined by the members as much as the officers. Demands for
equal pay arose from the perceived need for new detailed
bargaining methods to challenge a low pay and poverty amongst
the membership. Such demands, argued the division, came
best from the members directly affected. In this way, the debate
about low pay and equal pay initiated and continued to involve
an important political process within the union; that is, the
development of democratic, participatory structures for the
members through which to generate demands relevant to their
own lives.

Following the publication of NUPE's national discussion document on low pay and how to tackle it, the Northern Ireland division called together shop stewards and activities from the National Health and education services. They were asked to consider which of their members were particularly low-waged, the reasons for it and what could be done to alleviate low pay. These discussions initiated further discussions on pay and what members themselves wanted in terms of pay demands.

All members were supplied with job descriptions so that they, too, could understand the processes by which job evaluation was undertaken and so that they could make their contribution in understanding their own value. Meetings were held with the Northern Ireland Equal Opportunities Commission. At first, these involved men and women separately; then joint meetings were held. As a result of this, 400 initiating forms (IT1s) were filled in. It became clear that a strategic test case should be taken against the the biggest employer in the Province – the National Health Service (NHS) and, from the IT1s, potential test cases were selected. The case is dealt with in the next section; here, it is necessary to note that in continuing to press equal value through collective bargaining the union revolutionised traditional concepts of the going rate for the job.

Through the discussions among officers, stewards, the EOC and members, it became clear to members themselves that the lowest paid had actually financed past pay claims by cuts in part-timers' working hours and their increased productivity. Previously, part-timers' demands had often been seen as divisive by full-timers who had continued to seek traditional pay demands; for example, longer holidays, shorter working hours, etc., but the new agenda for bargaining that resulted from the discussions sought to incorporate a common interest in equal pay, better basic rates, minimum hours and proper protection for part-time workers.

The equal-pay claim has been made with a realistic appraisal of the pitfalls of campaigning for equal pay alone

> The Council and the committees felt that the fight for equal value was in fact a fight against low pay for the majority of our members. They stressed that it was paramount that grading structures were re-evaluated using equal-value mechanisms and that minimum earnings and protection clauses must be

integrated into the bargaining process. Otherwise workers would lose out by the very mechanism which was designed to attack low pay and raise their value. There is no point being upgraded if your hours are cut to pay for the upgrading and you subsequently fall once more outside superannuation rights and national insurance entitlements.

Full-time workers would then also lose out because of the employers' determination to create an army of flexible, cheap part-time labour which then attacks the security of full-time jobs (NUPE, Northern Ireland Division, 1986).

Since the legal approach ran contrary to that of the then national NUPE policy, since the experience of it reveals deficiencies in legislation but, since it also contributed to the consciousness of members, it is important to deal with it in some detail.

THE LEGAL CASE

Five part-time ancillary workers employed as domestics at the Royal Victoria Hospital submitted their still unfinished case as long ago as January 1985. They were then and are still paid on the lowest of the NUS ancillary grades. They compared their jobs to those of grade 4 porters and groundsmen. Significantly, one of the women who took the case was a NUPE steward. This helped to create a strong link between NUPE's full-time officers and the workers. Before the case Ms Davidson, the steward, commented that as night-workers, as ancillary workers working on women's work and as part-timers their work was largely invisible not only to Health Board officials but even to their own membership. The case changed all this – at the very least, it created a public and visible profile for an underrated group of workers.

Despite the fact that the original case was submitted in January 1985, the independent expert has not yet made any assessment. In December 1985 the tribunal ordered the appointment of an independent expert to carry out an independent assessment. But the appointment was stayed pending a preliminary hearing.

In January 1986 the employers wrote to the industrial tribunal saying that they had been advised by Counsel that the appointment of an independent expert was premature as the tribunal had given no ruling in relation to a pre-existing job-evaluation scheme. Under equal-value legislation, where a dispute arises as to whether work is of equal value, the tribunal shall not resolve that question where it is satisfied that there are no reasonable grounds for determining that the work is of equal value. A tribunal *must* find that there are no reasonable grounds for an equal-value claim where the woman's work and the man's work have been given different values on a job-evaluation study that is valid under the Act and where there are no reasonable grounds for determining that the evaluation discriminates on grounds of sex. In a leading case, *Bromley and others* v. *H. & J. Quick (1988)*, the Courts of Appeal held that for a job-evaluation scheme to comply with that Act it must measure the demands made by a job under various headings such as skills, responsibility and physical and mental demands. The employers, in the Northern Ireland case, argued that the National Health Service job-evaluation scheme, which had been implemented by the Department of Health in London, had been applied to health service workers in the province. Thus it was argued that the women were debarred from taking an equal-pay claim because their jobs had been properly evaluated.

In Northern Ireland, the Ancillary and General Staffs Joint Council (Northern Ireland) is the body responsible for determining pay and conditions for ancillary workers in the province. Its counterpart in Britain is the Great Britain Ancillary Staffs Council. Under the Finance Act (Northern Ireland), 1971, there are guarantees to keep the scale and standard of health services in Northern Ireland in general conformity with the scale and standard of services in Britain and to keep rates of pay as closely as possible in line with Britain. The Ancillary and General Staffs Joint Council (Northern Ireland) has, in fact, adopted a position of parity in relation to the pay and conditions of service for ancillary workers in Northern Ireland. In 1968 the staffs council in Britain had accepted the initiation of a job-evaluation study governing ten regions in the country. A lengthy and contorted process of job evaluation was implemented, but at no time was any analysis done in Northern Ireland. The employers argued that although no analysis had been carried out in Northern Ireland, its position was similar to other regions where no analysis had been carried out. Throughout the legal proceedings, they have used a wide range of delaying tactics and there have been major problems in getting discovery of documentation. The employers refused to allow entry to the experts and asked for a preliminary hearing to be delayed three times.

Despite the fact that the hearing was set for August 1988, it was not till March 1989 that the preliminary hearing was resolved. The applicants' case was supported by the EOC who provided an alternative expert who worked positively to support the union case. The initial upshot was favourable. Lengthy evidence was heard from both sides about the nature of the job-evaluation study carried out in Britain. In March 1989, the tribunal found that the evaluation had *not* been applied in Northern Ireland and was never applied to Northern Ireland 'other than indirectly' through the notion of parity with Britain. There was no evidence to suggest that it had been applied to Northern Ireland workers and the joint council in Northern Ireland was neither involved with nor had participated in the study. Nor did the Department of Health have any jurisdiction in Northern Ireland. The tribunal confirmed its order of December 1985 appointing an Independent Expert. The employers appealed to the Court of Appeal on this point and it has taken until the summer of 1991 for it to authorise an independent expert to proceed. It will be several more months before his or her report is considered by the tribunal.

The need for change

There is little doubt that this experience of a long drawn-out process and others in Northern Ireland (Maxwell, 1988 reporting research carried out by McCartan[3]) have done much to alter the strategy of the Equal Opportunities Commission. With a reputation for innovative approaches to litigation, it is now, however, attempting to encourage alternative ways of processing the implementation of equal pay; through the systematic implementation of non-discriminatory analytical schemes in a variety of industrial sectors and, following a staff review, it has created the structure to do this. This strategy is not seen as a 'soft option' or resorted to because it is all that is possible; it relies heavily upon the threat of legal action or formal investigation in the event of non-cooperation by employers (EOC, Northern Ireland, 1989).

The Northern Ireland experiences also corroborate the view that the job-evaluation defence should be removed from all UK legislation. The Trades Union Congress (TUC) in Britain has made a strong argument for its removal (TUC, 1989). Not only does it provide employers with the opportunity of introducing complex job-evaluation schemes as a way of avoiding equal-value claims, but it also provides women with no opportunity of demonstrating equal value. It diverts the tribunal from the main task of establishing whether two jobs are equal even where no direct comparison of jobs has been made. As the TUC points out, job evaluation is not objective and scientific. The TUC proposes that the job-evaluation defence should be permitted only *after* the independent expert has reported and even then it should not automatically put a brake on the case. The respondent would be required to show that the job evaluation scheme was non-discriminatory in application. Recently, the European Court of Justice has given some guidance about the minimising discrimination in the conception and execution of schemes (see Gregory in Chapter 2 of this volume) which may help to circumvent the deficiencies of British law.

Notwithstanding the difficulties of litigation, the thought that went into bringing the case and in formulating collective bargaining demands has led to a novel, third strategic approach and it is to this that I now turn.

EQUAL VALUE AND VALUING PUBLIC SERVICES

The Union has used equal value to highlight the importance, not only of the workers themselves, but of the value of effective NHS provision. In recent years, national legislation has required health authorities and local governments to submit service provision to competitive tendering. This means that services may well be provided by private contractors instead of by workers employed directly in the public sector. Once employed by 'model employers', public-sector workers are now threatened by job losses if service provision is 'contracted out' and poorer conditions of employment if 'in-house' bids are to compete successfully with those from outside. Thus, public-sector unions have had to try to combat privatisation. In Northern Ireland, the demand for equal value was used in a weapon in this fight. In raising the profile of the value of ancillary workers' work, the union was attempting to raise the value of the services themselves. This also helped to expose cuts in budget allocations to ancillary work which have taken place and continue to take place. NUPE appears to have had some success. In April 1988, a government circular was issued advising the four Northern Irish health boards to draw up tendering timetables by June of that year. But by December 1988, only nine contracts had been put out to tender and only two awarded to private contractors.

The union has rejected the strategy of 'in-house' bids winning at any price, with domestics paying the price in fewer jobs and reducing earnings and with patients paying the price in poorer services. Equal value has been incorporated into the unions' demands:

> The challenge mounted by these domestics whose jobs are directly under threat from cuts and privatisation is the best response to the view that you fight the problem by competing downwards. They are challenging on the basis of their value as workers, the value of their services and their value as human beings and they believe strongly that the fight against cuts and privatisation is best fought by ascertaining their value (NUPE, Northern Ireland Division, 1986).

Responding to members and the community

For the women who have taken cases there has inevitably been stress but a sense of satisfaction that they have played a central part in the union's strategy. The applicants reported that they felt excluded from the legal process, found the law difficult to understand and required the strong and supportive network of the union to continue. The case not only helped the union's members to be clearer about the concept of equal value but also made it more responsive to women-members' demands and, as the union was seen to be doing something positive for women, so, too, did those demands increase.

There is a strong sense of solidarity between the comparators and applicants and their high public profile, at least in Northern Ireland, has helped the workers to draw on support from the local community. Not much has been published yet on the effectiveness in the UK as a whole of the efforts of public-sector unions to fight privatisation through allying themselves with consumers to protect service quality by maintaining reasonable conditions of employment (Foster, 1991). But in this case the main users of the hospital service – women and children – have staged sit-ins to support the ancillary workers fighting privatisation and cuts in their budgets. The importance of taking the battle out into the local community should not be underrated. Hundreds of meetings have been organised with local residents and tenants' groups, voluntary organisations and women's groups. What has been created is a two-way relationship between the community and the hospital workers – with union-members supporting local campaigns and calling upon the community to help them with their campaign. The union, for its part, has put money, resources and people into supporting small campaigns.

CONCLUSION

A clear conception that equal value must be used within an overall strategy against low pay has united union members on the divisive issue of equal value. Equal pay has been used as a powerful weapon in a campaign against poverty and low pay which is endemic in Northern Ireland. The union has not only sought to make its demands relevant to its own members but has raised the profile of public services to make its campaign relevant to the community as a whole.

The test-case strategy has been used alongside collective-bargaining strategies and the law and legal action have not been used to substitute the process of collective bargaining but to augment it. Since equal-value legislation is controlled by the male-dominated judiciary it can hardly be surprising that the snail-like processes of the legal system have not led to a success-ful outcome of the case, but the union and its members have not made the mistake of relying solely on the outcome of the case.

Success cannot only be measured in the outcome of a par-ticular case but in the way that those processes have been instigated. Facing intense difficulties of privatisation and cuts in services the union has worked with its membership, with the EOC and with the public to carry out a high-profile campaign making invisible workers visible. It has also hit on the head the notion that the low-paid are difficult to organise and unwilling to participate in union struggles. If the law was led by public opinion there is little doubt that ancillary workers in the NHS would have won their claim to equal pay, paving the way for a wave of demands from Northern Ireland health service workers.

The lessons from Northern Ireland and the struggle of the health workers are clear. Whatever reforms there may be in equal-pay legislation, the law will never, on its own, eradicate fully the pay inequalities and poverty that women face in society. Used in the context of a broader strategy concerned with minimum-pay demands and challenging low pay, it may be a powerful weapon in mobilising the energies, enthusiasm and passions of workers living on poverty-line wages.

Notes

1. NUPE is one of the four largest unions in the UK and 67 per cent of its members are women. Its membership is almost exclusively public-sector employees primarily divided between the National Health Service, local government, water authorities and university non-teaching staff. Its members include ancillary workers in the NHS, home helps and care attendants as well as groundsmen, porters and workers in refuse. In 1975 the structure of the union was recognised and a system of district committees, area committees, divisional councils and divisional conferences initiated. These are based on over 20 000 stewards with the aim of extending the democratic base of the union and securing greater participation in the decision-making process. In Northern Ireland, in particular, the union has been keen to expand its membership into the voluntary sector and this has helped it to forge links with the wider community.

2. This average conceals the fact that the middle classes have a high disposable income because of salaries that are similar to those in the rest of the UK combined with much lower property prices than in England and, hence, lower mortgage repayments. Thus the position of the poor is even worse than indicated.

3. Pat McCartan, then Northern Ireland Regional Secretary of the staff union APEX, undertook his research as part of an M.Sc. in Manpower Planning at the University of Ulster.

References

Boyle, K. and Hadden, T. (1988) 'Options for Northern Ireland' in H. Drucker, P. Dunleavy, A. Gamble, and G. Peele (eds) *Developments in British Politics* (London: Macmillan).

Central Statistical Office (1989) *Regional Trends* 24 (London: HMSO).

Department of Employment (1989) *Family Expenditure Survey* (London: Department of Employment).

Department of Employment (1990) Press Release, 8.3.90. (London: Department of Employment).

Equal Opportunities Commission, Northern Ireland (1987) *The Aftermath of Recession: Changing Patterns in Female Employment and Unemployment in Northern Ireland*, Womanpower, no 4 (Belfast: NI EOC).

Equal Opportunities Commission (NI) (1989) *Annual Report* (Belfast: NI EOC).

Foster, D. (1991) *Privatisation: Local Government and Trade Union Responses* (provisional title) thesis submitted for the degree of Ph.D., Bath University.

Heery, E. and Kelly J. (1988) 'Do Female Representatives Make a Difference?: Women Full-time Officials and Trade Union Work', *Work, Employment and Society*, 3(4).

Heery, E. and Kelly, J. (1989) ' "A Cracking Job for a Woman" – a Profile of Woman Trade Union Officers', *Industrial Relations Journal*, 20(3), pp. 192–62.

Incomes Data Service (1986) *Study*, 359, April.

McKeown, P. (1988) 'Tipping the Scales', *Marxism Today*, September.

Maxwell, P. (1988) 'The Impact of Equal Value Legislation in Northern Ireland', paper presented at conference at Bath University, sponsored by the Public Administration Committee.

Maxwell, P. (1989) 'The Impact of Equal Value Legislation in Northern Ireland' (shorter version of Maxwell, 1988), *Policy and Politics*, 17(4).

National Union of Public Employees, Northern Ireland Division (1986) *Review* (NUPE: Belfast).

New Earnings Surveys of Great Britain and Northern Ireland (1989) (London: Department of Employment).

Townsend, P. (1979) *Poverty in the United Kingdom* (Harmondsworth: Penguin).

Trades Union Congress (1989) 'Comments of the TUC General Council on "Equal Pay . . . Making it Work – EOC Consultative Document" ' (London: TUC).

9 Comparable Worth and Nurses in the USA
Roslyn L. Feldberg

Comparable worth began attracting the attention of American advocates between 1976 and 1978. At the same time, articles explaining comparable worth and arguing for its importance began to appear in nursing journals. As early as 1978 the American Nurses Association, the primary professional organisation for registered nurses in the USA, was contributing funds to support the plaintiffs in what is widely considered to be the first comparable-worth case for nurses, *Lemons* v. *City and County of Denver*.[1]

In many ways, comparable worth seems tailor-made to address the problems of low wages in all female-dominated professions in the USA: elementary-school teachers, nurses, social workers and librarians.[2] These low-wage, female-dominated occupations could not benefit from the 1963 Equal Pay Act because there were no better-paid men doing the same work. In these professions workers are highly educated, have considerable technical skills and accept a high level of responsibility for the people they help, despite their low pay. Comparable worth addresses precisely these features of work in seeking to eliminate sex, race and other forms of bias in wage-setting. It requires that workers be paid according to the value of their jobs to their employers, without regard to the sex, race, age or other personal characteristics of the workers. Value is measured by responsibility, skill, effort and other 'compensable factors' associated with the job.

While many of these professions have embraced the concept of comparable work, nurses have brought more comparable-worth cases to court through their professional association and have more consistently supported comparable worth as a basic strategy for raising wages than have other professions.[3] Comparable worth appealed strongly to nurses for several reasons. First, nursing is the most sex-segregated female profession. Over 96 per cent of registered nurses are female. At the highest administrative and educational levels, where men are found in significant numbers among teachers and librarians, nursing is female-dominated. There are no male-dominated sub-specialities. For nurses to compare their pay with that of male-dominated jobs, they required a system which looked at 'compensable factors' across different jobs and professions.[4] Second, because they are women, nurses' work has been invisible and devalued. Their abilities have been seen not as acquired skills but as expressions of their female 'nature', similar to the caring and caretaking of wives, mothers or servants.[5] Yet nurses have retained the conviction that their skills and knowledge are vital to their patients' health and well-being. The women's liberation movement, changing gender roles and ideologies, and a growing awareness of women's contributions, strengthened nurses' belief in the value of their work. When comparable worth entered public discussion, nurses were ready for it.[6]

Third, nurses work in bureaucracies that are highly status-conscious and hierarchical. Especially in hospitals, where over two-thirds of RNs work, nurses often come into contact with administrators and doctors who devalue their work. On the one hand, nurses are treated as if their work was only to 'carry out orders'. On the other, nurses are held legally responsible, and hold themselves morally responsible, for the care of their patients. Moreover their knowledge develops in a context in which they rely on each other for support and assistance, forging strong networks and a sense of group professional identity, while confronting the limits of their autonomy and authority. Finally, the nursing profession is highly differentiated, by clinical speciality, work-setting, administrative position, class and educational background. Comparable worth mobilised this diverse membership around common goals: increased respect for their work and better wages.[7]

In addition, comparable worth was a different type of strategy. It relied heavily on data and technical experts: personnel specialists, comparable-worth experts and lawyers. As experts themselves, nurses are likely to be comfortable relying on experts. In addition, comparable worth offered nurses a chance to 'prove' to themselves and their supporters that their demands were just and that they were asking only for what 'even the experts' found was their due. Nurses learned early on that those technical analyses did not guarantee success. But for a female-dominated profession undervalued since its inception, the legitimation of their demands by experts was in itself a substantial victory.

In this chapter, I explore some aspects of the history of nursing and health care to provide a context within which to examine particular comparable-worth cases. I argue that comparable worth has provided nurses with a new visibility and a new framework in which to locate their demands. It has added to the impact of unionisation and consciousness-raising, amplified their voices, recast their claims to better pay as a matter of social justice and created a new arena in which nurses can press these claims. However, the problem of respect and pay for nurses is not yet solved, and comparable worth's potential for contributing to a solution must be carefully assessed.

THE WAGES OF NURSING: A BRIEF HISTORY

The beginnings of nursing as an occupation in the USA are found in two locations: in the homes of patients who could afford to hire a nurse and in the fledging hospitals established in the nineteenth century initially as charitable institutions. In the former wages varied considerably, depending in large part on the ability of the patient to pay; in the latter, the work was seen as providing a home (room and board), a small recompense and a chance for a respectable life for poor women. By the mid-1870s nurses' training begins. With it comes an effort to separate poor women working as nurses from their 'respectable sisters' who enter the training programmes and become known as graduate nurses.

By the 1920s, most graduate nurses worked as private-duty nurses in patients' homes or in hospitals. Graduate private-duty nurses earned approximately $1300 year (Reverby, 1987). When they worked, they earned more than many other women. But often they did not work. Weeks of employment alternated with weeks of unemployment. The pay of graduate staff nurses employed by hospitals, averaged $96 per month, plus room and board. They were few in number as most hospitals were staffed with untrained workers or nursing students, who worked for room and board as part of their training. Public health nurses also earned an average of $96 a month, but did not receive room and board.[8]

The Depression brought strong economic pressures on an already changing structure. With many patients unable to afford their services, private-duty nurses had difficulty finding enough work to earn their living. Hospitals, which had expanded rapidly in the 1920s, were faced with demands for more skilled nursing care as a result of changes in medical practices (Reverby, 1987; Kalisch and Kalisch, 1986). Graduates nurses, unable to survive in private duty, began to seek employment in hospitals as staff nurses, and by 1940 more than half of all nurses were employed in hospitals. As staff nurses in hospitals, nurses had steady employment, very low pay and rigidly structured work, in which nurses (women) were 'ordered to care' by (male) physicians and administrators. They also had a chance to work together and develop a new work culture and an awareness of shared concerns (Melosh, 1982).

The Second World War brought new opportunities for women's employment. Better pay and less-restrictive working conditions attracted nurses away from hospitals into public health, industrial nursing, armed-forces nursing and, in many cases, into non-nursing jobs. A wartime hospital-nursing shortage was alleviated by the introduction of 'volunteer' nurses' aides, part-time nurses and a growing number of the new 'practical nurses'. But neither wages nor working conditions for graduates nurses in hospitals improved during the war. By 1946, nurses wages averaged $0.87 an hour, the same as wages of women factory workers, with one nurse in four earning less than $0.75 an hour. By comparison, typists averaged $0.97 an hour and bookkeepers $1.11 (Reverby, 1987, p. 192)

As the post-war period began, surveys found that nurses who had left the hospitals for armed-forces nursing were reluctant to return (Kalisch and Kalisch, 1986, p. 544). The smaller cohort of young women leaving the high schools was turning to other fields. By 1951, the American Nurses Association publication, *Facts on Nursing*, declared a serious shortage of nurses.

Over the next twenty-five years the real wages of hospital staff nurses rose, paralleling those of other workers (Harrison and Bluestone, 1988). From 1960 to 1972, wages for hospital staff nurses increased rapidly, to an average of $180 per week or

$4.50 per hour in the major urban areas (Table 9.1).[9] In constant dollars, 'average' wages rose 60 per cent approximately three times faster than the rise in real wages for all workers. By 1972 'average' wages for staff nurses were slightly ahead of the median wages of all professional women (an inconsistent comparison, but the only one permitted by the data) and were 72 per cent of the median wages of professional men.[10]

Until recently, that marked the highpoint of staff nurses average wages. As Table 9.1 indicates, for the next nine years, staff nurses' real wages declined and remained below the 1972 level. Only in 1985, a full thirteen years later, did average real wages regain the 1972 level.

The last national industry wage survey for hospitals offers data for 1985, so we cannot track exactly how nurses' wages have increased through the late 1980s. However evidence from wage reports and smaller surveys shows sharp increases in the wages of staff nurses since 1985. For example, in Boston, the average wages of staff nurses in private hospitals increased 44 per cent in three and a half years from $485.50 a week (August, 1985) to $700 a week (January, 1989). Moreover, there has been a change in the wage structure. Previously, nurses had a very flat earnings curve, with experienced staff nurses earning little more than new graduates. Now the earnings curve has steepened somewhat. In one Boston area hospital contract, staff nurses with ten years experience earn 50 per cent more than nurses just entering the profession.

Much of the increase in the average and much of the steepening of the earnings curve has occurred since 1987, the year when a nursing 'shortage' of crisis proportion began to be reported throughout the USA (Aiken and Mullinix, 1987). Yet the pressure for wage increases came not only from the shortage, but also from a restructuring of health care that had left nurses, and other care-givers in hospitals, with greatly increased workloads and responsibilities, without commensurate increases in power, autonomy, respect or wages.

POLITICAL ECONOMY AND COST CONTAINMENT

Both the 'shortage' and the restructuring resulted from hospital managements' responses to the cost-containment measures

Table 9.1 Average[1] weekly wage for hospital[2] general duty[3] nurses in major urban areas, 1960–85 in current and constant[4] dollars (1960 = 100)

Year (n = number of cities)	Average wage median city		Range of average wages	
	Current $	Constant $	Constant $	Range
1960 (n = 15)	79.50	79.50	65–89	(D = 24)
1963 (n = 15)	86.50	83.76	72–95	(D = 23)
1966 (n = 16)	103.50	94.42	86–111	(D = 25)
1969 (n = 22)	144.50	116.39	94–137	(D = 43)
1972 (n = 21)	178.50	127.56	117–150	(D = 33)
1975 (n = 22)	220.40	121.37	107–155	(D = 48)
1978 (n = 22)	264.80	121.02	107–152	(D = 45)
1981 (n = 22)	373.60	121.71	107–150	(D = 43)
1985 (n = 23)	469.60	129.37	111–171	(D = 60)

Notes:
1. See note 9 for a definition of 'average'.
2. Hospital inclusiveness varies by year of survey. 1960, 1969, 1975, 1978 = all non-federal; 1972 = non-governmental; 1981, 1985 = non-federal, full-time employees.
3. General duty means staff nurses. Where male and female wages are given separately, female wages are used.
4. Constant dollars were calculated using the consumer price index.
   D = Difference.

Sources: US Department of Labor, Bureau of Labor Statistics, *Industry Wage Surveys: Hospitals* (various years); American Nurses Association, *Facts About Nursing* (various years)

of the 1980s, which were, in turn, responses to a thirty-year expansion of the health-care industry. The expansion, stagnation and then rapid rise of nurses' wages over the past thirty years must be viewed in this context.[11]

From 1960 to 1982, the percentage of GNP spent on health care doubled. The incredible growth of the health-care industry, especially the hospital sector of it, was fuelled by the introduction of two new federal policies which aimed to expand access to health care for the elderly and the poor. Medicare, a social insurance programme for the elderly enacted in 1965, and Medicaid, means-tested medical assistance for a substantial number of the poor, also enacted in 1965, channelled new monies into the health care system, without fundamentally altering its private, fee-for-service character. While post-war UK and Canada developed public-health systems (the one national, the other provincial) that guaranteed health-care access to the entire population and controlled to some extent both the practice and cost of health care, in the USA public monies were spent within a private system, paying the going rates and bidding those up.

While hospitals and the health-care industry expanded throughout the 1970s, nurses' wages, like those of other health-care workers, stagnated. The money that flowed into health care was spent on constructing modern hospitals, acquiring new technology, paying higher fees for surgical specialists, and meeting increased demands for health care. These developments were interrelated. The shift to high-technology medicine required expensive equipment and complex monitoring and treatment that could only occur in hospitals. Hospitals and doctors strove to develop or retain prominence in new procedures. As they did so, the use of new technology spread, driving up the demand for its promised benefits and adding its associated costs to health-care expenditures.

By the late 1970s, these rising costs catalysed a reaction. With the shift to conservative political control in the 1980s, the policy emphasis shifted from expanding access to health care to controlling health care costs. 'Cost containment' became the watchword of both governmental and private industry efforts to restructure health care. Hospitals were no longer reimbursed for the cost of treating each patient. Instead, 'Diagnosis Related Groups' or DRGs, were established that 'pre-set' the amount

Medicare would pay the hospital for treating a particular illness. If the treatment cost less money, the hospital pocketed the difference, if the treatment cost more, the hospital absorbed the loss. This new system, known as the prospective-payment system, was supposed to limit public spending on health care and encourage hospitals to operate efficiently.

Hospitals responded to DRGs by cutting the size of the hospital labour force, especially those involved in patient care. The most common strategy was to lay off ancillary personnel (e.g. respiratory therapists), licensed practical nurses, nurses' aides, orderlies, housekeepers and messengers and hire a few more nurses to cover their work, all in the name of creating a more professional, qualified and flexible staff. One analyst saw registered nurses as wonderfully versatile. For a couple of thousand dollars more a year, a hospital could have a much more highly qualified and versatile worker (Sparks, 1988). Presumably a nurse could – when needed – fill in for either a housekeeper or a physician. As long as nurses' pay was low, they would be in great demand. Meanwhile their workloads increased and their working conditions deteriorated, as fewer staff cared for sicker patients who were sent home as quickly as possible to minimise hospital costs.

The business orientation of hospitals became more pronounced. As hospital administrators cut back on patient-care staff, they were hiring new business staff to enable them to use the DRG system to greatest advantage (Applebaum and Granrose, 1986) and retraining patient-care staff in record-keeping to assure payment. They were also investing: in more-sophisticated computer systems, which enabled them to track more exactly and bill for the supplies used and the time nurses spent in caring for each patient; in new corporate structures, which established separate affiliated entities for profitable support services (for example, parking, laboratory analysis, management) that would not be subject to government regulation; and in aggressive advertising campaigns for new 'products' – These included, for example, birthing rooms (spaces for labour, delivery *and* recovery that are more homelike than traditional delivery rooms); gourmet dining-rooms; specialised substance-abuse clinics; weight-loss clinics. They were supposed to use existing space and personnel in ways which generated higher returns and attracted new patients.

These strategies developed in the context of a politics that promoted consumerism and privatisation. Each person, group, organisation was to choose (its own insurance) and to pay for its own health care. While these changes in financing and delivery limited access to health care, especially for the poor, they have not lessened health-care costs.

Nurses have experienced hospitals' shifts to greater reliance on 'high-tech' medicine and tighter staffing, while watching hospitals come to resemble corporations. They have voiced increasing doubts about hospital managements' commitment to good patient-care and increasing anger over being asked to stretch themselves to the detriment of both themselves and their patients.

THE NURSING 'SHORTAGE'

Nursing shortages are not new. They have occurred cyclically throughout the period immediately after the Second World War. Yet the 'shortage' of the 1980s was different (Aiken and Mullinix, 1987; Prescott, 1987). For a start, this 'shortage' developed at a time when more nurses than ever before were employed in hospital nursing. The 'shortage' was also part of the complex restructuring of the health-care system. DRGs brought increased demand for nurses (partly as a result of hospitals' own decisions to change their employment mix). At the same time more skilled nursing was needed, in part because DRGs meant that patients were in hospital only when they were most seriously ill and in part because high-tech medicines relies more heavily on skilled nursing care. The sense of urgency about the 'shortage' was heightened because it was already known that the number of nursing students had plummeted and that new graduates would not be available in large enough numbers to fill the vacancies. And finally, demographic changes, especially a rapid increase in the number of persons over 75, implied a growing demand for health care.

In past shortages, employers had moved quickly to expand the hospital labour pool by training more nurses, substituting less-skilled personnel and by recruiting foreign nurses. In the context of the late 1980s, these strategies were less available to hospital administrators. Moreover, nurses had changed too. As part of the societal change in women's consciousness, nurses were thinking differently about their work. Their critical contribution to the running of hospitals now stood out in clear relief. Juxtaposed to it were their low wages, limited futures and the lack of understanding of and respect for their work.[12] This time nurses responded to the 'shortage' with a new militancy and concrete demands for better pay and better conditions of work.

EMPLOYMENT AND COLLECTIVE BARGAINING

Hospitals employ over two-thirds of registered nurses (American Nurses Association, 1988, p. 101). In the USA, most hospitals are of two types: government hospitals (primarily state and local), which employ about one-third of hospital nurses, and private hospitals which employ the other two-thirds. Private hospitals, primarily non-profit-making, are usually single facilities, operating independently, although most are members of various hospital associations. Recently, many hospitals have affiliated into groups and, in some regions, 'for-profit' hospital chains are strong. The implications of these corporate changes for nurses' wages, working conditions and employment are not yet clear.

In the absence of a national health system or nationwide hospital chains, wages are set or bargained locally. There is considerable variation in wages by city and by region of the country, although over-all, wages in US hospital nursing were historically very low. Indeed, the outstanding characteristics of nurses' wages nationwide are low pay and little salary growth with years of service and increasing skill.

Wage-setting has been structured primarily by two forces: the power of hospitals both as 'single' employers and members of employers' associations, and the relatively slow growth of collective bargaining in health care.

Hospitals are powerful employers in many communities because there are few employers of registered nurses. Furthermore, through their associations, hospital managements have long shared wage- and benefit-information, a practice which keeps compensation within a narrow range. Indeed, one recent study of a hospital employers' association suggests that these practices have violated anti-trust laws and seriously depressed wages for nurses (Friss, 1988). Moreover, employers have been quick to use their charitable mission and the ideology of the profession, that nurses were dedicated to patient care and not 'just doing a job for money', to support lower wages.

In contrast to employers' power, collective bargaining is still new for US nurses. As recently as 1965, nationwide less than 5 per cent of nurses employed by private hospitals and less than 15 per cent of those employed by state and local government hospitals nationwide were covered by collective bargaining contracts (US Department of Labor, 1967, pp. 4–5). The next twenty years raised the coverage to roughly two-thirds of nurses in state and local government facilities and nearly one-fourth of nurses in private hospitals, a three-to four-fold increase in the percentage of organized nurses (US Department of Labor, 1987, p. 4–5). But large numbers of hospital nurses remain unorganised.

There have been several main impediments to nurses' engaging in collective bargaining (Miller, 1980). First, the structure of the hospital industry has made organising gains difficult. Because hospitals are independent entities, each must be organised separately. Second, legal barriers to organising employees of non-profit-making hospitals have also slowed organising. The National Labor Relations Act, 1935 mandated that employers engage in collective bargaining with elected representatives of employees. The 1947 Taft–Hartley Act, however, exempted non-profit-making hospitals from the obligation to bargain collectively. As a result, through much of the 1950s and 1960s, nurses were organised only in states that had enacted their own laws to protect the bargaining rights of hospital employees. These were states in which unions were generally strong: the North-eastern, Western and Great Lakes states. Bargaining rights were not restored at national level until the exemption was removed in 1974.

Third, collective bargaining has had to be established as appropriate for nurses (Flanagan, 1989a; Kalisch and Kalisch, 1986; Melosh, 1982). Historically, the American Nurses Association and many of its members saw unions as 'unprofessional' and incompatible with 'caring', and, at the same time, opposed 'outside unions' representing hospital nurses. However, as employers failed to respond to 'persuasion' and as conditions deteriorated during the Second World War the ANA endorsed collective bargaining for the state nurses' associations in 1946.

Fourth, there was and is no one organisation dedicated solely to organising nurses. The state nurses associations of the ANA represent nurses for collective bargaining and also represent the professional interests of all nurses. That dual function is a strength, because the associations understand many of the professional concerns of nurses, and a weakness, because they have been charged with conflict of interest due to the membership of supervisory as well as staff nurses within associations. Nurses have turned most often to the associations to represent them. Although only twenty-two state associations engage in collective bargaining and only ten of these represent more than 5000 nurses each, the state associations are the primary representatives of nurses. Together they represent more nurses than any one national union (140 000 in 1987), accounting for roughly 60 per cent of the unionised nurses in private hospitals and 50 per cent of their counterparts in state and local government hospitals (US Department of Labor, 1987). Still, their dual function means that their energies and resources are not focused solely on the concerns of staff nurses.

The commitment of the unions has been similarly fragmented, although for different reasons (Miller, 1980). While several unions, most notably American Federation of State, County and Municipal Employees (AFSCME), Service Employees International Union (SEIU) and District 1199, Retail, Wholesale and Department Store Union (known as 1199) have been involved in organising hospital nurses for over thirty years, many other unions have also organised nurses when the opportunity presented itself. The unions have not cooperated with each other nor has any one union traditionally focused on nurses as a priority constituency to be organised. Most union organising efforts have been parts of other campaigns, responses to requests, or attempts to add nurses to already organised hospital workforces. Within the unions nurses are usually a very small group and the unions lack the structures or the expertise to address many of their particular concerns.

ANA and the major unions involved in hospital organising have announced major organising initiatives within the past year. They will face stiff opposition as employers engage in

sophisticated 'anti-union' campaigns in which large wage increases are often given to prove to the nurses that they 'don't
need a union'. Indeed, during the height of the nursing 'shortage' of the late 1980s, one organiser from a state nurses' association joked that the fastest way for unorganised nurses to get
a rise was to meet with her two or three times and make sure
that hospital management knew about the meetings.

Although many nurses remain outside collective bargaining,
the relationship of nurses to collective bargaining is growing
steadily stronger. That growth, coupled with the changing political economy of health care and with nurses' frustration with
hospital working conditions and wages, has contributed to a
militancy that is likely to result in further organisation in the
near future. All these changes are reinforced by nurses growing
awareness of the value of their work and its central importance
to health care and to hospitals. For the present, limited collective bargaining and organisational fragmentation of nurses also
help to explain the localised and uneven nature of comparable
worth initiatives.

CAMPAIGNS, LAWSUITS AND LEGISLATION: CASES ON COMPARABLE WORTH FOR NURSES

Politics of caring and comparable worth

Nurses had been taught to 'care'. As they re-examined their
education and training and their jobs in light of the women's
liberation movement, they came to see their situation as a result
of 'the politics of caring'. Nurses saw that defining their work as
'care-giving' trivialised that work and ensured its invisibility.
Nursing was accorded as little respect and as little pay as other
'women's work'. The skills and responsibilities it entailed remained unnoticed and unnamed.

As nurses began to question their low wages, they decided
that the theory of comparable worth offered a good strategy for
comparing their pay with 'men jobs'. Needed information was
most readily available in the public sector, where nurses were
already more often organised. In contrast to the behind-the-
scenes strategies of private-hospital employers, public employers typically rely on established systems for classifying jobs and

setting wages. In addition, salary ranges for public job classes are public information. These differences, and the susceptibility of public employers to public scrutiny and political pressure, made public employers more frequent targets of comparable-worth campaigns.

The case examples that follow are all public-sector cases. Yet, as some of these cases show, the effect of comparable worth is not confined to the public sector. It seems to affect the entire local labour market. In much the way that wage and benefit increases in unionised hospitals drive up the rates in their unorganised counterparts, as these seek to 'remain competitive' and to prevent unionisation, so comparable-worth actions spill over from public to private sector.

Denver case[13]

The direct history of nurses and comparable worth begins with *Lemons* v. *City and County of Denver, 1978* which was a frustrating legal defeat. Judge Winner of the US District Court, District of Colorado, began his oral opinion by noting, 'This case is a case certainly of substantial importance to the plaintiffs . . . it is a case of substantial importance to the entire community, it is a case which is pregnant with the possibility of disrupting the entire economic system of the United States of America'. He went on to say that the plaintiffs' 'skills are such that in a truly egalitarian society, they would receive more money . . . I think that they have established that, by and large, male-dominated occupations probably pay more for comparable work than is paid in occupations dominated by females . . .' But he argued that Congress did not require such comparisons, and therefore that he would not make them. He would make only the narrower comparison of equal pay for equal work. 'I expressly find that the plaintiffs failed to prove any pay-differential based on sex for the performance of substantially equal work.' With that reasoning, the judge ruled against Mary Lemons and the nurses working for the city and county of Denver.

The circuit court of appeals upheld his decision and, two years later, the Supreme Court refused to review it. So ended the legal case of *Lemons* v. *City and County of Denver*. Yet the issues of that case for nursing and for comparable worth are not yet resolved.

The case began quietly enough, when the nursing administrators of Denver began to look at the issue of salary discrimination and saw what they felt was clear evidence of lower salaries
for nursing administrators than for male administrators with
similar levels of responsibility. The more they looked, the more
they saw discrimination, not only against themselves, but also
against staff and licensed practical nurses who worked under
them. The matter quickly became a matter of principle, involving the nursing profession as a whole.

It was the view that the nursing profession was a connected
whole, suffering discrimination at all levels, that led the nurses
to the path they followed. They wanted not merely to achieve a
salary increase, but to challenge and change the whole system
by which salaries were set. To do that they needed both a
systematic analysis of the salary-setting system used by the city
and county of Denver and, they believed, a court order to
change it.

The salary-setting system was a difficult one to study. It was
not a point system, which provides an immediate basis for
comparison through total points for each job compared with
salary ranges for each job. It was a key class system, in which jobs
are grouped into job families and salaries are set by tying the
key jobs to the prevailing wages in the local labour market
(Hutner, 1986; Kurtz and Hocking, 1983). Once the salaries of
the key jobs are set, all jobs in the family are paid in relation to
that salary. For nurses the key job was Graduate Nurse I, the
entry-level staff-nurse position. All other jobs for nurses, and
many other female-dominated jobs which had nothing to do
with health care, were included in the class. Indeed one of the
nurses' basic arguments in the case was that there were no
clear-cut criteria by which jobs in this class were grouped, except that the jobs were typically held by women. Thus nurse-
administrators were grouped in this class, without regard to
their administrative tasks, while male administrators were
grouped by educational requirements and administrative tasks,
not the tasks of the employees whose work they oversaw. The
city's defence was that there were no hard-and-fast rules about
how to classify jobs and that the jobs were reviewed not by tasks
but as 'whole jobs' and placed where the director of the system
was 'most comfortable' in placing them.

Once the jobs were in those classes, the starting-point for

salary-setting was the annual market survey. The market survey for Graduate Nurse 1 was a survey of the surrounding private hospitals, which met annually under the auspices of the Colorado Hospital Association to discuss wages. The situation was one in which a few employers controlled the market for all nurses working in hospitals and in the community. Their annual meetings eliminated wage competition among those employers and perpetuated the historically low wages of nurses. As long as nurses were compared with other nurses in the same labour market, their wages would remain substantially below what might be expected on the basis of their educational and training requirements, responsibility for patients' well-being and even lives, their physically demanding, often hazardous, dirty work, and their off-shift, often unpredictable hours.

While the City explained that it did not compare across job classes in its wage-setting system, the nurses did compare. What they found is history, most often remembered as 'nurses make less than tree-trimmers'. In fact, according to the city wage scale for 1977, Graduate Nurse 1 was paid less than many male-dominated jobs which required less education, training or responsibility (Hutner, 1986, p. 136). The entry-level monthly salary that year for Graduate Nurse 1 was $929; meanwhile Tree-Trimmer 1 was paid $1040, Painter 1 was paid $1088 and Sign Painter 1 was paid $1245 for the month. These male-dominated jobs were paid at $111–$316 more per month – which amounted to $1121–$3792 per year.

The nurses' case was based on the argument that the salary-setting system classified jobs in a sex-stereotyped way and relied on market surveys which incorporated historic patterns of sex discrimination. The evidence of discrimination was the system of lower wages for nurses than for groups of male employees who also worked for Denver and whose jobs were of lesser or equal value and requirements. The legal theory behind the case was 'disparate impact'. 'Disparate impact' means that a practice, which appears neutral, results in a different and disadvantageous impact on a protected group. In *Griggs* v. *Duke* the courts found that tests which appeared neutral had screened out black applicants for training by the employer and therefore were discriminatory. What had worked in *Griggs* v. *Duke* had not worked for the nurses.

The impact on comparable worth strategy

The Lemons case spurred a new round of analysis of among lawyers and scholars of the grounds on which sex-discrimination cases could be won. In particular the case established that, in the absence of a job evaluation conducted by the employer which established the worth of jobs in a common measure (e.g. points), the market defence was acceptable to the courts. Later in *Briggs* v. *Madison* it appeared that even where a job-evaluation study showed that a female-dominated job was worth more than a male-dominated job being paid at a higher rate, the market defence could be accepted if the employer argued that the male job was 'overpaid', but had to be paid at the higher rate to recruit workers to a distasteful job (Bellak, 1984). One result, to date, is that cases which have been won in the courts are those which show that the employer decided to pay the female-dominated job less than an employer-sponsored study showed to be its value. However, the argument that value is, or should be, the primary basis of assigning salaries has not been clearly established.

Implications for nursing

Lemons v. *City and County of Denver* ended as a legal case when the Supreme Court declined to review it, but the impact of this case on nursing's relation to comparable worth continued. The case had brought the American Nurses Association (ANA) and the Colorado Nurses Association into a much closer relationship with comparable worth than might otherwise have developed. Both groups contributed money to conduct the Lemons case and publicised it widely amongst their members. Most importantly, despite its loss, every aspect of the case, including the judge's negative ruling, affirmed the nurses' contention that their work was worth more than they were paid. The case brought to the fore nurses' complaints that they were underpaid and documented that underpayment in a way that convinced nurses across the country that they were discriminated against. It provided a new method for nurses to use in assessing what their pay 'ought to be' and showed the limitations of comparing themselves only with other nurses, although that remains a common method of setting salaries.

In the aftermath of the case, there were some interesting changes in Denver. Predictably, the nurses who filed the suit were pressured by their employer. Several left their jobs, one was demoted for 'budgetary' reasons. The employer claimed complete victory and a vindication of the salary-setting system. Yet within a year, the staff nurses at some of the private hospitals in Denver threatened to strike. Staff nurses who had been very supportive of the Lemons case were said to be involved. They received a major salary increase. Between 1979 and 1980 the entry-level salary for the city's Graduate Nurse 1 rose almost 20 per cent (Kurtz and Hocking, 1983, p. 380). By the mid-1980s nurses in the Denver area believed that the city nurses were now paid more at entry than the tree-trimmers.

A city spokesperson from the salary-setting board claimed that the case had had no impact (Kurtz, 1989). The salaries of city nurses went up, she claimed, because the private-hospital job action led to an increase in the wages which showed up in the city's market survey. That is probably correct. But it may be that the lesson in relative wages that nurses in Denver learned from the Lemons case created a climate in which nurses were ready to fight directly for wage increases and knew how much those wage increases should be.

Participants and observers have drawn many lessons from the Lemons case. First, they have argued that the legal case was 'too early', as the courts had not yet interpreted Title VII of the Civil Rights Act to go beyond 'equal pay for equal work'. Second, the nurses tried to present too much material and too complex a case covering the entire class of nurses, rather than specific groups of them. That assessment may be correct but, given the struggles of nursing leaders to define nursing's common ground, it is not surprising that nurse administrators chose to develop a case to represent the interests of all nurses. Third, the nurses most directly involved in the case felt they had relied on the courts to be 'fair', rather than relying on the political process. Their reliance on the judicial system and its inability or failure to reach a finding which nurses and others saw as promoting social justice may have been an important factor in leading later groups to fight for better wages through collective bargaining and legislative campaigns, which often focused on comparable worth but used a variety of tactics for achieving it.

Washington case[14]

The Washington case was not about nurses *per se*. It was about all women employed by the State of Washington, although two of the nine individual plaintiffs were nurses (Willborn, 1989). It was, however, important in its implications for nursing.

In 1974, at the request of the largest state employees' union, Washington Federation of State Employees (American Federation of State, County and Municipal Employees), and the Washington State Women's Commission, the governor authorised a study of the salaries of sex-segregated (at least 70 per cent male or female) jobs. The study, which used a point-evaluation system, showed virtually no overlap in the salaries of male-dominated and female-dominated jobs with the same number of points. Overall female-dominated jobs were paid an average of 80 per cent of the salaries of male-dominated jobs with the same points. A Nurse Practitioner II, at 385 points, had average monthly earnings of $832, the same as those of a Boiler Operator with only 144 points. Extrapolating from the male salary line of the 1974 Washington study, I found that average compensation for a job with 385 points was slightly over $1000 per month (Remick, 1984b, p. 103). This meant that Nurse Practitioner II was almost 20 per cent below the salary line.

The Washington state legislature did not accept the results of the study. For the next six years the union sought to have the study updated and implemented. During this period, there was continual political struggle over the concept of comparable worth. In October, 1981 AFSCME filed an EEOC (Equal Employment Opportunity Commission) complaint on behalf of all women employed by the State of Washington. In July 1982 AFSCME filed suit against the state. In June 1983 two bills which had passed the state legislature were signed into law. One committed the state to comparable worth. The other appropriated funds to begin implementation of comparable worth for state employees.

The lawsuit, *AFSCME* v. *State of Washington*, went to trial in August 1983. Judge Tanner ruled that the question was not whether comparable worth was an appropriate way of setting salaries, because the state legislature had already established that method as legally required in Washington. Instead the question was whether the State had practised discrimination in past and present salary-setting. Judge Tanner found the State guilty of intentional discrimination based on its sex-segregated job advertisements and its failure to correct the disparate impact of its salary setting procedures as revealed in the 1974 study. Correction and back pay were ordered.

The State appealed against the ruling to the Ninth Circuit Court of Appeals. Here the decision was reversed. In the interim, before the case was heard at the Appeals Court, AFSCME and the State of Washington began negotiating an out-of-court settlement. By the time the Appeals Court ruled in favour of the State, negotiations for a settlement were almost complete and continued until a settlement was reached. The settlement involved defining a comparable-worth pay-line based on the average actual salaries of benchmark jobs and bringing all undervalued job classes to within two ranges (5 per cent) of the comparable-worth line by 1993 (Settlement, 1985; Willborn, 1989). This average actual salary line included female-dominated and mixed jobs and so was lower than the male line used in earlier analyses. Since all jobs were included, gender could no longer be a basis of comparison. All undervalued jobs, male-dominated and mixed jobs as well as female-dominated ones, would receive equity adjustments.[15] Salaries of job classes above the line would not be reduced or frozen to implement comparable worth. Comparable-worth increases would not be diminished by general salary increases. The State committed itself to raising all the undervalued jobs to within two ranges of the average comparable-worth line.

There were no provisions for back pay. Former state employees received no money under this agreement. Those groups furthest from the comparable-worth average pay line would reach their guaranteed position, 5 per cent below the line, last. The groups closest to the line would reach that position first. No group was guaranteed to reach the line.

The nurses in the State of Washington received salary increases through the settlement, not as nurses or as members of a female-dominated job class, but as part of an underpaid class of workers. The suit succeeded initially in part because of changes in legal interpretation and in part because the State of Washington had its own study documenting sex-discrimination in salaries for jobs of comparable worth. Yet those features were not sufficient to maintain a legal victory. The settlement that was achieved was reached in large part in response to political pressures. These pressures, generated by a 1982 Democratic election victory in both houses of the legislature, a successful unionisation drive among the 3000 clerical workers of the University of Washington, and by intense lobbying for comparable worth by women's groups and some unions, including AFSCME and the Washington Nurses Association (Remick, 1984b), had earlier led the legislature to appropriate money for comparable worth. Now they supported the move to a settlement. The route that the nurses in *Lemons* v. *City and County of Denver* had eschewed was the path to pay increases in *AFSCME* v. *State of Washington.*

From the standpoint of nursing, as well as the other female-dominated jobs, the unanswered question of the Washington case remains – how well did the job-evaluation study measure the worth of 'women's work'?[16] The study found that female-dominated jobs were systematically underpaid, using an unmodified set of factors and weights that may not have given female-dominated jobs full credit for the responsibility and difficulty of their work. For women employed by the State of Washington, any further remedy for bias remaining in the job-evaluation system will be outside the legal system, since the settlement relinquishes AFSCME's right to further legal action.

If there is a lesson in the AFSCME settlement, it may well be that nurses and others should not rely exclusively on courts or on expert studies. The former are unlikely to rule in nurses' favour, the latter, although potentially useful, are unlikely to prove decisive in achieving victory. Salaries are not set directly on the basis of abstract principles of equity. They are won through political struggles. It was politics and fear of liability that most likely brought the State of Washington to bargain with AFSCME even after the State had won in the courts.

Pennsylvania case[17]

On 5 May 1987, the Pennsylvania Nurses Association (PNA) announced what it called 'the largest pay equity award in the history of nursing' for state employees represented by the Association. The award was a settlement of the pay portion of a sex-discrimination lawsuit filed in Federal District Court in

November 1986. As in the Washington case, the lawsuit itself was the culmination of over six years of negotiation with the state over the classification and pay of all major nurse classifications.

An analysis of sex segregation and salary differences for male-dominated and female-dominated classifications was done by the PNA in 1985, using data supplied by the state. The evidence showed that 84 per cent of the job classifications were sex-segregated (at least 70 per cent incumbents of one sex), and that half of the job classes had 'no women in them at all' (PNA, 1985). Furthermore, PNA found that male-dominated jobs had higher pay ranges than female-dominated jobs doing similar work or having similar entry requirements. For example the 'male' job Revenue Field Auditor 2 had a salary range of $18 875 – $25 624, while the salary range of the comparable 'female' job, Registered Nurse 2, was only $16 567 – $21 477. Details of pay ranges and job classifications for health-care jobs indicated that male-dominated positions were routinely classified in higher pay grades than female-dominated ones. Finally PNA produced evidence that women were denied equal promotional opportunities.

Despite the analysis prepared by PNA, the Commonwealth refused to grant wage increases to remedy the situation. In June 1985 PNA filed a complaint with the Equal Employment Opportunity Commission (EEOC). In that complaint, PNA argued that sex segregation 'inevitably leads to wage discrimination against the less-favored group'. It based its claim on the disparate impact of sex-segregation on the wages of female-dominated job classes. The EEOC complaint emphasised that PNA had 'repeatedly requested the State to conduct a study of sex-based wage discrimination, but the State has repeatedly refused' (Barnett, n.d.). It also pointed out that the State had refused to supply PNA with the results of state's own job evaluations, based on the Hay system, which were said to be the basis of its wage-setting.

While the suit was pending, negotiations on a new contract continued. In January 1986, PNA members conducted a nine-day strike, in which the main issue was pay equity. In May and June 1986 PNA again met with the Commonwealth to discuss pay ranges for classes in the PNA bargaining unit. No action was taken. One month later the Commonwealth reclassified psychiatric nurses downward by two pay grades. In August PNA received its 'right to sue' letter, the letter issued by EEOC which allows a party charging discrimination to file legal suit when EEOC has not acted within six months but has not dismissed the charge. In November 1986 PNA and fifty individual members filed a sex-discrimination suit against the Commonwealth of Pennsylvania.

In its lawsuit, PNA argued that not only were there inequities in salaries but also that these inequities carried over into workers' compensation coverage and retirement benefits. In particular, PNA claimed that incumbents of several male-dominated jobs (including Psychiatric Security Aides and Correctional Officers) who were temporarily incapacitated as a result of any work-related injury or illness received their salaries as long as they were disabled, had the right to return to their jobs whenever they were able and did not have their time out of work deducted from their sick-leave entitlement. Nurses working in the prisons were eligible for these benefits only if their disability was caused by the act of an inmate. In all other circumstances, they received full pay during disability leave for a maximum of 12 months over a three-year period. Once they had used the maximum disability leave, they had to use their sick time or take unpaid leave, during which time they did not receive state coverage for medical or life insurance. Finally, the nurses' rights to return to their positions ended three years from the date of their disability, even if they had not fully recovered. In addition, the same male-dominated jobs were eligible for retirement at age 50 after three years of service, while nurses who worked in the prisons and forensic units were not eligible for retirement until age 60.

The Commonwealth of Pennsylvania claimed that nurses working in the prisons and forensic units were not subject to the same levels of stress and the same risk of assault as the male-dominated job classes in these settings.

As this suit went forward, an out-of-court settlement was reached on the pay claims put forward by PNA. Over six years registered nurses and medical technologists represented by PNA would receive an aggregate of $16 million in wage increases. The basic nursing classifications (Nurse 1, Nurse 2 and Nurse Supervisor) moved up three to four pay ranges, increases of $3000 – $4000 annually, in May 1987, while other classifications moved up one to two pay ranges. In addition, other in-range step increases were negotiated so that over 70 per cent of the bargaining unit would receive pay-equity increases within the first year of the settlement.

While the wage portion of the suit was settled out of court in May 1987, an out of court settlement of the suit over discrimination in retirement benefits was approved by the Federal District Court in October 1990.[18] As the first US suit to claim sex discrimination in benefits, the PNA case demonstrates the breadth of the comparable-worth analysis.[19] If comparable worth is to be an effective tool for redressing inequity, it must include benefits and other advantages such as health insurance pensions, disability and other allowances. More and more women depend solely on their own jobs as their economic base and we must ensure that these are as good as good 'men's jobs'.

The separation of nurses from other female-dominated classifications in Pennsylvania, however, meant that only nurses and other health care classes represented by PNA benefited directly from the settlement of the wage claim. Although the initial PNA complaint and suit charged sex discrimination in all female-dominated classes, no support was forthcoming from unions which represented other female-dominated classifications. Here the long-standing distance between the state nursing associations as collective bargaining agents and union bargaining agents limited the gains for other female-dominated classes. Whether the other unions will press sex-discrimination wage claims on behalf of the women they represent remains to be seen.

Minnesota case[20]

The State of Minnesota is a direct contrast to other comparable-worth cases which have affected nurses. Without a major conflict between female state employees, their unions and the State, the State initiated a programme to evaluate and address pay inequities in female-dominated job classes.

According to its official history, pay equity in Minnesota began in the autumn of 1975 when AFSCME and the state negotiated a contract that called for a study of state jobs and a comparison of salaries in clerical and non-clerical jobs (Commission on the Economic Status of Women, 1988). By May 1979 the study of state and local jobs, using the Hay evaluation system, was completed. Two and a half years later, a Task Force on Pay Equity was established to examine salary differences between male and female jobs. Its reports, 'Pay Equity and Public Employment' (March, 1982) was translated into action that same spring through a state law which established both a pay-equity policy and a procedure for awarding pay-equity salary increases. One year later the legislature allocated over $20 million for these increases. In the next three years, legislation requiring local governments (towns, school committees, etc.) to implement pay equity or face financial penalties was enacted.

About half of the health-care professionals employed by the state received wage increases under this scheme. Relative to similarly valued male-dominated jobs, nurses moved from roughly 80 per cent to 90 per cent of maximum salaries. State nurses thus received a marked increase in their wages during the period 1983–6. At the same time, Minneapolis–St Paul nurses in private hospitals also experienced greater wage increases than their counterparts in other major cities, even as nursing as a whole lost ground.

While the Minnesota case illustrates that comparable worth can be achieved through legislation without major political struggle, it also raises some important questions. The consciousness-raising which had been so important a benefit of other comparable-worth campaigns may not have occurred in the quieter movement in Minnesota (Evans and Nelson, 1989). Will this make it harder to maintain the advances? Will as yet unaddressed biases in the evaluation system be less likely to gain public attention? Will nurses and other women working in female-dominated jobs be certain of the value of their work?

WHAT HAS COMPARABLE WORTH MEANT FOR NURSES?

The impact of comparable worth on US nurses' wages cannot be assessed outside the context of the changing organisation of health care and of the economy. As this is written in 1989, hospitals in the USA, where over two-thirds of US nurses are working, are experiencing the most acute 'shortage' of nurses in recent decades. On the one hand, one immediate result of the current 'shortage', unlike many in the past, is higher nurses' wages. On the other hand, it is not yet clear whether nurses' wages are finally beginning to rise relative to those of comparable male-dominated professions.

The question is, is comparable worth helping to institutionalise higher nurses' wages or are the current wages increases merely a result of market forces? If it is the former, we can expect hospital nurses to show increased militancy on economic issues and to insist on wages and benefits comparable to those in male-dominated occupations. If it is only the latter, then the increases in nurses wages may turn out to be temporary, and to disappear.

There have been many attempts to evaluate comparable worth. These attempts generally take one of two forms: a review of court cases or a review of campaigns. The evaluations can be predicted from the starting perspective. Those who look primarily at comparable-worth cases as legal cases find comparable worth a 'failure' in the courts. Those who review comparable-worth cases as political campaigns find comparable worth a powerful strategy. Both are right, and both are too narrowly focused to be satisfying.

The courts have consistently ruled against comparable-worth cases. In the unfavourable political climate of the late 1970s and especially the 1980s no legal strategy aimed at overcoming discrimination against people of colour or against all women succeeded. Comparable worth is a prime example of the category. Social change has rarely succeeded in the US courts before it was accomplished in other arenas. Not surprisingly, the tradition was upheld during the period in which comparable worth reached the courts. It was a period in which there was no longer a social consensus aimed at ending discrimination and its effects. Indeed, the earlier consensus that supported civil rights victories had begun to compete with the concept 'reverse discrimination'. Even in the earlier period, none of the principles which supported that consensus had ever been applied primarily to end discrimination based on sex.

Moreover, comparable-worth cases required judges to find discrimination underlying practices which were viewed as outcomes of the working of the market-place. It would have been much more surprising if comparable worth had won in the courts.

In contrast, comparable-worth campaigns have more often succeeded, even when the lawsuits they generated failed. They have raised wages for particular groups of female-dominated jobs (even if only as part of a correction of wage-inequities) and at times have challenged taken for granted conceptions of 'women's work'. These campaigns were all conducted by state nurses' associations and other unions, in collaboration with women's advocacy groups and civil rights organisations. However, looking only at the organised political forces that mobilised around comparable worth is also too narrow a view of comparable worth's impact.

Amongst nurses, comparable worth remains attractive even though few of the successful comparable-worth campaigns in the USA centred on nurses. Comparable worth alone did not *cause* the dramatic increase in nurses' wages at the end of the 1980s. Yet, I would argue, it contributed significantly to that increase. Around the concept of comparable worth, strategies crystallised for raising nurses' wages.

What comparable worth did for nurses was to bring a new visibility to their work. It also brought their potential power to disrupt hospital care to the attention of their employers. The analyses done in the name of comparable worth illuminated the work of nursing: its skills, its demands, its responsibilities and its working conditions. It showed dramatically the full scope of a job that had previously been trivialised and taken for granted. It gave names to aspects of nurses' jobs that had never been named, much less acknowledged. Comparable worth created a climate and provided a tool, imperfect but still revealing, for re-evaluation. Through it, nurses came to *know* that their work was worth much more than they were being paid and that, whatever the rulings of the courts, the public sympathised with and supported their claims. With new confidence, nurses presented their demands for higher wages in the courts, in the legislatures, at the bargaining table and, when necessary, on the picket line. They made it clear to hospital administrators, to politicians and to themselves and their families that they were no longer willing to work for less than they were worth.

The impact of comparable worth can be seen in all those arenas. Only when we look broadly do we begin to see what comparable worth has really meant for nurses and to understand why nurses respond to comparable worth.

Comparable worth is not a magic technique. Proving that nurses' jobs are as valuable as those of other better-paid, hospital employees will not sweep away the opposition of physicians and hospital administrators to nurses' higher wages. What it offers is a new ground from which nurses can launch a struggle. The success of that struggle depends on nurses' ability to seize these new grounds and use them to win the wage, benefits and conditions of work that they want. Once having won these, it will be a daily struggle to maintain them.

Notes

Acknowledgements. Thanks to Mary Fillmore, Nona Glazer, Susan Reverby and Ronnie Steinberg for reading earlier drafts of this chapter. Peggy Kahn's editorial work greatly improved the narrative. The chapter also benefited from conversations about comparable worth with Carolyn Magid and from my work as a member of the Pay Equity Advisory Committee of the Commonwealth of Massachusetts. Finally thanks are due to the Massachusetts Nurses Association which encouraged my interest in this topic. The views stated are the author's and do not reflect the opinions of the Massachusetts Nurses Association.

1. In the USA, registered nurse (RN) is the title of a nurse who is licensed to perform the most extensive range of general nursing care. In this chapter the terms registered nurse and nurse are used interchangeably.

2. For a brief introduction to the concept of comparable worth see Feldberg (1984). For discussions of technical and political issues see Acker (1987 and 1989); Remick (1984a and 1984b); Steinberg and Haignere (1987); Treiman and Hartmann (1981).

3. American Library Association (ALA) has also been committed to comparable worth, but has not emphasised litigation as part of its strategy (Steinberg, 1990a). See Kenady (1989) for ALA's approach. For the American Nurses Association (ANA) approach to comparable worth, see Flanagan (1986 and 1989b).

4. It has been estimated that nurses' wages would be at least 18 per cent higher if nursing were a male-dominated occupations (Flanagan, 1989b, p. 3). That is consistent with findings that female-dominated occupations are typically paid 20 per cent less than their value as measured by traditional job-evaluation instruments.

5. For discussions of the skills and knowledge involved in nursing see Benner (1984) and Benner and Wrubel (1989). For example, nurses' skills in interpreting changes in patient's skin tone, breathing and emotional state often enable them to anticipate a problem before electronic monitors indicate irregularity (Benner, 1984).

6. There is a rich recent literature on the work of nurses in the USA. See Benner (1984); Benner and Wrubel (1989), Melosh (1982) and Reverby (1987). Gray (1989) argues, on the basis of an Australian study, that changes in sex roles and gender ideology have contributed more to nurses' militancy than have changes in the organisation of their work.

7. See Friss (1981 and 1988) for discussions of the problems which nurses face in trying to raise their wages. Friss (1988) argues that challenges to hospital employers' actions to restrict wage increases are likely to be more useful than comparable-worth campaigns.

8. For historical data on nurses' income see Reverby (1987, especially pp. 98–111) and Kalisch and Kalisch (1986).

9. Hospital staff nurse is the largest category of nurses. It excludes head nurses and other designations. The term 'average' refers to an estimated average wage calculated for this chapter. There are no annual average wages reported for hospital staff nurses. The University of Texas Medical Branch at Galveston conducts an annual national survey of hospitals, medical schools and medical centres. It reports average monthly starting and maximum salary ranges. It does not report the overall average or the distribution of nurses' wages across the entire salary range. Therefore I developed an estimated average weekly wage for hospital staff nurses working in non-federal hospitals from the Industry Wage Survey (US Department of Labor, 1987 and other years). This series provides actual average wages for hospital staff nurses by city for particular years. The series does not provide an average across the cities. Therefore, the 'average' used in Table 9.1 to represent average staff nurse wages is the average of the median city for the year indicated.

10. Professional includes professional and technical workers. During this period the largest occupation of professional women was elementary-school teacher. Relative to elementary-school teachers, nurses 'average' wages rose from 86 per cent of teachers in 1959 to 98 per cent in 1985–6. This increasing percentage can reflect either real gains by nurses or a relative decline in teachers' salaries. In any case, since elementary-school teachers officially work a shorter day and short year, their hourly rate remains above that of nurses for this period. Teachers salary estimates are from US Department of Education (1987).

11. There is an enormous literature on US health care and its costs. Sources for this analysis include Starr (1982) and the National Health Accounts of the United States for various years, for example, Gibson and Waldo (1982).

12. For a discussion of how nurses develop their skills with experience but are not rewarded, see Benner (1984). For a further discussion of nurses' skills see Steinberg (1990b).

13. *Lemons* v. *City and County of Denver* US District Court, District of Colorado, no. 76-W-1156, 17 April 1978 as corrected 28 April 1978, FEP Cases, pp. 906–14. There have been many discussions and interpretations of *Lemons* v. *City and County of Denver*. Among those used in this analysis are Hutner (1986), Barnes (1980), Bullough (1978) and Kronstadt (1978). Almost every discussion of comparable worth and nurses mentions this case.

14. Sources for my analysis of the Washington case are largely Remick (1984b) and Hutner (1986). This section was written before Willborn (1989) was published but was modified where new information suggested revision.

15. Most US unions face serious dilemmas in dealing with comparable worth. They have predominantly male members or leaders or both. Some pressures to limit comparable-worth adjustments are generated by whatever threats to their masculinity or their privileges these men see in 'women's work' being valued as 'equal to' or 'of greater worth than' their own work. In addition, these forces have led many union activists to recast 'comparable worth' as 'pay equity' emphasising its potential for achieving equitable pay for all work rather than its potential for eliminating gender, race and/or age bias in wage-setting.

16. There is a thought-provoking literature on the adequacy of job-evaluation studies as a technique for identifying sex bias in wage-setting. See Remick (1984a and 1984b), Steinberg and Haignere (1987), Acker (1987 and 1989), Treiman and Hartmann (1981) and Treiman (1984). A thorough discussion of these issues in analysing the work of nurses is found in Steinberg (1990b).

17. The Pennsylvania case did not go to trial and did not receive extensive attention. My main sources for this case are materials prepared by the Pennsylvania Nurses Association (PNA), legal documents, and personal communications with both Edith Barnett, the attorney who represented PNA in this case, and Richard Stober, the Director of Professional, Economic and General Welfare for PNA. My thanks to both of them for answering my questions graciously and supplying materials promptly.

18. The settlement gives nurses working in the prisons the same retirement benefit – as that available to correction officers (i.e. retirement at age 50 after three years of service at the same pension rate) and gives nurses credit for service toward that pension back to the 1986 date of the filing of the lawsuit. It affects only current employees. The suit on disability was dropped after it was discovered that nurses were covered under a work-related disability plan that was just about equivalent to that of the correction officers.

19. See Willborn (1989) for benefit issues in the Hayward case in England. These are the only two cases I know of in which benefits have been the main focus of attention after a wage adjustment has been settled.

20. Sources for this case are primarily the documents prepared by the Minnesota Council on the Economic Status of Women. Nina Rothschild, Commissioner of Employee Relations, answered many questions and supplied the pay plan for the State of Minnesota. Minnesota is unique among the states in providing primary data about its pay plan to interested citizens. The State relied on the Hay evaluation system, apparently without fundamentally modifying the factors or their definitions. The question of whether the evaluation system fully credits female-dominated job classes for their work has not yet been addressed publicly by the Commission on the Economic Status of Women. The book by Evans and Nelson (1989) appeared after this section was drafted. Their account confirms the factual record as reported here and the

explores many of the questions raised here about the limitations of comparable-worth adjustments which do not result from a grassroots campaign. However, I would maintain that increasing women's salaries towards equity is valuable in itself.

References

Acker, Joan (1987) 'Sex Bias in Job Evaluation: A Comparable Worth Issue', in C. Bose and G. Spitze (eds) *Ingredients for Women's Employment Policy* (Albany, NY: State University of New York Press).
Acker, Joan (1989) *Doing Comparable Worth* (Philadelphia: Temple University Press).
Aiken, Linda H. and Mullinix, Connie F. (1987) 'The Nursing Shortage, Myth or Reality?', *New England Journal of Medicine*, vol. 317, no 10 (3 September) pp. 641–5.
American Nurses Association (1951) *1951 Facts About Nursing* (New York: American Nurses Association).
American Nurses Association (1961) *Facts About Nursing*, 1961 edn. (New York: American Nurses Association)
American Nurses Association (1964) *Facts About Nursing*, 1964 edn. (New York: American Nurses Association)
American Nurses Association (1967) *Facts About Nursing*, 1967 edn. (New York: American Nurses Association).
American Nurses Association (1971) *Facts About Nursing*, 1970–71 edns. (New York: American Nurses Association).
American Nurses Association (1974) *Facts About Nursing*, 1972–73 edn. (New York: American Nurses Association).
American Nurses Association (1977) *Facts About Nursing, 1976–77* (Kansas City, Mo: American Nurses Association).
American Nurses Association (1983) *Facts About Nursing, 1982–83* (Kansas City: Mo: American Nurses Association).
American Nurses Association (1987) *Facts About Nursing, 1986–87* (Kansas City, Mo: American Nurses Association).
American Nurses Association (1988) *Collective Bargaining Data*, unpublished.
Applebaum, Eileen and Granrose, Cherlyn S. (1986) 'Hospital Employment under Revised Medicare Payment Schedules', *Monthly Labor Review*, vol. 109, no 8 (August) pp. 37–45.
Barnes, Craig (1980) 'Denver: A Case Study', in B. Bullough (ed.) *The Law and the Expanding Nursing Role* (New York: Appleton-Century-Crofts).
Barnett, Edith (1988) Telephone interview.
Barnett, Edith (No date) 'Pennsylvania Nurses Association Memorandum in Support of EEOC Charges'.
Bellak, Alvin (1984) 'Comparable Worth: A Practitioner's View', prepared at the request of the US Commission on Civil Rights for Consultation on Comparable Worth, Washington, DC, 6–7 June.
Benner, Patricia (1984) *From Novice to Expert* (Menlo Park, Cal: Addison-Wesley).

Benner, Patricia and Wrubel Judith, (1989) *The Primacy of Caring* (Menlo Park, Cal: Addison-Wesley).

Bullough, Bonnie (1978) 'The Struggle for Women's Rights in Denver: A Personal Account', *Nursing Outlook*, vol. 26, no 9 (September) pp. 566–7.

Commission on the Economic Status of Women (1988) *Pay Equity: The Minnesota Experience* (revised) (St Paul: Commission on the Economic Status of Women).

Cook, Adele (1990) 'Comparable Worth: An Economic Issue', *Nursing Management*, vol. 21, no 2 (February) pp. 28–30.

Evans, Sara M. and Nelson, Barbara J. (1989) *Wage Justice: Comparable Worth and the Paradox of Technocratic Reform* (Chicago: University of Chicago Press).

Feldberg, Roslyn L. (1984) 'Comparable Worth: Toward Theory and Practice in the United States', *Signs*, vol. 10, no 2 (Winter) pp. 311–28.

Flanagan, Lyndia (1986) *Pay Equity, What It Means and How It Affects Nurses* (Kansas City, Mo: American Nurses Association) (pamphlet).

Flanagan, Lyndia (1989a) *Braving New Frontiers, ANA's Economic and General Welfare Program, 1946–1986.* (Kansas City, Mo: American Nurses Association) (booklet).

Flanagan, Lyndia (1989b) *Earn What You're Worth* (Kansas City, Mo: American Nurses Association) (booklet).

Friss, Lois (1981) 'Work Force Policy Perspectives: Registered Nurses', *Journal of Health Politics, Policy and Law*, vol. 5 (Winter) pp. 696–719.

Friss, Lois (1988) 'Why Don't Nurses Demand More Pay?', in R. M. Kelly and J. Bayes (eds) *Comparable Worth, Pay Equity and Public Policy* (New York: Greenwood Press).

Gibson, R. M. and Waldo, D. R. (1982) 'National Health Expenditures, 1981', *Health Care Financing Review*, vol. 4 (September) pp. 1–35.

Gray, David (1989) 'Militancy, Unionism and Gender Ideology, A Study of Hospital Nurses', *Work and Occupations*, vol. 16, no 2 (May) pp. 137–52.

Harrison, Benjamin and Bluestone, Barry (1988) *The Great U-Turn: Corporate Restructuring and the Polarizing of America* (New York: Basic Books).

Hutner, Frances (1986) *Equal Pay for Comparable Worth* (New York: Praeger).

Kalisch, Philip and Kalisch, Beatrice (1986) *The Advance of American Nursing* (Boston and Toronto: Little, Brown & Co.) 2nd end.

Kenady, Carolyn (1989) *Pay Equity: An Action Manual for Library Workers* (Chicago: American Library Association).

Kronstadt, Sylvia (1978) ' "New Frontier" for Equal Rights', *The Nation*, vol. 226 (29 April) pp. 505–6.

Kurtz, Maxine (1989) Telephone interviews (29 August and 6 September).

Kurtz, Maxine and Hocking, E. (1983) 'Nurses *vs* Tree Trimmers', *Public Personnel Management Journal*, vol. 12, no 4 (Winter) pp. 369–81.

McKibbin, Richard (1988) 'Limited Pay Growth Thwarts Nursing', *American Nurse*, vol. 20, no 5 (May) p. 3.

Melosh, Barbara (1982) *'The Physician's Hand'*, *Work Culture and Conflict in American Nursing* (Philadelphia: Temple University Press).

Miller, Richard (1980) 'Hospitals', in G. Somers (ed.) *Collective Bargaining: Contemporary American Experience* (Madison, Wis: Industrial Relations Research Association).

Minnesota Department of Employee Relations (no date) *Salary Plan, Effective July, 1988*, supplied by Nina Rothschild, Commissioner of Employer Relations.

Newman, Winn and Vonhof, Jeanne (1981) ' "Separate but Equal" – Job Segregation and Pay Equity in the Wake of Gunther', *University of Illinois Law Review*, vol. 2, pp. 269–331.

[The] Pennsylvania Nurse (1987) 'PNA Files Sex Discrimination Suit against Commonwealth', (January) pp. 4, 14.

[The] Pennsylvania Nurse (1987) 'PNA's Sex Discrimination Suit Against the Commonwealth Moves Closer to Court', (February) p. 1.

[The] Pennsylvania Nurse (1987) 'PNA Reaches Sex Discrimination Settlement', (June) pp. 1, 8.

Pennsylvania Nurses Association (1985) 'PNA Sex Discrimination Charges against the State of Pennsylvania', *Fact Sheet* (7 June).

Pennsylvania Nurses Association (1987) ' "Historic" Settlement Reached in PNA's Sex Discrimination Lawsuit', *Contact: Educational News of the Commission on Economic and General Welfare*, vol. 15, no 3 (June) pp. 1, 3, 8.

Pennyslvania Nurses Association v. Commonwealth of Pennyslvania, 1988, third amended complaint, filed 16 March.

Prescott, Patricia (1987) 'Another Round of Nurse Shortage', *Image: Journal of Nursing Scholarship*, vol. 19 (Winter) pp. 204–9.

Remick, Helen (1984a) 'Dilemmas of Implementation: The Case of Nursing', in H. Remick (ed.) *Comparable Worth and Wage Discrimination, Technical Possibilities and Political Realities* (Philadelphia: Temple University Press).

Remick, Helen (1984b) 'Major Issues in *a priori* Applications', in H. Remick (ed.) *Comparable Worth and Wage Discrimination, Technical Possibilities and Political Realities* (Philadelphia: Temple University Press).

Reverby, Susan (1987) *Ordered to Care, The Dilemma of American Nursing, 1850–1945* (Cambridge, London, New York: Cambridge University Press), pp. 215–48.

Settlement Agreement between the State of Washington and AFSCME, the Washington Federation of State Employees and nine individually-named plaintiffs in the case, *American Federation of State, County and Municipal Employees v. State of Washington*, 578 F. Supp. 846 (W. D. Wash. 1983), 1985.

Sparks, Patricia (1988) 'Gender Issues in the Nurturing Occupations: Focus on Nurses and Health Care Professionals', unpublished; on file at the School of Social Work, CUNY – Hunter College, New York.

Starr, Paul (1982) *The Social Transformation of American Medicine* (New York: Basic Books).

Steinberg, Ronnie (1990a) personal communication (April).

Steinberg, Ronnie (1990b) *Report Concerning the Proposed Testimony of Dr Ronnie Steinberg PHD [sic] Concerning the Appropriateness of the Respondent Hospital's Proposed Comparison System*, presented to the Pay Equity Hearings Tribunal for a Hearing between the Ontario Nurses Association and Women's College Hospital.

Steinberg, Ronnie and Haignere, Lois (1987) 'Equitable Compensation: Methodological Criteria for Comparable Worth', in C. Bose and G. Spitze (eds) *Ingredients for Women's Employment Policy* (Albany, NY: State University of New York Press).

Treiman, Donald (1984) 'Effect of Choice of Factors and Factor Weights in Job Evaluation', in H. Remick (ed.) *Comparable Worth and Wage Discrimination, Technical Possibilities and Political Realties* (Philadelphia: Temple University Press).

Treiman, Donald and Hartmann, Heidi (eds) (1981) *Women, Work and Wages: Equal Pay for Jobs of Equal Value* (Washington, DC: National Academy Press).

US Department of Education (1987) *Digest of Educational Statistics* (Washington, DC: Government Printing Office).

US Department of Labor (1967) 'Industry Wage Survey: Hospitals, July, 1966', *Bureau of Labor Statistics Bulletin*, No. 1553 (June).

US Department of Labor (1971) 'Industry Wage Survey: Hospitals, March 1969', *Bureau of Labor Statistics Bulletin*, no 1688 (May).

US Department of Labor (1980) 'Industry Wage Survey: Hospitals and Nursing Homes, September 1978', *Bureau of Labor Statistics Bulletin*, no 2069 (November).

US Department of Labor (1983) 'Industry Wage Survey: Hospitals, October 1981', *Bureau of Labor Statistics Bulletin*, no. 2204.

US Department of Labor (1987) 'Industry Wage Survey: Hospitals, August 1985', *Bureau of Labor Statistics Bulletin*, no. 2273 (February).

US Department of Labor (1989) 'Industry Wage Survey: Hospitals, Boston, Mass., January, 1989', *Bureau of Labor Statistics Summary* (August).

Willborn, Steven (1989) *A Secretary and a Cook* (Ithaca, NY: ILR Press).

10 Equal Value in the Local Authorities Sector in Great Britain

Sue Hastings

INTRODUCTION

This chapter examines the impact of the Equal Value (Amendment) Regulations on the local authority sector in Great Britain.[1] It does so in two distinct sections – one covering the manual workers employed by local authorities, the other dealing with the authorities' white-collar, or non-manual, employees. The distinction is made partly because the collective-bargaining arrangements are different for the two groups and involve, in the main, different unions; but more importantly because the concept of 'equal value' has impacted very differently on the two parts of the sector. The final section of the chapter consists why this may have been the case.

LOCAL AUTHORITY MANUAL WORKERS

In spite of being relatively lower paid than their male colleagues, female local-authority manual workers had no claim for equal pay under the Equal Pay Act as it was originally passed in 1970 and implemented in 1975.

They had no 'like work' claims because of the very high degree of occupational segregation within this million-strong group of workers. Female manual workers for local authorities were, and largely still are, home helps, care assistants in old people's homes, school-meals cooks and assistants, and office and school cleaners. Male manual workers were, and are, refuse-collectors and drivers, road-menders and street-sweepers, and parks and gardens staff (although the male predominance in this latter area has become somewhat diluted in recent years,

215

especially in the south-east of England where acute labour shortages have contributed to greater integration.)

Nor had the women any 'work rated as equivalent' claims. This was because in the late 1960s a job-evaluation scheme had been agreed by the National Joint Council (NJC) for Local Authority Manual Workers and implemented to cover all one million jobholders, roughly three-quarters of whom were women, the great majority working part-time. The results of this exercise had been jointly and fairly implemented by the standards of the late 1960s and 1970s, and thus met the criteria which were used in assessing whether women had 'work rated as equivalent claims'.

It was apparent to both union and management representatives on the NJC in 1984 that some women manual workers would be able to pursue claims under the new 'equal value' procedure, which would involve a comparison of their work with that of a named male comparator under headings such as 'decision, skill and effort'. The negotiators were particularly concerned about the home helps whose jobs were generally agreed to be undervalued by the old structure. This was partly because the home helps' jobs had changed over the intervening years from being cleaners for elderly people in their own homes to being carers with responsibilities for, for example, collecting prescriptions from doctor or chemist, ensuring medication is taken, shopping and preparing meals, and reporting any medical or social problems to the relevant agencies. Their status too had been raised with the recognition of their role in enabling the elderly to stay in their own homes rather than be moved into communal old people's homes.

It was, therefore, agreed between the two sides of the JNC that a new job-evaluation exercise should be carried out. This would allow regradings of obviously undervalued female occupational groups in a systematic fashion, rather than in the *ad hoc* manner which would occur if individual women took their claims to Industrial Tribunals, with or without union support. Furthermore, if the scheme were a fair and non-discriminatory one it would provide a subsequent defence, under section 1(5) of the amended Equal Pay Act, against any later claims which would be seen as having a destructive effect on the new structure.

Rather than call in management consultants, as had been the case with the 1960s scheme, it was decided that the new scheme should be designed in-house and specifically for the group of workers in question. The burden of this work fell on the staff of the Local Authorities Conditions of Service Advisory Board (LACSAB), who provided the secretariat for the NJC, together with several of the relevant unions' paid officials. The new scheme thus had a major union input at the design stage as well as at the implementation stage. In this respect it differed significantly from most evaluation exercises undertaken in the UK, where there is commonly participation at the implementation stage, but much more rarely at the design stage.

The exercise was carried out with a view to producing an 'equal value' scheme,[2] although in retrospect it is not clear that anyone involved had a very clear idea of what that meant. In design terms, there were two major differences between the new scheme and the one it superseded. The first was that a factor for 'responsibility for members of the public' was introduced in addition to the more usual 'responsibility for supervising others' and 'responsibility for resources' factors. The new factor benefited jobs involving direct contact with local authority clients; it particularly advantaged the home helps, but to a slightly lesser extent also helped other female-dominated jobs, many of which also involved client contact, for instance, care assistants, school-crossing attendants and school-meals staff.

The second difference concerned the way in which the 'skills and knowledge' required for the job were measured. The old scheme had laid heavy emphasis on jobs where formal training courses and/or certification were provided by the local authorities – gardening and parks maintenance are examples of this system. The new scheme specifically allowed, in its factor and level definitions, for informally acquired skills such as caring, cleaning and cooking skills brought to the job to be taken into account at all levels.

In terms of the implementation of the scheme, a number of steps were taken to try to ensure that the exercise was carried out, and was seen to be carried out, in as fair and unbiased a manner as possible. For instance, 'equal value' consultants were commissioned to vet the scheme for gender bias and to oversee its implementation at national level. The consultants concerned,

David Wainwright and Lorraine Paddison of TMS Consultants, participated in the national training sessions for panel members and ran exercises on identifying and eliminating sex bias. They also checked the results of the preliminary evaluations.

It was agreed that women should make up at least half the eight-strong membership of each of the ten evaluation panels. Because most of the national and local officers of the manual workers' unions were male, the female panel-members came largely from the workforce. Special training sessions were provided for the union-side panel-members only, to avoid them being at a disadvantage when they came together with the management-side panel-members, who were often personnel-department staff or similar local authority non-manual employees with more experience of this type of activity.

There were some early problems over job descriptions, a crucial area in any job-evaluation exercise and one where there is clearly a danger of bias creeping in if women talk down their own jobs or interviewers are not sensitive to the need to draw out the interviewees. The union-only training sessions had included exercises on the importance of job descriptions and the need to avoid bias in their preparation. The actual preparation of the pilot job-descriptions was in the hands of staff of the Local Authorities' Management Services and Computer Group (LAMSAC). When the results began to come through it was clear that they were not satisfactory. Although it caused delay to the exercise, the LAMSAC consultants were replaced by a team of academics, led by Sidney Kessler, Professor of Industrial Relations at City University, who were provided with a detailed, 40-page job-questionnaire and instructions in order to ensure consistency of approach over the 540 job-descriptions to be collected around the country.

The national exercise, described above, covered thirty-seven 'benchmark' jobs, selected from all the main occupational groups and commonly found across the country. Once it was completed, joint teams at regional and local levels were instructed to match up jobs in their own areas to the relevant national description; where this could not be done the jobs were to be evaluated locally using the nationally designed scheme.[3]

The new structure, which was agreed in 1987, resulted in the upgrading of most of the predominantly female groups relative to the predominantly male groups. Home helps and the most senior of the cooks jobs evaluated moved up to the next to the top grade, alongside refuse drivers and the most skilled of the gardening jobs. In terms of basic pay, it can reasonably be argued that, as a result of the exercise, female local-authority manual workers have equal pay for work of equal value with their male counterparts.

However, the job-evaluation scheme only dealt with basic pay rates and did not affect bonus payments. Research undertaken by the LEVEL group of London local authorities since 1987 has shown that bonus payments skew total earnings to such an effect that gender rather than grade is the better indicator of earnings.[4] This occurs because more men have access to bonus schemes and even where there are bonus schemes for both male and female groups the payments to women are usually lower than the payments to men. The study also found that among the local authorities covered nearly all the high-earning bonus schemes, which could add up to 100 per cent on top of basic pay, were for 'male' jobs.

So in spite of the job-evaluation exercise, it would still be possible for a female manual worker to go to an Industrial Tribunal claiming equal total earnings with a male comparator on a bonus scheme. The local-authority employer would have to try to justify the additional bonus payments in terms of the increased performance required to achieve them and to show that they are not gender related. As many of the bonus schemes were introduced in the 1960s and no longer meet their original purposes, such justification might be difficult. Given this clear and widely acknowledged potential for challenging under the equal pay legislation, it is perhaps surprising that by 1991, over three years after the results of the job-evaluation exercise had been implemented and their effects digested, no claims had been registered with Industrial Tribunals by female local-authority manual workers.

Both sides of the JNC are well aware of the problem. To some extent, it is being reduced by the legislation requiring competitive tendering for many local-authority services – in order to retain the contract in-house groups of workers may negotiate reduced bonus levels or even their total elimination. On the other hand, there is also some anecdotal evidence that female-dominated groups such as school cleaners and meals staff are more likely to have had to give up their bonuses in order to retain their contracts than male groups, such as parks and gardening staff.

LOCAL AUTHORITY NON-MANUAL EMPLOYEES

The non-manual employees of local authorities, like their manual-worker colleagues, had also not been affected by the Equal Pay legislation as originally enacted in 1970. Equal pay, in terms of the same rate for the job whether undertaken by man or woman, had been negotiated by the relevant unions with the employers in the 1950s, so, in theory, there should not have been any possible 'like work' claims.

The non-manual group also had a job-evaluation scheme. The Purple Book Scheme,[5] as it was commonly called, because it was included in the terms-and-conditions manual for local-authority white-collar workers, which historically always had purple covers to distinguish it from the equivalent manuals for other groups, had been developed and agreed in the early 1970s. However, unlike the parallel 1960s scheme for the manual workers, its application to jobs was not compulsory.

Some local authorities adopted the scheme in its entirety and graded all non-manual jobs under it. Others used it only as an appeals mechanism to resolve grading disputes over particular jobs, so only jobs which had been subjects of appeal through their grading grievance system had been evaluated against its criteria. Other local authorities, many of them in the north of England, did not use it at all. It was thus not nearly such an all-embracing scheme as that for the local-authority manual workers.

The passing of the 'equal value' Amendment Regulations certainly raised questions in the minds of some of the relevant union officials, NALGO, the National Association of Local Government Officers, and ACTTS, as it was then called, the white-collar section of the Transport and General Workers' Union (TGWU), just as it had for their manual-worker colleagues. However, attempts to investigate a review of the Purple Book Scheme did not progress quickly. A number of reasons can be suggested for this:

- the secretariat officials from LACSAB, who were largely the same people for both white-collar and blue-collar negotiating bodies, rapidly became heavily involved in the new manual-workers' job-evaluation exercise and were unable to provide the resources for a similar exercise for non-manual staffs;
- even in 1985, and to a much greater extent than for the manual group, pressures were beginning to develop for the break-up of the national negotiating system. Labour-market pressures, especially in the south-east of England, were starting to cause some local authorities to offer pay and benefit incentives to specialists and top executives in order to recruit and retain them. In such circumstances a new nationally negotiated job-evaluation scheme may not have seemed appropriate to some management-side members of the JNC;
- because of labour-market forces in conjunction with pressures from Government to improve the efficiency of local authority service management, some authorities were beginning to bring in management consultants to examine aspects of their organisation. It was not long before the consultants, notably Hay–MSL with its off-the-shelf Guide Chart Profile System of Job Evaluation, were also conducting grading and salary reviews for authorities.

Criticism of, and dissatisfaction with, the Purple Book Scheme did develop, albeit gradually. The criticism was fuelled by a second report from LEVEL,[6] which identified areas within the scheme which could be open to challenge on grounds of bias against women's jobs. This study had been commissioned from Lorraine Paddison of TMS consultants, who, as well as having been involved in the 'equal value' training for members of the local authority evaluation panels, was, and is, also a member of the ACAS-appointed panel of Independent Experts for 'equal value' claims, so her views were regarded as influential.

Discussions over the Purple Book Scheme at national level eventually resulted in the scheme being formally abandoned in July 1990 'in view of the widespread doubts about the suitability of [the scheme] and its value given the developments in local authorities since the scheme was introduced and in employment law, particularly equal pay legislation',[7] but without agreement on how it should be replaced.

In the absence, in the period immediately following the passing of the Equal Value (Amendment) Regulations, of any significant activity on the 'equal value' front at national level, it was left to individual women to pursue their own claims. Initially at least, some of these were taken without, or with only limited, union support.

The first claim of note in the sector, however, was union-supported, the union involved being NALGO, which as well as organising local authority administrative staff also covers support and ancillary staff in schools. Mrs Leverton was a qualified nursery nurse working in a nursery attached to a school. Her husband was the local NALGO officer. Nursery nurses, in hospitals and day nurseries as well as in school nursery classes, have long been regarded as one of NALGO's lowest-paid groups. Unfortunately, however, the value of their work was never examined, because the case was delayed, and eventually dismissed, as a result of a number of legal issues raised by the Respondents, Clwyd County Council, the employer of both local authority administrative and education service staff.

As with many potential equal-value applicants in schools, Mrs Leverton had no obvious male comparator at her own workplace. With the assistance of her union, therefore, she identified a group of male clerical staff in the administrative section of the local authority who were known to be on higher salaries then her own. However, she did not have any job descriptions or other information which would have allowed her to decide which individual(s) would be the best comparator(s) and to name him/them. So she submitted her application form and went to the first hearing of the Industrial Tribunal without having named an individual comparator, as stipulated in the relevant regulations.

The Industrial Tribunal, after hearing evidence of a joint submission by the employers and local union branch asserting that the pay of nursery nurses compared unfavourably with the salary scales for clerical staff, accepted that there was a *prima facie* case and, therefore, granted discovery of the documents required by the Applicant and her representatives. The County Council appealed against this decision to the Employment Appeals Tribunal (EAT), but the EAT confirmed the Tribunal's decision.[8]

The County Council then argued that the Applicant and her comparators were not 'in the same employment', as required by the legislation, because of the substantial differences in hours and holidays between nursery nurses attached to schools and local authority clerical staff, which, it was argued, meant that common terms and conditions did not apply to the two groups. The Industrial Tribunal accepted this defence, as did the EAT and each appeal court up to the House of Lords,[9] when the matter was appealed by the Applicant and her union.

The appeal courts also made it clear that, had the claim not been dismissed on the 'same employment' argument, it would have failed because the difference in hours and holidays would also have constituted a 'material factor defence' on which the employers could rely. The decision of the House of Lords was that the lower courts were wrong in their interpretation of the 'same employment' provisions, but correct in holding that the difference in hours and holidays could, and did, constitute a 'material factor defence' against the claim.[10]

Probably the first of the perhaps-more-typical claims in the local authority non-manual sector was that taken by Mrs Elizabeth Smith, an ACTTS member, working for Avon County Council as a District Care Organiser. Her work involved assessing clients, mainly elderly people, for the provision of home assistance services in a defined area of Bristol and supervising the home helps who provided the care – and who were of course at the time benefiting from a review of their grading as part of the manual-worker group.

Mrs Smith did not in the first instance take her claim for equal pay to her union, but wrote to the Equal Opportunities Commission (EOC). The EOC having assessed her claim for parity with a male transport organiser and an administrative officer in the personnel department as a good one provided both legal and expert evaluation assistance. In fact, the Council settled Mrs Smith's claim in her favour before it get reached the point of being referred to an Independent Expert.[11]

It was emphasised by the Council that Mrs Smith's settlement was a personal one. This did not, of course, prevent more than sixty other District Care Organisers from pursuing their own claims. The Council refused to settle with them so they, too, submitted applications to the Industrial Tribunal. Interestingly, a small number of the applicants were men. The female applicants put in 'equal value' claims naming one of the same comparators as Mrs Smith had, plus an additional one. The male applicants claimed equal pay for 'like work' with Mrs Smith, herself. The EOC were again involved in supporting the applicants, but this time so were their unions, NALGO and ACTTS.

Six months after the Applicants had lodged their claims against Avon, the County Council committed itself to the introduction of a new job-evaluation scheme to cover all its non-manual employees. The scheme selected by the Council was a well-known management consultancy scheme, the Hay Guide Chart Profile System of Job Evaluation. Because of the scale of the exercise it could take up to two years to complete. The Council asked the Industrial Tribunal to grant a stay on hearing the claims until after the Hay exercise was complete, when, because of the way the British legislation is framed, the scheme could provide the Council with a defence against the applications. The Industrial Tribunal refused to grant the stay requested and the EAT confirmed its decision, on the grounds that the Applicants had a right to immediate determination of their claims.[12]

After this decision and in spite of their initial reluctance to negotiate, the Council eventually agreed to settle before the legal proceedings got under way, again resulting in the upgrading of all the applicants.[13]

A second case against the same local authority, Avon County Council, concerned three women whose jobs were, at the time of the claim, somewhat ambiguously entitled respectively 'Senior' and 'Assistant' Area Organisers. Their responsibilities included registering child-minders and overseeing the activities of voluntary playgroups in their allocated areas of the county. They brought claims comparing themselves with a male official responsible for the registration of residential homes for the elderly, and an officer in the social services department responsible for the allocation of teenagers in the care of the council to foster-homes or other accommodation.

This case was referred by an Industrial Tribunal to an Independent Expert. The Expert chose to use the Purple Book Job Evaluation Scheme in making her assessment and found that the Applicants' jobs were not of equal value to those of their male comparators. The choice was an unfortunate one, as one of the points made in criticism of the scheme was that it allowed no credit for responsibilities for individuals, such as child-minders, who are not actually employed by the local authority. This point, among a number of others concerning the methodology adopted by the Independent Expert, was made by the job-evaluation specialist commissioned by the EOC.[14] The issue was due to be dealt with at a further hearing of the Tribunal, but on the first morning of that hearing, the Respondents agreed to settle their claims, again in the Applicants' favour. Three of the Applicants received £5850 each in settlement of their claims, while the fourth received £1500.[15]

The original cases covering Home Care Organisers have sparked off other similar claims for those responsible for organising home care services in other authorities. There are a number of these at different stages of the legal procedure in different parts of the country. However, there has been no attempt, publicly at least, by either the unions or the employers to deal with this and related groups of jobs nationally.

One of the first claims initiated by one of the unions in the sector, in this case NALGO, was that of Mrs Siberry and Mrs Smith, both School Meals Supervisors and representing a larger group of women working for Sheffield City Council and undertaking the same functions. Their male comparators, who had been identified through NALGO, included officers in the Cleansing Department and one in the Recreation Department. Although the claim was lodged in 1985, it rapidly became bogged down in the series of legal arguments, some of which went to appeal, and it was not until 1989 that the case was even referred to an Independent Expert.[16]

A year later the Independent Expert's report found for the Applicant against one comparator, but against them on the other. The report was accepted by the Industrial Tribunal. Further legal arguments ensued, but before these were heard before the Tribunal, the case was settled between the parties with substantial cash settlements to the Applicants and smaller payments to their colleagues.[17]

Another set of claims concerning work done exclusively, or almost exclusively, by women is that of three Welfare Assistants representing a much larger group of Welfare Assistants, working in support of teachers in primary schools in West Sussex. They are claiming equal pay on a hourly basis (to avoid problems over hours and holidays – see the Leverton case above) with part-time male Messenger Drivers working for the Library Service, who are on an equivalent grade as themselves, but paid at higher points on the scale. The second Comparator is a Searchroom Supervisor in the County's Public Records Office, who is the equivalent of one grade above the Applicants.

The Welfare Assistants' claim is interesting, because, although the main hearing of the County Council's defence by the Industrial Tribunal took place after the distribution of the circular withdrawing the Purple Book Job Evaluation Scheme, the Authority nevertheless tried to use an assessment based on it as one of their arguments for not referring one of the two claims made by the Applicants to an Independent Expert. However, as a result of damaging cross-examination of a Local Authority witness, the evidence was withdrawn; and the Tribunal referred the claims to the Independent Expert, to whom it had already been agreed between the Parties that the first claim would be referred.

It is apparent from the above descriptions, that most of the claims by the local authorities women employed by non-manual job, involved client-oriented jobs, either organising or providing a service direct to members of the public, whether they be the elderly or children. This is unlikely to be a coincidence. One possible explanation lies in the historical development of these jobs as relatively recent additions to local authority bureaucratic structures. Because of their service-providing nature, they were seen as women's jobs and slotted in at the bottom of a structure designed to favour jobs with access to local politicians (councillors) and top executive positions. The other possible explanation lies in their relatively close association with women's jobs which had benefited from the restructuring of manual workers' jobs.

The only notable exception to this pattern is a claim taken by a group of audio-typists against Derbyshire Police Authority, and supported by their union, NALGO, claiming pay parity with a male photographic technician. The claims were referred to an Independent Expert, who took two years to produce a report, which was not admitted by the Tribunal because of the 'unprofessional' attitude of the Expert and his refusal to answer any questions on reports produced by the parties' experts. Under the relevant Regulations the only recourse for the Tribunal in such circumstances is to appoint another Independent Expert, which they did.

It is arguable that one of the reasons why the Respondent Police Authority has defended these claims so strongly is that, unlike the cases described previously, they challenge fundamental bureaucratic attitudes, which have traditionally always resulted in women's jobs being towards the bottom of the grading structures of large organisations, while the more 'administrative' and particularly 'executive' men's jobs are graded towards the top of the structure.

OBSERVATIONS AND CONCLUSIONS

Possibly the most important factors affecting the very different impact of the amended Equal Pay Act on the two parts of the local-government sector are the very different roles and status of the relevant job-evaluation schemes, in the context of the position awarded to job evaluation in the legislation.

The first 'equal value' case to have raised the issue of an existing job-evaluation scheme was that of the Ford sewing-machinists. Put briefly, the sewing-machinists had been trying to achieve an upgrading of their job ever since Ford had introduced a job-evaluation scheme for its production workers in 1968. When the Equal Value (Amendment) Regulations were implemented, they immediately put in claims to Tribunals. However, the Respondent company argued that under section 1(5) of the Act, there was a fair and non-discriminatory job-evaluation scheme covering both applicants and comparators and that there were therefore 'no reasonable grounds' for the claims to be referred to an Independent Expert.

The scheme covering Local Authority Manual Workers had, in fact, been introduced with the assistance of the same management consultants, Urwick Orr, only a year after the Ford Production Workers' Scheme; and it was quite similar in structure and method of implementation. Yet the Local-Authority employers do not appear to have recognised, or to have preferred not to recognise, that their scheme could provide an equally sound defence to any claim.

In contrast, individual local authorities have continued to use the Purple Book Scheme and, in isolated instances, even to raise it as a defence against 'equal-value' claims, when it must have been known to them that its validity was being questioned at national level.

A second and related factor must be the nature and level of union organisation in the two parts of the sector. By comparison with the private sector, the whole of the local-authority sector must be considered to be well-organised. However, there is no doubt that membership is higher and union strength correspondingly greater among the manual than among the non-manual employees of local authorities. It seems reasonable to conclude that this has contributed to the much more patchy response to the possibilities of 'equal value' among non-manual than among manual workers and their union officials.

The development of 'equal value' within the local authority sector clearly illustrates the reasons why most unions in Britain prefer to negotiate over the introduction of 'equal-value' pay structures rather than to follow the legal route. It also shows what happens when employers refuse to negotiate; and how the legal procedure is weighted in their favour thus encouraging such a refusal.

Even over one sector of employment, in what is effectively a random sample of all cases, a number of legal obstacles have been raised by local authorities to delay the resolution of claims. In spite of this, most of the claims have eventually been settled, usually in favour of the Applicants.

Notes

1. Most of what is said applies also in Northern Ireland, but as both the local authority structure and the Equal Pay legislation are slightly different from those in the rest of the UK, it is excluded to avoid confusion over terminology.

2. For a detailed description of the scheme and its implementation, see *Equal Opportunities Review*, no 13, May/June 1987, pp. 21–4. See also the scheme's manual, National Joint Council for Local Authorities' Services, Review of Grading Structure, Assimilation and Assessment, August 1987.

3. National Joint Council for Local Authorities' Services, Review of Grading Structure, Assimilation & Assessment, August 1987, pp. 2–7.

Sue Hastings

4. The London Equal Value Steering Group (LEVEL); *A Question of E̶ ings̶, a Study of the Earnings of Blue Collar Employees in London Loc̶ Authorities*; September 1987.

5. It is sometimes also known as the Appendix H scheme, because the description of it was to be found at Appendix H of the relevant manual!

6. LEVEL, Job Evaluation and Equal Value – a Study of White-Collar Job Evaluation in London Local Authorities, September 1987.

7. National Joint Council for Local Authorities' Administrative, Professional, Technical and Clerical Services, Advance Notification, Extract from Circular no 319, dated 2 August 1990, referring to a National Joint Council meeting of 5 July 1990.

8. *Equal Opportunities Review*, no 1, May/June 1985, pp. 38–40.

9. *Equal Opportunities Review*, no. 9, September/October 1986, pp. 36–8.

10. *Equal Opportunities Review*, no. 24, March/April 1989, pp. 38–40.

11. *Equal Opportunities Review*, no. 26, July/August 1989, p. 11.

12. *Equal Opportunities Review*, no. 26, July/August 1989, pp. 45–7.

13. *Equal Opportunities Review*, no. 26, July/August 1989, p. 11.

14. *Mrs. Amphlett, Rook, Thorne and Green v. Avon County Council, An Assessment of the Report Prepared by an Independent Expert in These Cases* (unpublished).

15. *Equal Opportunities Review*, no. 26, July/August 1989, pp. 11, 16.

16. *Equal Opportunities Review, Discrimination Digest*, no. 2, Winter 1989, pp. 2–3.

17. *Financial Times*, 5 December 1990.

...parable Worth for ...c Employees: ...plementing a New Wage Policy in Minnesota

Sara M. Evans and Barbara J. Nelson[1]

Minnesota is a state with a long history of social and economic policy innovation concerning women's issues. In the governmental sphere Minnesota was among the first states to adopt Mothers' Aid and, in the last decade, Minnesota led the nation in no-fault divorce reform and programmes for sexually abused children (Jacob, 1988). In the non-governmental sphere, women of the labour movement and the political left in Minneapolis were among the few who protested about the inadequacy of Aid to Dependent Children payments that were lower than work relief payments during the Depression (Faue, 1988). More recently, St Paul was the site of the first battered women's shelter in the USA (Gelb, 1983).

In this atmosphere of innovation, Minnesota was the first state to succeed in initiating and implementing a comparable-worth pay policy in public employment. This policy is controlled by two statutes, the 1982 State Employees Pay Equity Act, covering state employees, and the 1984 Local Government Pay Equity Act, covering employees of all types of local jurisdictions. Both laws were designed as 'process' bills, that is to say, they established in law the principle of paying public employees by a comparable-worth standard, and, for the local law, described a process by which jurisdictions can determine whether pay-equity bias exists.

Neither law carried an appropriation. The state pay-equity plan has been fully implemented by the Minnesota Department of Employee Relations (DOER) with funds from two legislative appropriations. The methods for financing pay-equity rises in local jurisdictions have not yet been worked out. Currently, each jurisdiction is paying for comparable worth with local funds. Localities have hoped that state government would help to finance part of local pay-equity rises from state general revenues and some legislators supportive of pay equity also support partial state assistance. But a shortfall in state revenues in 1986 (due in large part to a tax cut in 1985), and a projected shortfall of as much as $813 million in the 1987–8 biennium (much of which could be regained by bringing the state tax-code into conformity with the federal income-tax changes beginning in 1987) make asking for assistance problematic and receiving it unlikely.

This chapter is an analysis of Minnesota's pay-equity policy so far, a report of the first stages of the initiation and implementation processes. The objectives are to provide a chronology recounting the initiation of this policy in Minnesota, and to analyse the Minnesota experience against the backdrop of national efforts to adopt and implement this policy. The chapter has four sections: a short commentary on Minnesota's importance as a case study, a definition of the issue of comparable worth in Minnesota, the history and politics of pay-equity policy in Minnesota, and an analysis of Minnesota's role in a national campaign to change wage policy.

MINNESOTA AS A CASE STUDY: DELINEATING THE FACTORS AFFECTING IMPLEMENTATION

The information and analysis reported in this chapter are part of a multi-jurisdictional study of the political, economic, and social consequences of the initiation of comparable worth wage policies. The study, designed as a natural experiment, uses a variety of sources of data including interviews with participants in the policy process, public and private documents, newspaper accounts, and transcripts of the sessions at the national conference 'New Directions in Comparable Worth: Minnesota and the Nation' held in Minneapolis from 17 to 19 October 1985. This chapter does not afford us the opportunity to discuss in detail the methodology we have used. We can comment, however, on how Minnesota's experience is similar to or different from other jurisdictions, as a way of articulating some of the dimensions on which we have made comparisons. As Alexander George has suggested, the objective of case studies is 'to formulate the idiosyncratic aspects of the explanation for each case in terms of general variables' (George, 1979, p. 46; see also Verba, 1967; Eckstein, 1975).

Minnesota offers a useful and perhaps provocative case study, both for theorists of public policy and for practitioners. Part of the importance of the Minnesota experience is that Minnesota was the first state to pass and implement comparable-worth wage legislation for both state and local employees. (The efforts in Minnesota were aided by almost a decade of activism in Washington State and the presence of a national public interest group, the National Committee on Pay Equity.) As a result of Minnesota's success, many advocates of pay equity quite openly look to the state to be a model for the substance and process of initiating the policy in their jurisdictions. But when Minnesota passed both of its laws, the opposition was largely unorganised, and when it was vocal, not especially emotional or disparaging. Now, five years later, the policy-making milieu has changed. Critics are better organised and quite likely to use ridicule in an attempt to make the policy seem foolish or unworkable (Johansen, 1984; *Minneapolis Star and Tribune,* 17 November 1984).

This changed situation places Minnesota's experience with agenda-setting in the paradoxical position of being emulated but not easily replicable. But the existence of an organised opposition does not by itself foreclose future consideration of comparable worth. State legislatures are especially likely to consider comparable worth when the public workforce is unionised by unions supporting this issue, when organised feminists with governmental connections support the policy, when the civil service is amenable to this sort of change, and when the political culture combines moralism and a drive for technocratic excellence. In turn, all of these factors need to be consolidated by committed political leadership. When supporters hold both houses of the legislature and the executive branch (or often, even two of the three governmental bodies as in New York and New Jersey), it may be possible to overcome an increasingly hostile general environment (Johansen, 1984; Nelson, 1984).

The decision of Minnesota legislators to initiate a state law requiring *local* jurisdictions to adopt a comparable-worth wage standard for their employees has not yet been copied. To copy Minnesota's local pay-equity legislation would take an iron political will, nimble legislative skills, and a state constitution without strong home-rule powers (Evans and Nelson, 1988). Constitutionally, it appears that most states could pass such legislation, unless the home-rule (i.e. local control) sections of state constitutions specifically prohibit it. Certainly, if the professional associations representing the types of local jurisdictions – school boards, cities, counties and the like – oppose such legislation, it is less likely to pass. Examining the local comparable-worth legislation in Minnesota gives us a window on mandated implementation. If comparable worth is required of local governments by other states, or if it were required of private employers, the implementation processes might well resemble local compliance in Minnesota.

With almost 1600 local jurisdictions implementing comparable worth, it is difficult to categorise the implementation process as belonging to one specific model. We can note, however, those conditions that facilitate implementation and evaluate the Minnesota experience against them. Daniel A. Mazmanian and Paul A. Sabatier arrange the variables involved under three headings:

1. the tractability of the problem;
2. the ability of a statute to structure implementation;
3. non-statutory variables affecting implementation (Mazmanian and Sabatier, 1983, pp. 18–43).

State and local implementation of pay equity in Minnesota show rather significant differences in the factors impinging on implementation. Not surprisingly, the implementation of pay equity for state employees was easier because it encompassed only one government, employed an existing technology, required very little behavioural change and was led by the person who helped to draft the clear and straightforward statute. The new law made 'comparability of the value of the work' the primary consideration in setting salaries for state employees. In addition to establishing this as policy, procedures for implementation were also specified. They included the timing and methods of reviewing salaries, appropriating funds for comparability adjustments and distributing salary increases.

Implementation in the almost 1600 local jurisdictions has been more complicated. In particular, as a result of the local pay-equity law most jurisdictions had to choose or create a job-evaluation technology, and teach its application to any number from ten to forty people (while educating the workforce on pay equity in general) in situations where local leaders ranged from cautiously supportive to actively hostile. The state had no economic sanctions against localities that did not conform to the reporting requirements of the local pay-equity law, nor were citizen monitoring groups active in most jurisdictions. Like the state law, the local law also established both basic policy and procedures for implementation. But these procedures had to allow for the variety of local situations and gave local procedures had to allow for the variety of local situations and gave local officials a great deal of discretion. In addition, the language of the local law was not as clear as the state law. The local law made pay equity 'a' consideration rather than 'the' consideration when establishing public-sector wages.

A DEFINITION OF COMPARABLE-WORTH WAGE POLICY IN MINNESOTA

During the consideration of the state-employee pay-equity act, members of the Minnesota House and Senate government employee committees were presented with detailed information on the concept and process of establishing a pay-equity wage policy. Advocates of the state pay-equity bill came to its hearings armed with persuasive graphs showing that jobs of equal value to the State of Minnesota were not paid equivalently. Supporters argued for equivalent pay for *different* jobs that are judged to be equal on the basis of technical evaluations of skills, effort, responsibility, and working conditions. For example, an evaluation of Minnesota State Government jobs showed that secretaries, a predominantly female job class, had the same total job-evaluation points as did delivery-van drivers, a predominantly male job class. Secretaries were paid less than delivery-van drivers, however. The Minnesota State Employees Pay Equity Act required that the wages of secretaries be raised to those of delivery-van drivers.

A more technical description of the policy is useful to understanding its political history. Stated formally, comparable worth is a wage policy requiring equal pay within a jurisdiction or firm for job classifications that are valued equally in terms of skill, effort, responsibility, and working conditions. In practice, implementing this policy requires the application of a single job-evaluation system to all job-classifications within the jurisdiction or firm. The single job-evaluation system measures in detail the skill, effort, responsibility, and working conditions of every job classification and combines the scores in each area to produce a single overall score for every classification. Job classifications with equal overall scores are considered to have equal value to the jurisdiction or firm. Under a comparable-worth wage policy, classifications of equal value are paid equivalently. A large number of studies have shown, however, that many equally evaluated job classifications are not paid equivalently. In most workplaces, if two job classifications have the same value according to the job-evaluation system, but one is held primarily by men and the other is held primarily by women, the job held by men usually pays more (Nelson, 1985a).

The State of Minnesota used the results of an existing Hay Associates point-factor job evaluation to determine whether jobs evaluated equivalently were paid equivalently. As Figure 11.1 shows, at equal Hay Point values, jobs dominated by women often paid less than those dominated by men (Council on the Economic Status of Women, 1982). The State of Minnesota chose to use the male line (Line A on the diagram) as the measure of non-discriminatory salary practices, and raised the salaries of equivalent jobs dominated by women to that line. Balanced classes (not shown on the diagram) or male-dominated classes of equivalent value that fell below the male salary line, were *not* given pay-equity raises.

Although not all local jurisdictions have completed their pay equity analyses, preliminary information suggests that many localities will not use the male salary line in determining comparable-worth wage rates. Some localities plan to use an average between the male and female lines and others mentioned that

236

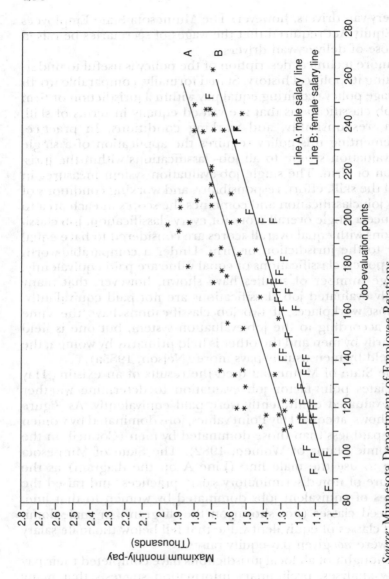

Source: Minnesota Department of Employee Relations

Figure 11.1 Minnesota State Government before pay equity

they plan to raise salaries within a range called an 'equity corridor' (*Minneapolis Star and Tribune*, 14 March 1985). The Hennepin County Board (greater Minneapolis), for example, will use a 'balanced class' pay line as the standard against which to measure salaries. Within an 'equity corridor' extending 10 per cent above or below the balanced line, salaries will be considered to be equitable. Low salaries will be raised to the bottom of the corridor, and 'reasonable restraint' will be exercised in containing the rise of salaries in classes above the corridor. But in no case will any job class be paid more than 10 per cent above or below market rates, as determined by a new area market-place study (*Minneapolis Star and Tribune*, 14 November 1986). The 'equity corridor' approach does not have the support of the Minnesota Department of Employee Relations even though it has been used in the State of Washington pay equity discussions since 1976. Minnesota employee relations officials believe that full pay equity requires the use of the male salary line in setting comparable-worth wages and that localities may be open to suit over the issue. Some localities clearly disagree. Local unions will ultimately have to decide whether they wish to press the issue.

In a number of jurisdictions outside Minnesota, pay equity analyses have investigated the effects of racial and ethnic job-segmentation in conjunction with gender-segmentation. Minnesota has focused its comparable-worth efforts solely on gender differences in equivalent work. When Minnesota began its pay-equity process, the racial and ethnic aspects of comparable-worth analysis were just beginning to be discussed widely. Minnesota was not a good place to apply such an analysis. Approximately 3.8 per cent of the state-level public work force consists of racial and ethnic minorities, a percentage slightly *above* the population average for the state as a whole (Minnesota Department of Employee Relations, 1985). For this reason, both state government and localities were required only to analyse gender differences in wage rates for equivalently valued jobs.

INITIATING COMPARABLE WORTH IN MINNESOTA

Political culture

The political culture and institutions of Minnesota have proved especially suitable for activity on the issue of comparable worth. Minnesota's political culture combines moralism and a drive for technocratic excellence to produce an interventionist and innovative public sector. Virtually every study shows Minnesota a leader in creating or quickly adopting new public policies, especially in social policy (Walker, 1969; Gray, 1973; Eyestone, 1977).

Political institutions – legislatures, executives, parties and interest groups – both reflect and create this activist political culture. The labor and feminist forces favouring comparable worth have historically been well-organised and sophisticated actors. Both are closely connected to Democratic party politics. Traditionally, the two major political parties define themselves as distinctly more liberal than the national bodies with which they are affiliated. The Democratic–Farmers–Labor Party (DFL) was formed in 1944 as a merger of the then-dominant Farmer–Labor Party and the struggling Democratic Party (Gieske, 1984). Until quite recently, the Independent Republican Party (IR), a name adopted in 1975, has traditionally portrayed itself as more sympathetic to the reform climate of Minnesota politics than to the current national Republican Party. A measure of the progressive nature of the political parties is that both have self-defined feminist (not women's) caucuses dating from the mid-1970s (Shrewsbury, 1984).

Not surprisingly, this climate has fostered a professionalised and highly unionised public workforce. In 1981, the year before pay equity achieved the legislative agenda, the State of Minnesota employed over 31 000 people; more than 29 000 (or roughly 93.5 per cent) were covered by union contracts. Employees were represented by eleven different unions, in sixteen bargaining units, but the most prominent union, then and now, was the American Federation of State, County, and Municipal Employees (AFSCME). Excluding University employees, AFSCME represented 61.9 per cent of state employees. Importantly, 49.9 per cent of AFSCME's members were women. AFSCME represented 75.0 per cent of the women covered by union contracts in state employment in 1981 (Council on the Economic Status of Women, 1982).

In the same year, women in state employment averaged $4929 less per year than men employed by the state. The average woman's wage was $13 874 and the average man's wage was $18 803 (Council on the Economic Status of Women, 1982, p. 17). Many factors accounted for the difference, including the fact that less than 1 per cent of women working for the state were employed in managerial positions. Advocates of comparable worth also suggested that jobs traditionally and heavily occupied by women were undervalued. An analysis of job evaluations done by Hay Associates demonstrated that this was true and formed the basis of legislative action.

History and politics

When the Minnesota Legislature in 1982 declared: 'It is the policy of this state to attempt to establish equitable compensation relationships between female-dominated, male-dominated, and balanced classes of employees in the executive branch', the issue of comparable worth had been recognised by some Minnesota leaders for at least eight years. Indeed, the evolution of comparable worth in Minnesota parallels its development as a national issue.

The immediate history of pay equity in Minnesota began in November 1974, when AFSCME Council 6, in a move paralleling its sister affiliate in Washington State, required that the state initiate a study to assess pay practices and promotional policies which discriminated against women. At the heart of its request was an assertion that male-dominated job classes were paid significantly more than the female-dominated classes. Executive Director of AFSCME Council 6, Paul Goldberg, noted, 'Salary rates for experienced, responsible clerical positions often requiring post-high-school business education are $10 to $150 less than the pay for inexperienced janitors, whose duties may be extremely limited' (*Minneapolis Star*, 15 October 1974). The following year they negotiated an agreement for such a study though, unlike that in Washington State, the study was never funded.

The context for successful action on comparable worth lay in the growing political influence of individual feminists within the state government and their successful alliances with both unions and women's groups. The legislature established the Council on the Economic Status of Women (CESW) in 1976 with a budget of $95 000 and a requirement to report by the end of 1977 regarding the 'laws and practices constituting barriers to the full participation of women in the economy' (*Minneapolis Tribune*, 11 February 1976). The council consisted of ten legislators and eight members of the public appointed by the Governor. From the outset, advocates such as Representative Stanley Enebo and Secretary of State Joan Growe emphasised the growing gap between men's and women's pay at the national level and the need for information about the situation in the state. The Council was similar to other Councils and Commissions on Women, which had their roots in the activism initiated by John Kennedy's Presidential Commission on the Rights and Responsibilities of Women (Johansen, 1984; Freeman, 1975). Without this permanent institutional base, it would have been very difficult for advocates to work on women's wage issues for the length of time necessary to develop a pay-equity approach.

Chaired by State Representative Linda Berglin, the Council hired Nina Rothchild, a suburban school-board member and political activist, to serve as its senior staff. The political expertise and energy of Berglin and Rothchild created a powerful mix. The Council began hearings immediately and produced a barrage of reports detailing the problems of women in the Minnesota labour force and specifically in state employment. Their early reports in 1977 provided a statistical profile on Minnesota women. Representative Berglin stated that, 'In compiling the chartbook, we were stunned by the inequities which still exist in Minnesota for women' (*Minneapolis Tribune*, 17 April 1977). They also documented state discrimination, finding that women were paid less than men in state employment and tended to cluster in a small number of job classes (*Minneapolis Star*, 23 March 1977).

Discrimination and gender-segregation of the labour force became constant refrains in the stream of reports issuing from the Council in subsequent years. Defining 'economic status' broadly, the Council examined and made legislative recommendations on issues such as sex discrimination in insurance, inheritance taxes, and housing; minimum wage and tip credits;

tax credits for child care; age discrimination; and family planning. In part by avoiding divisive issues such as abortion (which the Council declined to define as an economic issue) and by lobbying only *for* its own bills and not *against* bills of which it disapproved, the Council compiled a remarkably successful record in its first two and a half years, winning passage of twenty-one of thirty-two recommended bills. Legislators who agreed to sponsor Council legislation received copies of suggested wording for the bill, background information packets, and suggestions for persons who could be called upon to testify (*Minneapolis Tribune*, 5 February 1979).

At the same time, other groups within the state continued to press for action as well. Twin Cities NOW had presented statistics in 1976 which documented the deteriorating position of women in the Minnesota labour market (*Minneapolis Tribune*, 8 November 1976). Their assertion that women experienced greater discrimination than minority men generated intense debate and criticism from other women's groups and from the minority community. Activists within the union movement continued to press for comparable worth, drawing increasingly on statistics provided by the Council. In addition, Hennepin County Welfare Department eligibility technicians, predominantly women, conducted their own study to demonstrate that they were underpaid (*Minneapolis Tribune*, 26 August 1980).

Through the late 1970s the CESW clearly searched for policy responses to the wage gap between women and men and to growing female poverty, gradually documenting the insufficiency of traditional measures aimed at equal opportunity. A *Minneapolis Tribune* editorial in June 1979 noted the lack of improvement for women state employees in the two years since the first Council investigations: 'The [Council's] report underscores the need for state agencies to renew their long-standing commitment to job equality – and to look for new ways to achieve that goal' (*Minneapolis Tribune*, 11 June 1979). At the same time, the conditions for a comparable-worth study improved. In 1979 the Legislature funded a state job-evaluation study conducted by Hay Associates, thereby generating the necessary data-base for comparable-worth. While the impetus was apparently separate from pay-equity concerns, and indeed the initial Hay Associates report indicated that there was no significant disparity in state pay rates along gender lines, some of the legislative members of the CESW were no doubt aware of the potential uses of this data base. At the same time, the issue of comparable worth was emerging on the national level as a key policy innovation with the strong support of the Equal Employment Opportunity Commission under Eleanor Holmes Norton and the creation in 1978 of the National Committee on Pay Equity.

The changed political climate of the 1980s, however, made the pursuit of equity through governmental policies more controversial while at the same time, the concept of comparable worth had clearly filtered down to the local level, sparking labour disputes in Minnesota as elsewhere. Secretaries in Anoka-Hennepin Independent School District 11, members of the School Service Employees Union, struck over the wage gap between secretaries and custodians in June 1981 (*Minnesota Tribune*, 1 July 1981).

Despite conservative opposition to the Council on the Economic Status of Women, the legislature in 1981 granted it permanent status with an amendment that prohibited it from advocating abortion in any way. Newly-elected Independent Republican Governor Al Quie appointed several conservative members to the Council, including some who had worked to abolish it. Objections to the Council, however, revolved primarily around Council attention to what opponents deemed to be 'social' rather than 'economic' issues, such as battered women's shelters, child care, and programmes for displaced home-makers (*Minneapolis Tribune*, 19 November 1981). Even in the eyes of conservatives, pay equity fell into the legitimate purview of the Council.

In the autumn of 1981 the Council appointed a Pay Equity Task Force to re-analyse the Hay Associates data by comparing male- and female-dominated job classes. The composition of the Task Force built on the Council's own successful experience. It was composed primarily of legislators from both parties sympathetic to women and assigned to key committees. It also included representatives of key constituencies, most notably AFSCME. And the Council chose the rhetoric of 'pay equity' over that of 'comparable worth' to emphasise the issue of fairness.

The report, released in January 1982, documented pay disparities between male- and female-dominated job classes that received equivalent points under the Hay system. Council Executive Director Nina Rothchild, noting that 'using the Hay system, the state is clearly saying that women's jobs aren't worth as much as men's jobs', spelled out the Council's recommendation for legislation establishing a comparable-worth standard as a primary consideration for setting the salaries of female state employees (*Minneapolis Star and Tribune*, 22 January 1982).

The bill was shepherded through the legislature by Senator Linda Berglin (DFL) and Representative Wayne Simoneau (DFL) with a minimum of fanfare. The bill established the principle of pay equity as the primary basis of remuneration in state employment, spelled out a process by which it could be achieved, but did not carry an appropriation. In hearings, scattergrams (like Figure 11.1) graphically depicted the Task Force's findings while lobbyists quietly assured legislators that funding for the bill could wait another year.

Both press and opposition remained silent. In March the *Minneapolis Star and Tribune* barely noted passage of the bill. Buried in a longer article in the sixth page of the second section were a series of paragraphs under 'Other bills signed by the governor will . . . '. The second of five read: 'Establish a state policy of comparable worth in state employment, aimed at ensuring that so-called "women's jobs" carry salaries equal to comparable jobs usually reserved for men' (*Minneapolis Star and Tribune*, 24 March 1982). AFSCME political director Rick Scott, one of the key lobbyists on the issue, indicated later the conviction that establishing the policy was the most critical step (Scott, 1985). A policy and process bill, without funding, was all that was politically feasible in 1982, an election year in which state revenues experienced a serious shortfall, forcing painful cuts in state-funded social services. In the same session, abortion again proved to be a bitterly divisive issue. The 1982 pay-equity legislation allowed legislators to make a gesture toward the interests of women voters without becoming embroiled in fiscal difficulties or touchy issues like abortion. The bill passed easily in both houses and Governor Quie signed the legislation without hesitation.

Clearly economic justice for women held a privileged place on the state's political agenda by 1982. Local newspapers published editorials in favour of pay equity and offered scathing assessments of women's economic conditions. In July the Minnesota Women's Consortium, a broad coalition of women's groups across the state, introduced a 'Women's Economic Action Plan' with the endorsement of all but one major candidate for state-wide office. Bridging local and national concerns, Independent Republican US Senator Dave Durenberger also cast himself as a champion of women's rights. Early in 1983 he announced the introduction of national economic-equity legislation to end discrimination in pensions, taxes, insurance, child-support and alimony, dependent-care services and government regulations. The bill, whose House sponsor was Representative Geraldine Ferraro, did not include a pay-equity provision.

At the same time the cultural conflict over women's place in society continued to be played out in the Council on the Economic Status of Women. Republican citizen appointees joined with the single Republican legislator to oust Senator Berglin and elect a new chair (*Minneapolis Star and Tribune*, 20 March 1983). The DFL-dominated legislature then voted to change the Council into a legislative commission whose members would all be drawn from the legislature itself. Yet this conflict did not detract from the implementation of pay equity, which proceeded apace.

Newly-elected DFL Governor Rudy Perpich included in the biennial budget submitted to the 1983 legislature $21.7 million specifically for pay equity, allocated to bargaining units based on each unit's cost to achieve pay equity. The total inequity was estimated at $26 million, and this first appropriation represented 1.25 per cent of payroll per year for the first two years of implementation. Of the total allocation, $7 million was spent to reduce inequities in the first year of the biennium; $7 million was spent to maintain this level of funding in the second year; and $7 million was used to reduce inequities further during the second year of the biennium.

The easy and virtually unremarked appropriation of funds for comparable worth was a function of three facts. First, the state economy had begun to emerge from recession and budgetary constraints were no longer as severe as they had been. Second, the initial bill spelled out a clear process which had firm support from the principal labour unions representing state employees. In effect, the state appropriated salary increases for state employees in two parts. The first represented traditional cost-of-living and merit increases. The second provided a pot of money for the purpose of achieving pay equity.

Whether the total available for general cost-of-living and merit rises was lower because of the existence of the pay-equity appropriation is debatable. Finally, Governor Perpich had appointed Nina Rothchild to serve as State Commissioner of Employee Relations, the official responsible for administering such appropriations and implementing pay equity.

When the State Department of Employee Relations began its negotiation with AFSCME Council 6 in July 1983, both sides were firmly committed to the idea of pay equity. They bargained in the traditional manner over the basic appropriation and the day after they concluded that agreement they re-entered negotiations on the allocation of pay-equity funds. The appropriation for 1983–5 represented just over half the money needed to achieve pay equity as defined in the task-force report. The Department of Employee Relations, under Nina Rothchild, identified female-dominated classes that fell significantly below the pay line established by male-dominated classes and bargained with the union over the specific allocations which would be made (*Minneapolis Star and Tribune*, 26 July 1983).

Inspired by progress at the state level and by rising awareness of pay discrepancies, employees in several local jurisdictions increased their pressure for pay equity. In the summer of 1983 Minneapolis Working Women (a clerical workers' organisation) released a study of city employees that showed that the majority of male employees earned more than $20 000 per year while most female employees earned considerably less. The city councils of both Minneapolis and St Paul made initial gestures toward investigating pay equity. Three women employees of Hennepin County undertook a pay equity study on their own time using the state's Hay system and information from county files to demonstrate that women employees earned less than men in comparable county jobs. AFSCME used the study to demand that the county establish a job-evaluation system and a policy commitment to comparable worth (*Minneapolis Star and Tribune*, 8 June 1983). AFSCME also initiated a study in St Paul and joined Minnesota Working Women in placing pressure on the Minneapolis City Council. The local unions were not sure, though, whether pay equity would be better achieved by legislation or by collective bargaining.

The pressure from the grass roots further increased with the announcement of Judge Jack Tanner's federal district court decision in the *AFSCME* v. *State of Washington* case, which reorganised comparable worth as a valid complaint under Title VII (452 US 161, 1981). Rising expectations and slow responses at the local level led representatives of clerical employees in September 1983 to ask the Commission on the Economic Status of Women to propose legislation requiring local governments to implement pay equity as well. They criticised city and county governments, the University of Minnesota, and local school boards for failing to follow the state's lead. Hennepin County Commissioner Mark Andrew indicated that he would be the only one on his county board willing to adopt a pay-equity policy. Others would probably oppose such a measure on the grounds of cost. Minnesota Working Women's director, Wendy Robinson, testified that there 'probably are grounds for a lawsuit' in Minneapolis (*Minneapolis Star and Tribune*, 23 September 1983). During the summer and autumn Linda Berglin (now a Senator) began to canvass the professional associations representing public managers and officials, including the Association of Minnesota Counties (AMC), the Minnesota League of Cities (MLC), and the Minnesota School Boards Association (MSBA).

By October the Minnesota School Employees Association, representing clerical workers in Anoka-Hennepin Independent School District 11, had filed a complaint with the EEOC because the school board refused to accept the concept of comparable worth. And clerical workers in suburban St Louis Park schools were deadlocked in negotiations with their school board over the same issue. Unions in several other districts indicated their intention to introduce comparable worth into the bargaining for their next contract (*Minneapolis Star and Tribune*, 22 February 1984). By contrast, the city of Princeton, Minnesota, (population 3259) led by Mayor Faith Zwemke, conducted its own pay-equity study in 1983 and implemented pay equity for three of the thirty-three city employees in 1984 at a cost of roughly $10 000 (*Minneapolis Star and Tribune*, 29 April 1984).

The new legislative session began in January 1984, and efforts on behalf of local legislation began in earnest. Although the Local Government Pay Equity Act passed in both houses by an overwhelming margin, its legislative history was more conflictual than that of the earlier state law. Early in 1984, IR Representative David Bishop proposed a bill to make pay equity voluntary for local governments, rather than offering a state-mandated local-governments wage policy. At first, many legislators were hesitant to require local pay-equity policy, aware of the unease of local governments and perhaps of gathering national opposition. The Reagan Administration, for example, announced in January its intention to challenge the Washington State decision and Linda Chavez, staff director of the US Commission on Civil Rights, suggested that the commission should investigate the premises of comparable worth: 'The principle that underlies "comparable worth" is a fundamentally radical one that would alter our existing market-place economy' (*Minneapolis Star and Tribune*, 6 January 1984).

Yet the issue remained relatively uncomplicated in Minnesota, particularly in the light of the apparent ease with which it had been implemented at the state level. While the House held the line on legislation requiring pay equity for all localities, Senate backers were not able to control the issue at each stage of the legislative process. For instance, in March the Minnesota Senate voted 'to encourage counties, municipalities and school districts to pay men and women equally', but balked at requiring them to do so. With adroit lobbying by AFSCME political action director Rick Scott, Senator Berglin's bill was heard and passed the following month, again with little or no publicity. The Minnesota Association of Counties testified against the bill, but other associations remained neutral on the issue and the vote was overwhelmingly favourable. As in the case of the 1982 bill, 1984 was an election year and one in which the 'gender gap' had become a subject of much discussion. And this was a bill that initially at least required no commitment of funds from state coffers.

Newspapers gave the consideration of the local bill only perfunctory coverage. Occasional stories on librarians' wages and brief notices of the bill's progress through the legislature constituted the only reporting. When the Local Government Pay Equity Act passed, however, coverage intensified, in part because proponents announced their victory. On 29 April the *Minneapolis Star and Tribune* ran a feature story on page 1 of the second section, highlighting the history of the issue and comments by Senator Linda Berglin and others. 'It works', declared Commissioner Rothchild. 'I'm bombarded with calls and letters from all over. It's surprising that something we've had to invent ourselves has had no major problems.' On the same day, the paper featured a longer companion story, 'Fair pay/work-ers' suit sparks nationwide revolution', concerning the Washington State case.

The content of the local jurisdiction law followed the pattern set by the state with one important exception. As mentioned before, instead of using the language of the state law designating 'equitable compensation relations' as '*the* primary' wage-setting consideration, the local law made equitable compensation '*a* primary' consideration. This language has been interpreted by some local managers as *requiring* that jurisdictions connect pay levels to market wages (the common practice in public employment in Minnesota) as well as using a comparable-worth analysis. Advocates of comparable worth believe that this interpretation weakens the comparable-worth provision and violates comparable-worth theory.

The local law was more explicit in articulating the process by which jurisdictions determined possible wage biases. The law required local governments to conduct job-evaluation studies, to examine those studies for discrepancies in the pay of similarly evaluated male- and female-dominated job classes, to estimate the cost of remedying the discrepancies, and to propose a plan for implementation. Such reports were due by October 1985 in the Department of Employee Relations, which would then recommend further steps to the Legislature in 1986. Clearly the Washington case provided impetus for the bill and an environment for its implementation. Responding to concerns that job-evaluation data could give rise to suits, the bill provided protection from suit in state courts until 1 August, 1987, in order to give local governments time to deal with the fiscal implications. The local pay-equity legislation could not, of course, protect a locality during the grace period from being sued in federal court under Title VII of the Civil Rights Act. And soon after its passage local governments began to voice fears that implementation 'may invite lawsuites from employees who do not get raises [rises]' (*Minneapolis Star and Tribune*, 31 July 1984).

The extent of innovation required by the bill generated substantial national attention. Governor Perpich trumpeted Minnesota's success at the National Governors' Association and succeeded in winning broad endorsement of pay equity. Nina Rothchild received a distinguished service award at the same meeting, but Perpich apparently lost his position on the executive board of the association because of his vigorous lobbying (*Minneapolis Star and Tribune*, 1 August 1984).

The law also forced new kinds of cooperation between state and local governments and among similar types of jurisdictions, none of which were without tension. Department of Employee Relations personnel under Nina Rothchild travelled around the state in the summer, autumn, and winter of 1984–5 explaining the issue. Bonnie Watkins and David Lutes, DOER pay-equity specialists, produced 'A Guide to Implementing Pay Equity in Local Government', followed by four technical booklets on the implementation process for counties, school boards, small and medium cities, providing step-by-step advice. Lutes also produced software for microcomputers to assist in the process. At the same time, local jurisdictions resisted state intrusion and asserted that the process of job evaluation imposed unique problems for each type of jurisdiction. Most had no job-evaluation system at all and they turned for advice primarily to sister jurisdictions through such organisations as the Association of Minnesota Counties, the League of Minnesota Cities, the Metropolitan Area Management Association (MAMA, representing mid-size cities in the Twin Cities area), and the Minnesota School Boards Association.

The Department of Employee Relations urged jurisdictions to use a 'job match' with the state's Hay point system, and most of the jurisdictions which did so were relatively small. Larger jurisdictions wanted their own systems for reasons of defensibility, to ensure broad employee participation in implementation procedures, and because their jobs were felt to be too different from the list of state jobs to use the match effectively. They wanted a system that would be acceptable to all employees, and the hope that a professional reclassification based on employee input would encourage employees to 'buy in' and see the process as fair acted as a strong incentive to hire outside consultants.

The School Boards Association and the Counties Association each interviewed and hired outside consultants (Arthur Young & Co.) to conduct pilot studies and train member-organisations who chose to use their services. Immediately employee groups expressed discontent on two issues. First, a number of unions felt that Arthur Young's Decision Band method did not adequately value working conditions. Second, problems over the choice of job-evaluation methodology were exacerbated by the fact that the unions could only 'meet and confer' over them. At the end of the discussion, management retained the sole right to choose the job-evaluation system.

Suburban middle-sized cities joined together to hire Control Data Corporation to develop a job-evaluation system suited to their needs. But conflict in places like Hennepin County, where the local board and personnel staff remained sceptical of the concept, continued. Board members criticised comparable worth for 'bureaucratic wage-setting' comparing 'tree-trimmers with secretaries' and a 'shift away from the market-place, into a subjectively determined set of debated standards' (*Minneapolis Star and Tribune*, 24 August 1984). Public debate on comparable worth in the second half of 1984 began to include oppositional rhetoric similar to that generated at the national level by the Reagan Administration.

Early in implementation, the cities of Minneapolis and St Paul ran into political conflicts over the issue of job evaluation, though few leaders publicly opposed pay equity. In Minneapolis, the pay-equity committee split over whether to conduct a pay-equity analysis of existing job classifications or to hire a consultant to restudy the entire classification system. City-Council-member Kathy O'Brien worried that the general upheaval and dissatisfaction caused by a reclassification would be blamed on comparable worth, as turned out to be the case. Participatory reclassification systems were time-consuming, because of the large number of players and need for male- and female-dominated unions to work out an accord on the practical issues. Citing the danger of lawsuits, proponents of the full outside study prevailed (*Minneapolis Star and Tribune*, 16 August 1984). For similar reasons, St Paul had hired an outside consultant to conduct a pay-equity study. Several employee groups, particularly police and firefighters, reacted angrily to the study results, leading Mayor George Latimer to initiate a second study which superseded the first.

In the first months of 1985 there were several attempts in the courts and in the legislature to alter implementation of pay equity at the local level. In February the Minnesota School Employees Association and the International Union of Operating Engineers filed suit in Hennepin County District Court to prevent the use of the Decision Band system. The suit was dismissed in March. At the same time, police and firefighters approached the state legislature in an attempt to remove themselves from the job-evaluation process. They claimed that such studies failed to evaluate their jobs fairly and that, by comparing them internally to other job classes rather than externally to other police or firefighters, the labour arbitration process would be compromised.

State associations of police and firefighters succeeded in introducing legislation in both state houses to exempt them from job evaluations and pay-equity studies. The bills enjoyed a brief success in committee until AFSCME, women's groups (notably the League of Women Voters), and the League of Cities mobilised a significant lobbying effort to defeat them and obtained a public *veto* threat from the governor. These groups concentrated on the Senate, which had remained in DFL hands, after the legislative elections of November 1984 gave the House of Representatives to the IRs. A final compromise gesture amended the law slightly. Under the new amendment, if police or firefighters' wage negotiations went to binding arbitration, the arbitrators would allow employees to present their objections to the job-evaluation system in the arbitration process (*Minneapolis Star and Tribune*, 10 May 1985). An attempt to extend the deadline for local-government pay-equity plans two years beyond 1 October, 1985, failed completely.

While opponents of pay equity were increasingly vocal in 1985, bipartisan support remained strong. Independent Republican Senator Dave Durenberger, the senior US senator from Minnesota, included in his 'Economic Equity Act of 1985' a provision to initiate a comparable-worth study at the national level. He said, 'The state of Minnesota studied it and came up with a pay-equity system for state employees that many consider a success story. It's time for Congress to meet the pay-equity problem head-on, and begin studying its implications and proposed solutions' (*Minneapolis Star and Tribune*, 15 May 1985). At the same time, local-level opponents shifted their ground from outright opposition to debate over the technician definition of pay equity. In March 1985, after hiring a consultant and proceeding with a job-evaluation study, Hennepin County Labor Relations Director Rolland Toenges indicated that the county would continue to adhere to market wages and restrict salaries to within 10 per cent of market rates. In contrast to the state practice of raising female salaries to the male salary line, he proposed that attentiveness to market rates would raise salaries within a range he called an 'equity corridor' (*Minneapolis Star and Tribune*, 14 March 1985).

By the summer of 1985 most local jurisdictions in Minnesota were well into the process of conducting pay-equity studies. The state had appropriated and negotiated the allocation of a second two-year appropriation of $22.2 million for pay equity for state employees. When the US Circuit Court of Appeals over-turned the *AFSCME* v. *State of Washington* case in September 1985, pay equity in Minnesota appeared to be a foregone con-clusion at both state and local levels. School boards for the most part were prepared to meet the 1 October deadline. Cities and counties indicated that many would be late but that studies would be completed in time for the next legislative session. The *Minneapolis Star and Tribune* reported that opponents like Rep-resentative Terry Dempsey, IR–New Ulm, had no expectation of changing the law any more: 'While [Demsey would] like to repeal the law, the chances of doing that are zero' (*Minneapolis Star and Tribune*, 6 September 1985).

The local pay-equity law required that the Department of Employee Relations report to the legislature by 30 January 1986, the reslts of the pay equity analyses done by localities and forwarded to it. As of 15 January 1986, the Department had received 1090 of 1583 pay equity reports from local govern-ments. Its summary stated that '80 per cent of school districts, 63 per cent of cities and townships, 37 per cent of counties, and 74 per cent of all other jurisdictions . . . [had reported]. The reports cover[ed] 75 994 employees statewide, accounting for about 42 per cent of the estimated total number of employees in local governments.' For reporting jurisdictions, local govern-ments estimated that the cost of pay-equity rises would average 2.6 per cent of payroll and would take 2.3 years to implement (Minnesota Department of Employee Relations, 1986, report summary, unnumbered page).

Nine months later, in September 1986, the numbers had inched upwards, with 87 per cent of school districts, 68 per cent of cities and townships, and 51 per cent of counties having reported (Bonnie Watkins, Department of Employee Relations, 25 September 1986). St Paul had completed its study and bar-gained over it, raising the salaries of 600 of the 3000 city em-ployees retroactively to 31 March 1985. The costs were estimated at $2.2 million in 1986, and the city's annual base pay was expected to rise by $1 million (*St Paul Pioneer Press and Dispatch*, 17 October 1986). In contrast, Minneapolis became disappointed with its attempt to redo its existing classification system and implement comparable worth using a newly-devised system. Rejecting its initial plan, the city decided to use its old classification system to determine comparable jobs and pay equity raises. Other Twin Cities governments contributed to this patchwork response. The Minneapolis School Board implemented a plan raising salaries of 700 of the district's 5500 employees. The cost, $900 000 over four years, is being contained by a guideline that no salary will be set at more than 15 per cent above market wage (*Minneapolis Star and Tribune*, 30 April 1986). Although Hennepin County and the jurisdictions represented by the MAMA study have not completed their analyses, they too will limit pay-equity rises through the use of an equity corridor or a cap on public wages in relationship to private-sector wages.

As the localities were implementing their plans in 1986, the State Employees Pay Equity Act faced a last challenge in the legislature. A shortfall in state revenues led to a situation where the budget-makers in the IR-controlled House considered 'unallocating' the last year of state-employee comparable-worth rises. Local women's groups saw this as part of a three-pronged attack against women's issues that included not only comparable-worth cuts but also significant reductions in AFDC and the serious underbudgeting of the CESW. All three efforts were checked, but the restoration of most of the AFDC budget took the combined efforts of all the major religious leaders in the Twin Cities plus labour, women's, and civil rights groups. In November 1986 the DFL retook the House of Representatives, extending Democratic control of the state house and the governor's mansion through 1988. Both the local and state laws should be safe from unfriendly changes through this period.

NATIONAL LESSONS FROM THE MINNESOTA EXPERIENCE

Two lessons can be drawn from the Minnesota experience that can help to locate this state's efforts in a national context. The first lesson is that the content and process of adoption and implementation change as a policy diffuses from place to place and from one level of government to others. The diffusion of innovation literature often emphasises the process of adoption at the expense of noting differences in content (Walker, 1969, but also see Gray, 1973, and Eyestone, 1977). The differences within and outside Minnesota in defining comparable worth and applying it demonstrate that a wide variety of practices are now subsumed under the pay-equity rubric. The State of Minnesota uses the male-job line in defining the wage targets for underpaid, equivalently-evaluated jobs. Most large localities in Minnesota use a balanced-class or all-job wage line, often with equity corridors. This formula is also employed in San Jose and Washington State. These corridor definitions raise the question of whether this policy, rather than eliminating bias, formalises a percentage difference in the wage of equivalently-valued and male- and female-dominated jobs. New Jersey's 1985–6 comparable-worth policy was more a solidarity wage than formal comparable worth because the policy was not based on job evaluations.

These differences deserve the attention of scholars and activists on both sides because they raise important and provocative questions. Are the differences important and if so why? How do supporters view these differences and should they publicise them given the existing difficulty in explaining even the basic technical aspects of comparable worth? Would opponents find one or more practices more acceptable and modify their stand or would they use the differences to suggest that comparable worth is a confused issue?

The second lesson from the Minnesota experience focuses on the transformation of comparable worth from an issue primarily controlled by a small group of highly placed advocates to a practical political and managerial issue directly affecting thousands of implementors. The success of initiating the Minnesota state law depended on a few supporters moving quickly, reducing conflict by keeping initiatives relatively quiet, and using one of the authors of the policy as its chief implementor. Such a scenario defines a policy controlled by a small group of professional leaders (interest groups, legislators and bureaucrats) interacting in their institutional roles. State-level pay-equity policy exemplifies a small iron-triangle of almost classical description.

The move to local pay equity transformed the issue. *Thou-*

sands of elected and appointed officials, managers, union officials and employees became involved in implementing comparable worth. This transformation leads to something more than the classical 'complexity of joint action' observation made of most implementation studies (Pressman and Wildavasky, 1979). Certainly, by engaging so many new participants the local law allowed for variations in interpretations, slow-downs, and the contribution of the legislative conflict in new arenas. But the local law also changed comparable worth from an issue controlled by political élites to one which took on more popular-level characteristics. Comparable worth not only became more administratively complex, but also entered a new stage where it had to be considered by individuals who might not have paid any attention to it, had it not become part of their work environment. Thus the extension of comparable worth to the local level in Minnesota alerts us to the paradoxical nature of reforms that rest on technocratic change. The implementation of this equity issue rests in the hands of public managers who are often ambivalent about its goals. If this continues to be the case around the country, comparable worth may routinely be implemented as a professional personnel-management issue rather than an equity issue. The equity characteristics of the policy are likely to remain more evident when comparable worth retains its political character, but ironically, that controversial quality may limit the possibility for any action at all.

Note

1. This research was supported by grants from the North-west Area Foundation, and from the Office of the Academic Vice-President, the Center for Urban and Regional Affairs, the Graduate School and the Hubert H. Humphrey Institute, all at the University of Minnesota. We would like to thank Lavon Anderson, Liz Conway, and Nancy Johnson Haggmark for research assistance, and Linda Baumann, Donna Kern, Louise Straus and Debra Tornes Leon for secretarial support.

References

Council on the Economic Status of Women (1982) *Pay Equity and Public Employment* (St. Paul, MN).

Eckstein, H. (1975) 'Case Study and Theory in Political Science', in F. I. Greenstein and N. W. Polsby (eds) *Handbook of Political Science* (Reading, Mass.: Addison-Wesley) pp. 79–138.

Evans, S. and Nelson, B. (1988) 'Mandating local change in Minnesota: State-required implementation of comparable worth by local jurisdictions', in Ronnie Steinberg (ed.) *Comparable Worth: A View From the States* (Philadelphia, Pa: Temple University Press).

Eyestone, R. (1977) 'Confusion, Diffusion, and Innovation', *American Political Science Review*, no 71, pp. 441–7.

Faue, E. (1990) 'Women, Family and Politics: Farm-Labor Women and Social Policy in the Great Depression' in Patricia Gurin and Louise Tilly (eds) *Women in Politics and Change* (New York: Russell Sage Foundation).

Freeman, J. (1975) *The Politics of Women's Liberation* (New York: McKay).

Gelb, J. (1983) 'The Politics of Wife Abuse', in Irene Diamond (ed.) *Families, Politics and Public Policy* (New York: Longman) pp. 250–62.

George, A. L. (1979) 'Case Studies and Theory Development: The Method of Structured, Focused Comparison', in Paul Gorden Lauren (ed.) *Diplomacy: New Approaches in History, Theory, and Policy* (New York: Free Press) pp. 43–68.

Gieske, M. L. (1984) 'Minnesota in Midpassage: A Century of Transition in Political Culture', in M. L. Gieske (ed.) *Perspectives on Minnesota Government and Politics* (Minneapolis, Minn.: Burgess Publishing Company) pp. 1–34.

Gray, V. (1973), 'Innovation in the States: A Diffusion Study', *American Political Science Review*, no 67, pp. 1174–85.

Jacob, H. (1990) 'Women and Divorce Reform', in Pat Gurin and Louise Tilly (eds) *Women, Politics and Change* (New York: Russell Sage Foundation).

Johansen, E. (1984) '*Comparable Worth: The Myth and the Movement.* (Boulder, Colo.: Westview Press).

Mazmanian, D. A. and Sabatier, P. (1983) *Implementation and Public Policy* (Glenview, Ill.: Scott, Foresman).

Minneapolis Star (1974) 'State-job Sex Bias Suspected', 15 October, 7C.

Minneapolis Star (1977) 'Study Says State's Job Policy Full of Sex Bias', 23 March, 9A.

Minneapolis Star and Tribune (1982) 'Group says 'Female' Jobs Pay Less than 'Male' Jobs', 22 January, 1A.

Minneapolis Star and Tribune (1982) 'Quie Vetoes Bill Establishing 'Job Creation Conference', 24 March, 6B.

Minneapolis Star and Tribune (1983) 'Squabble in the Sisterhood', 20 March, 2C.

Minneapolis Star and Tribune (1983) 'County Pays Women Less, Study Indicates', 8 June, 12B.

Minneapolis Star and Tribune (1983) 'State Closing Gender Gap on Salaries', 26 July, 1A.

Minneapolis Star and Tribune (1983) 'Legislation Requested to Equalize Public Wages', 23 September, 17A.

Minneapolis Star and Tribune (1984) 'Civil Rights Panel to Study Major Program Changes', 6 January, 3A.

Minneapolis Star and Tribune (1984) 'School Clerical Workers Fight Equal Pay Issue', 22 February, 4B.

Minneapolis Star and Tribune (1984) 'Minnesota's Comparable Worth Plan was the First in Nation, and 'It Works', 29 April, 1B.

Minneapolis Star and Tribune (1984) 'Comparable Worth Raises [rises] Concerns', 31 July, 1B.

Minneapolis Star and Tribune (1984) 'Perpich Loses Spot on Group's Board', 1 August, 13A.

Minneapolis Star and Tribune (1984) 'Disagreement over Methods Stalls City's Pay Equity Project', 16 August, 20A.

Minneapolis Star and Tribune (1984) 'A Hennepin County Comparable-Worth Study', 24 August, 8B.

Minneapolis Star and Tribune (1984) ' "Comparable Worth" a Loony Idea, Says Rights Panel Chief, 17 November, 1A.

Minneapolis Star and Tribune (1985) 'Local Governments Tackle Issue of Comparable Worth', 14 March, 1Y.

Minneapolis Star and Tribune (1985) 'Comparable-Worth Bill Passes', 10 May, 20B.

Minneapolis Star and Tribune (1985) 'Durenberger Set To Introduce Comparable Worth Legislation', 15 May, 10A.

Minneapolis Star and Tribune (1985) 'State's Comparable Worth Law a Model', 6 September, 1A.

Minneapolis Star and Tribune (1986) 'School District Approves Comparable Play-Plan', 30 April, 6B.

Minneapolis Star and Tribune (1986) 'County Study Finds Inequities in Women's Pay', 14 November, 7B.

Minneapolis Tribune (1976) 'State Panel on Women's Pay is Backed', 11 February, 6B.

Minneapolis Tribune (1976) 'Study: Women Suffer Job Bias', 8 November, 1B.

Minneapolis Tribune (1977) 'Economic Status of Women Profiled', 17 April, 17E.

Minneapolis Tribune (1979) 'Women's Council Strives to Continue Record of Success', 5 February, 2B.

Minneapolis Tribune (1979) 'Women in Minnesota Still Lag in Pay', 11 June, 10A.

Minneapolis Tribune (1980) 'Union, Feminist Leaders See Bias in Pay Differences', 26 August, 1A.

Minneapolis Tribune (1981), '230 Secretaries Strike in Area School District for Custodian Salaries', 1 July, 6A.

Minneapolis Tribune (1981) 'Some on Women's Economic Council Object to Social Issues', 19 November, 8D.

Minnesota Department of Employee Relations (1985) *Biennial Work Force Report* (St Paul, Minn. MDOER).

Minnesota Department of Employee Relations (1986) *Pay Equity in Minnesota Local Governments* (St Paul, Minn. MDOER).

Nelson, B. J. (1985a) 'Comparable Worth: A Brief Review of History, Practice, and Theory', *Minnesota Law Review*, no 69, pp. 1199–216.

Nelson, B. J. (1985b) 'Popular Misperceptions of Comparable Worth Policies and Their Political Consequences', presented at the Western Political Science Association meetings, March.

Nelson, B. J. (1984) *Making an Issue of Child Abuse: Political Agenda Setting for Social Problems* (Chicago: University of Chicago Press).

Pressman, Jeffrey L. and Wildavsky, Aaron (1979), *Implementation* (Berkeley, Cal.: University of California Press) 2nd edn.

St Paul Pioneer Press and Dispatch (1986) 'Council OKs Comparable Worth Pact', 17 October, 4C.

Scott, Rick (1985) 'Comments at the Conference, New Directions in Comparable Worth: Minnesota and the Nation', University of Minnesota, Minneapolis.

Shrewsbury, C. M. (1984) 'Women in Minnesota Politics: A Preliminary Sketch', in M. L. Gieske (ed.) *Perspectives on Minnesota Government and the Politics* (Minneapolis, Minn.: Burgess) pp. 44–52.

Verba, S. (1967) 'Some Dilemmas in Comparative Research', *World Politics* no 20, pp. 111–27.

Walker, J. (1969) 'The Diffusion of Innovations among the American States', *American Political Science Review*, no 63, pp. 880–900.

AFSCME v. *State of Washington*, 452 US, 161, 1981.

Watkins, Bonnie (1986) Phone interview, 25 September.

Bibliography

ACAS (1990) 'Developments in Payment Systems: The 1988 ACAS Survey' (London: Advisory, Conciliation and Arbitration Service).

Acker, J. (1989) *Doing Comparable Worth: Gender, Class and Pay Equity.* (Philadelphia: Temple University Press).

Acker, J. (1987) 'Sex Bias in Job Evaluation: A Comparable Worth Issue', in Bose, C. and Spitze, G. (eds), *Ingredients for Women's Employment Policy* (Albany, NY: State University of New York Press).

Aiken, L. H. and Mullinix, C. F. (1987) 'The Nursing Shortage, Myth or Reality?', *New England Journal of Medicine,* 317 (10), 641–5.

American Nurses Association (1951) *1951 Facts About Nursing,* (New York: American Nurses Association).

American Nurses Association (1961) *Facts About Nursing,* 1961 edn (New York: American Nurses Association).

American Nurses Association (1964) *Facts About Nursing,* 1964 edn (New York: American Nurses Association).

American Nurses Association (1967) *Facts About Nursing,* 1967 edn (New York: American Nurses Association).

American Nurses Association (1971) *Facts About Nursing,* 1970–1 edn (New York: American Nurses Association).

American Nurses Association (1974) *Facts About Nursing,* 1972–3 edn (New York: American Nurses Association).

American Nurses Association (1977) *Facts About Nursing, 1976–7* (Kansas City, MO: American Nurses Association).

American Nurses Association (1983) *Facts About Nursing, 1982–3* (Kansas City, MO: American Nurses Association).

American Nurses Association (1987) *Facts About Nursing, 1986–7* (Kansas City, MO: American Nurses Association).

American Nurses Association (1988) 'Collective Bargaining Data' (unpublished).

Applebaum, E. and Granose, C. S. (1986) 'Hospital Employment Under Revised Medicare Payment Schedules', *Monthly Labor Review,* 109(8), 37–45.

Armstrong, P. (1982) 'If It's Only Women's Work It Doesn't Matter So Much' in West, J. (ed.) *Work, Women and The Labour Market* (London: Routledge & Kegan Paul).

Barnes, C. (1980) 'Denver: A Case Study', in Bullough, B. (ed.) *The Law and the Expanding Nursing Role* (New York: Appleton-Century-Crofts).

Barnett, E. (1982) 'Comparable Worth and the Equal Pay Act – Proving Sex-based Wage Discrimination Claims after *County of Washington* v. *Gunther*', *Wayne Law Review,* 28, 1669–1700.

Barnett, E. (undated) 'Pennsylvania Nurses Association Memorandum in Support of EEOC Charges' (Pennsylvania Nurses Association).

259

Beatty, R. W. and Beatty, J. R. (1984) 'Some Problems with Contemporary Job Evaluation Systems' in Remick, H. (ed.) *Comparable Worth and Wage Discrimination: Technical Possibilities and Political Realities* (Philadelphia: Temple University Press).

Bell, D. (1988) 'Unionized Women in State and Local Government, in Milkman, R. (ed.), *Women, Work and Protest* (Boston: Routledge and Kegan Paul), pp. 280–99.

Bellak, A. (1984) 'Comparable Worth: A Practitioner's View', prepared at the request of the US Commission on Civil Rights for Consultation on Comparable Worth (Washington, DC, 6–7 June).

Benner, P. (1984) *From Novice to Expert* (Menlo Park, CA: Addison-Wesley).

Benner, P. and Wrubel, J. (1989) *The Primacy of Caring* (Menlo Park, CA: Addison-Wesley).

Blackburn, R. M. (1967) *Union Character and Social Class* (London: Batsford).

Blum, L. M. (1991) *Between Feminism and Labor: The Significance of the Comparable Worth Movement* (Berkeley: University of California Press).

Blum, L. M. (1987) 'Possibilities and Limits of the Comparable Worth Movement', *Gender & Society*, 1, (4), 381–99.

Bourn, C. and Whitmore, J. (1989) *Discrimination and Equal Pay* (London: Sweet & Maxwell).

Boyer, R. O. and Morais, H. (1955) *Labor's Untold Story* (New York: Cameron Associates).

Boyle, K. and Hadden, T. (1988) 'Options for Northern Ireland' in Drucker, H., Dunleavy, P., Gamble, A. and Peele, G., (eds) *Developments in British Politics* (London: Macmillan).

Braverman, H. (1974) *Labor and Monopoly Capital: The Degradation of Work in the Twentieth Century* (New York: Monthly Review Press).

Brenner, J. (1987) 'Feminist political discourses: Radical versus liberal approaches to the feminization of poverty and comparable worth'. *Gender and Society*, I(4), 447–65.

Brown, A. and Sheridan, L. (1988) 'Pioneering Women's Committee Struggles with Hard Times', *Labor Research Review*, 11, 63–78.

Bullough, B. (1978) 'The Struggle for Women's Rights in Denver: A Personal Account', *Nursing Outlook*, 26(9), 566–7.

Bureau of National Affairs (BNA) (1984) *Pay Equity and Comparable Worth* (Washington, DC: BNA).

Bureau of National Affairs (1981) *The Comparable Worth Issue: A BNA Special Report* (Washington, DC: BNA).

Burnham, L. (1985) 'Has Poverty been Feminized in Black America?' *The Black Scholar*, March/April, 14–24.

Cameron, I. (undated) 'Equal Opportunities for Women: A Challenge for the Finance Industry and BIFU' (Banking Insurance and Finance Union: unpublished manuscript).

Carey, M. A. (1988) 'Union Negotiators Quietly Crow Over Gains at Yale', *New Haven Register*, 31 January.

Carden, M. L. (1978) 'The Proliferation of a Social Movement: Ideology and Individual Incentives in the Contemporary Feminist Movement', *Research in Social Movements, Conflict and Change*, 1, 179–96.

Carden, M. L. (1974) *The New Feminist Movement* (New York: Russell Sage).

Central Statistical Office (1989), *Regional Trends* 24 (London: HMSO).

Charles, N. (1986) '*Women and Trade Unions*', in *Feminist Review* (ed.), *Waged work: A Reader* (London: Virago), 160–35.

Cockburn, C. (1989) 'Equal Opportunities: The Short and Long Agenda'. *Industrial Relations Journal*, 20(3), 213–25.

Colling, T. and Dickens, L. (1989) *Equality Bargaining – Why Not?* (London: HMSO).

Colling, T. and Dickens, L. (1990) 'Why Equality won't Appear on the Bargaining Agenda', *Personnel Management*, April, 48–53.

Commission on the Economic Status of Women (1988) *Pay Equity: The Minnesota Experience*, revised (St Paul: Commission on the Economic Status of Women).

Comparable Worth Project (1982) *First Steps to Identify Sex- and Race-based Pay Inequities in a Workplace* (Oakland: Comparable Worth Project).

Cook, Adele (1990) 'Comparable Worth: An Economic Issue', *Nursing Management*, 21(2), 28–30.

Cook, Alice (1984) 'Developments in Selected States', in Remick, H. (ed.), *Comparable Worth and Wage Discrimination* (Philadelphia: Temple University Press, 1984).

Contra Costa Times (1972) 'CCC Clerical Employees Ponder Strike Over Wage, Benefit Offer', 20 June.

Council on the Economic Status of Women (1982) *Pay Equity and Public Employment* (St Paul, MN).

Coyle, A. (1982) 'Sex and Skill in the Organisation of the Clothing Industry' in West, J. (ed) *Work, Women and the Labour Market* (London: Routledge & Kegan Paul).

Coyle, P. (1988), 'Yale Unions to Rally with Jackons', *New Haven Register*, 19 January.

Craig, C., Garnsey, E. and Rubery, J. (1985) *Payment Structures in Small Firms: Women's Employment in Segmented Labour Markets* (London: Department of Employment Research Paper 48).

Crompton, R. (1989) 'Women in Banking: Continuity and change since the Second World War', *Work, Employment and Society*, 3, 141–56.

Crompton, R. and Jones, G. (1984) *White-Collar Proletariat Deskilling and Gender in Clerical Work* (London: Macmillan).

Cupo, A., Ladd-Taylor, M., Lett, B., and Montgomery, D. (1982) 'Beep, Beep, Yale's Cheap: Looking at the Yale Strike'. *Radical America*, 18(5), 7–19.

Darity, W. and Myers, S. (1980) 'Changes in Black–White Income Inequality, 1968–1978: A Decade of Program?' *Review of Black Political Economy*, 10, 354–79.

Davies, M. (1974) 'Women's Place Is at the Typewriter: The Feminization of the Clerical Workforce' in *Radical America*, 3, 1–28.

Davies, M. (1982) *Women's place is at the typewriter: Office work and office workers 1870–1930*. (Philadelphia: Temple University Press).

Dean, V., Roberts, P. and Boone, C. (1982) 'Comparable Worth Under Various Federal and State Laws' in Remick, H. (ed) *Comparable Worth and Wage Discrimination, Technical Possibilities and Political Realities* (Philadelphia: Temple University Press).

Department of Employment *Family Expenditures Survey* (1988) (London: Department of Employment).

Department of Employment (1989) *New Earnings Survey* (London: Department of Employment).

Department of Employment Press Release, 8 March 1990 (London: Department of Employment, 1990).

Dex, S., and Walters, P. (1989) 'Women's occupational status in Britain, France, and the USA', *Industrial Relations Journal*, 20(3), 203–212.

Dickens, L., Townley, B. and Winchester, D. (1988) *Tackling sex discrimination through collective bargaining* (London: HMSO).

Dickens, L. (1989) 'Women – A rediscovered resource?', *Industrial Relations Journal*, 20(3), 167–175.

Dowd, N. (1986) 'The Metamorphosis of Comparable Worth', *Suffolk University Law Review*, XX, 833–865.

Eckstein, H. (1975) 'Case study and theory in political science', in Greenstein, F. I., and Polsby, N. W. (eds.) *Handbook of Political Science* (Reading, MA: Addison-Wesley Publishing Company).

Egan, A. (1982) 'Women in Banking: A Study in Inequality', *Industrial Relations Journal*, 13, 20–31.

Ehrenreich, B. (1987) 'The Next Wave'. *Ms. Magazine*, no. 1–2, July-August.

Eisenstein, Z. R. (1987) *The Radical Future of Liberal Feminism* (New York: Longman).

England, P. (forthcoming) *Comparable Worth: Theories and Evidence* (New York: Aldine).

Epstein, C. F. (1981) *Women in Law* (New York: Basic Books).

Equal Opportunities Commission (1990) *Equal Pay for Men and Women: Strengthening the Acts* (Manchester: EOC).

Equal Opportunities Commission (EOC) (1989a) *Equal pay . . . making it work. Review of the equal pay legislation: Consultative document* (Manchester: EOC).

Equal Opportunities Commission (EOC) (1989b) *Towards equality: A casebook of decisions on sex discrimination and equal pay 1976–1988* (Manchester: EOC).

Equal Opportunities Commission (1985) *Job evaluation schemes free of sex bias* (Manchester: EOC).

Equal Opportunities Commission for Northern Ireland (1990) *The Equal Pay Legislation: Recommendations for Change* (Belfast: EOC (NI)).

Equal Opportunities Commission, Northern Ireland (1989) *Annual Report* (Belfast: EOC (NI)).

Equal Opportunities Commission, Northern Ireland (1987) *The Aftermath of recession: Changing Patterns in Female Employment and Unemployment in Northern Ireland*. Womanpower, No 4. (Belfast: EOC (NI)).

Equal Opportunities Review (1989) *Discrimination Digest, No 2*, Winter.

Equal Opportunities Review (EOR) (1989a) 'Attracting and retaining women workers in the finance sector'. (EOR) (28), 10–20.

Equal Opportunities Review (EOR) (1989b) 'Equal value update'. (EOR) (26), 10–25.

Equal Opportunities Review (EOR) (1989c) 'Criteria for Cross-establishment equal pay claim', (EOR) 24, 38–40.

Equal Opportunities Review (EOR) (1989d) 'Profile: Kay Carberry, Head, Equal Rights Department, TUC'. (EOR), (23), 26–27.

Equal Opportunities Review (EOR) (1989e) 'Equal value update'. (EOR) (26), 10–25.

Equal Opportunities Review (EOR) (1989f) 'Equal value: A union update'. (EOR) (22), 9–15.

Equal Opportunities Review (EOR) (1988) 'Equal value update'. (EOR) (18), 8–17.

Equal Opportunities Review (EOR) (1987a) 'Equal value: The union response'. (EOR) (11), 10–19.

Equal Opportunities Review (EOR) (1987b) 'Local authority job revaluation' (EOR) (13), 21–24.

Equal Opportunities Review (EOR) (1986a) 'Hours and holiday differences bar cross-establishment equal value claim' (EOR) (9), 36–38.

Equal Opportunities Review (EOR) (1986b) 'Equal value survey'. (EOR) (6), 2.

Equal Opportunities Review (EOR) (1986c) 'Two years of the equal value law'. (EOR) (6), 6–16.

Equal Opportunities Review (EOR) (1985a) 'Unions' experience of equal value'. (EOR) (4), 12–17.

Equal Opportunities Review, (EOR) (1985b) 'Employer ordered to disclose job description to equal value applicant' (EOR) (1), p. 38–40.

Evans, S. M. and Nelson, B. J. (1989) *Wage Justice, Comparable Worth and the Paradox of Technocratic Reform* (Chicago: University of Chicago Press).

Evans, S. M. and Nelson, B. J. (1988) 'Mandating local change in Minnesota: State-required implementation of comparable worth by local jurisdictions', in Steinberg, R. (ed.) *Comparable Worth: A View From the States* (Philadelphia, PA: Temple University Press).

Eyestone, R. (1977) 'Confusion, diffusion, and innovation'. *American Political Science Review,* 71, 441–117.

Faue, E. (1990) 'Women, Family and Politics: Farm–Labour Women and Social Policy' in the Great Depression', in Gurin P. and Tilly L. (eds.) *Women, Politics & Change Century American Politics* (New York: Russell Sage Foundation).

Feldberg, R. L. (1986) 'Comparable worth: Toward theory and practice in the United States', in Gelp, B., Harstock N. C. M., Novak C. and Strober M. (eds.) *Women and poverty* (Chicago: University of Chicago Press), 163–180.

Feldberg, R. L. (1989) 'Comparable Worth: Toward Theory and Practice in the United States'. *Signs,* 10, (2), 311–28.

Feldberg, R. L. (1980) 'Union Fever: Organizing Among Clerical Workers, 1900–1930'. *Radical America,* 14(3).

Feldberg, R. L. and Glenn E. N. (1984) 'Clerical Work in Female Occupations', in Freeman J. (ed.) *Women: A Feminist Perspective* (Palo Alto, CA: Mayfield Publishing Company).

Ferber, M. (1982) 'Women and work: Issues of the 1980's'. *Signs: Journal of Women in Culture and Society* 8(2), 273–295.

Flammang, J. (1987) 'Women Made a Difference: Comparable Worth in San Jose'. In Katzenstein, M. F. and Mueller, C. M. (eds.) *The Women's Movements of the United States and Western Europe* (Philadelphia: Temple University Press), 290–312.

Flammang, J. (1986) 'Effective Implementation: The Case of Comparable Worth in San Jose'. *Policy Studies Review,* 5(4), 815–837.

Flammang, J. (1985) 'Female Officials in the Feminist Capital: the Case of Santa Clara County'. *Western Political Quarterly*, 38(1), 94–118.

Flanagan, L. (1989) *Braving New Frontiers, ANA's Economic and General Welfare Program*, 1946–1986. (Kansas City, MO: American Nurses Association (booklet)).

Flanagan, L. (1989) *Earn What You're Worth* (Kansas City, MO: American Nurses Association (booklet)).

Flanagan, L. (1986) *Pay Equity, What It Means and How It Affects Nurses* (Kansas City MO: American Nurses Association (pamphlet)).

Flexner, E. (1975) *Century of Struggle: The Women's Rights Movement in the United States* (Cambridge: Harvard University Press).

Foner, P. S. (1980) *Women and the American Labor Movement: From World War I to the Present* (New York: The Free Press).

Foster, D. (1991) *Privatisation: Local Government and Trade Unions Responses* (provisional title). (Thesis submitted for the degree of PhD, Bath University).

Freeman, J. (1987) 'Whom You Know Versus Whom You Represent: Feminist Influence in the Democratic and Republican Parties', in Katzenstein, M. F. and Mueller, C. M. (eds.), *The Women's Movements of the United States and Western Europe* (Philadelphia: Temple University Press), 215–44.

Freeman, J. (1975) *The Politics of Women's Liberation* (New York: Longman).

Freeman, R. B. and Leonard, J. S. (1985) 'Union Maids: Unions and the Female Workforce'. National Bureau of Economic Research, Working Paper Number 1652. (Cambridge, MA: June).

Friss, L. (1988) 'Why Don't Nurses Demand More Pay?' in Kelly, R. M. and Bayes, J. (eds.) *Comparable Worth, Pay Equity and Public Policy* (New York: Greenwood Press).

Friss, L. (1981) 'Work Force Policy Perspectives: Registered Nurses'. *Journal of Health Politics, Policy and Law*, 5, 696–719.

Gelb, J. (1987) 'Social Movement "Success": A Comparative Analysis of Feminism in the United States and the United Kingdom', in Katzenstein, M. F. and Mueller, C. M. (eds.) *The Women's Movements of the United States and Western Europe* (Philadelphia: Temple University Press).

Gelb, J. (1983) 'The Politics of Wife Abuse', in Diamond, I. (ed.) *Families, Politics and Public Policy* (New York: Longman).

Gelb, J. and Palley, M. L. (1987) *Women and Public Policies* (New Jersey: Princeton University Press).

George, A. L. (1979) 'Case studies and theory development: The method of structured, focused comparison', in Lauren, P. G. (ed.) *Diplomacy: New Approaches in History, Theory, and Policy* (New York: Free Press).

Ghobadian, A. and White, M. (1986) 'Job evaluation and equal pay' Policy Studies Institute (London: Department of Employment Research Paper No. 58).

Gibson, R. M. and Waldo, D. R. (1982) 'National Health Expenditures, 1981', *Health Care Financing Review*, 4, 1–35.

Giddings, P. (1984) *When and Where I Enter: The Impact of Black Women on Race and Sex in America* (New York: William Morrow and Company).

Gieske, M. L. (1984) 'Minnesota in medpassage: A century of transition in political culture', in Gieske, M. L. (ed.) *Perspectives on Minnesota Government and Politics* (Minneapolis, MN: Burgress Publishing Company).

Gilpin, T., Isaac, G., Letwin, D., McKivigan, J. (1988) *On Strike for Respect: The Yale Strike of 1984–85* (Chicago: Charles H. Kerr Publishing Company).

Golden, D. (1988) 'Taking on Harvard', *The Boston Globe Magazine*, August 7).

Goldman, D. (1989) 'Women in the public sector', *The Illinois Public Employee Relations Report*, 6(3–4), 4–9.

Gray, D. (1989) 'Militancy, Unionism and Gender Ideology, A Study of Hospital Nurses', *Work and Occupations*, 16(2), 137–52.

Gray, V. (1973) 'Innovation in the states: A diffusion study', *American Political Science Review*, 67, 1174–1185.

Gregory, J. (1989) *Trial by Ordeal: a study of people who lost Equal Pay and Sex Discrimination cases in the Industrial Tribunals during 1985 and 1986* (London: Her Majesty's Stationery Office).

Gregory, J. (1987) *Sex, Race and the Law: Legislating for Equality* (London: Sage).

Gregory, J. and Stoddart, J. (1987) 'Equal Pay: Out of the Ghetto?' (*International Labour Reports No. 23*).

Grune, J. A. (1980) *Manual on Pay Equity: Raising Wages for Women's Work* (Washington D. C.: Committee on Pay Equity, Conference on Alternative State of Local Policies).

Harrison, C. (1988) *On account of sex: The politics of women's issues 1945–1968* (Berkeley: University of California Press).

Harrison, B. and Bluestone, B. (1988) *The Great U Turn: Corporate Restructuring and the Polarizing of America* (New York: Basic Books).

Hartman, H. (1976) 'Capitalism, patriarchy, and job segregation by sex', in Blaxall, M. and Reagan, B. (eds.), *Women and the workplace: Implications of occupational segregation* (Chicago: University of Chicago Press), 137–70.

Heen, M. (1984) 'A Review of Federal court decisions under Title VII of the Civil Rights Act of 1964', in Remick, H. (ed.), *Comparable worth and wage discrimination* (Philadelphia: Temple University Press).

Heery, E. and Kelly, J. (1980) 'A cracking job for woman' A profile of women trade union officers. *Industrial Relations Journal*, 20(3), 192–202.

Heery, E. and Kelly, J. (1988) 'Do Female Representatives Make a Difference: Women Full-time Officials and Trade Union Work', *Work, Employment and Society*, 2(4).

Hole, J. and Levine, E. (1971) *Rebirth of Feminism* (New York: Quadrangle/ New York Times).

Horrell, S., Rubery, J. and Burchell, B. (1989) 'Unequal jobs or unequal pay?' *Industrial Relations Journal* 20(3), 176–191.

Horrell, S., Rubery, J. and Burchell, B. (1990) 'Gender and Skills', *Work, Employment and Society* 4(2), 189–216.

Hurd, R. (1986) 'Bottom-Up Organizing: Here in New Haven and Boston' in *Labor Research Review*, 8, 4–19.

Hutner, F. (1986) *Equal Pay for Comparable Worth* (New York: Praeger).

Huws, U. (1989) 'Negotiating for equality'. *Studies for Trade Unionists*, 15(59) (London: Worker's Education Association).

Incomes Data Service (1986) *Study 359*, April.

Industrial Relations Services (1989) 'Job evaluation: the road to equality?' *Industrial Relations Review and Report 448*, 5–10.

Industrial Relations Services (1990) 'Job evaluation and equal value: recent developments' *Industrial Relations Review and Report 455* (January), 11–14.

Industrial Relations Services (1990) 'Conflicting pressure evident in retail pay awards' *Pay and Benefits Bulletin 255*, 5–9.

Jacob, H. (1990) Women and divorce reform, in Gurin, P. and Tilly, L. (eds.) *Women in Twentieth Century American Politics* (New York: Russell Sage Foundation).

Johansen, E. (1984) *Comparable Worth: The Myth and the Movement* (Boulder, CO: Westview Press).

Justice (1987) *Industrial Tribunals* (London: Justice).

Kalisch, P. and Kalisch, B. (1986) *The Advance of American Nursing*. 2nd ed. (Boston and Toronto: Little, Brown & Co).

Katzenstein, M. F. (1987) 'Comparing the Feminist Movements of the United States and Western Europe: An Overview'. In Katzenstein, M. F. and Mueller, C. M. (eds.), *The Women's Movements of the United States and Western Europe*. (Philadelphia: Temple University Press).

Kauffman, M. and Citron, R. (1988) 'Yale Unions Say Four Year Contract Opens a New Era', *The Hartford Courant*, January 27.

Kautzer, K. (1988) 'Charting a New Course for the American Labor Movement' in Gil, E. and Gil, D., *Toward Social and Economic Justice* (Cambridge: Schenkman).

Kautzer, K. (1985) 'University of Hard Knocks, Lessons from the Yale Strike'. *Dollars and Sense*, May.

Keegan, C. (1987) 'How Union Members and Nonmembers View the Role of Unions', *Monthly Labor Review*, August.

Kenady, C. (1989) *Pay Equity: An Action Manual for Library Workers*. (Chicago: American Library Association).

Keppel, B. (1981) 'San Jose on New Ground in Women's Wage Debate'. *Los Angeles Times*, June 30.

Kessler-Harris, A. (1990) *A Woman's Wage: Historical Meanings and Social Consequences* (Lexington: The University Press of Kentucky).

Killingsworth, M. (1985) 'The economics of comparable worth: Analytical, empirical, and policy questions' in Hartmann, H. (ed.) *Comparable worth: New directions for research* (Washington, D. C.: National Academy Press).

Kirkby, D. (1987) 'The Wage Earning Woman and the State: the National Women's Trade Union League and Protective Legislation, 1903–1923'. *Labor History*, 28(1), 54–74.

Klein, E. (1987) 'The Diffusion of Consciousness in the United States and Western Europe'. In Katzenstein, M. F. and Mueller, C. M. (eds.), *The Women's Movements of the United States and Western Europe* (Philadelphia: Temple University Press).

Kronstadt, S. (1978) ' "New Frontier" for Equal Rights'. *The Nation*, 226 (April 29), 505–06.

Kumar, V. (1986) *Industrial Tribunal Applicants under the Race Relations Act 1976* (London: Commission for Racial Equality).

Kurtz, M. and Hocking, E. (1983) 'Nurses vs. Tree Trimmers'. *Public Personnel Management Journal*, 12(4), 369–81.

Labor Research Review (1988) Issue on *Feminizing unions 11* (Spring).

Labour Research Department (1989) 'Unions and part-timers – Do they mix?' *Labour Research*, (March) 19–22.

Labour Research Department (1990) 'Union reserved seats – Creating a space for women', *Labour Research*, 79(3) (March), 7–8.

Labour Research Department (1989) 'TUC reports: Congress looks forward to the 1990's'. *Labour Research*, 78(1) (October 5).

Labour Research Department (1990) 'Equal pay claims on the move'. *Bargaining Report*, (June), 12–17.

Lacombe, J. J. and Sleemi, F. R. (1988) 'Wage Adjustments in Contract Negotiations in Private Industry in 1987', *Monthly Labor Review*, May.

Ladd-Taylor, M. (1985) 'Women Workers and the Yale Strike'. *Feminist Studies*, Fall, 465–89.

Leonard, A. M. (1987) *Judging Inequality: The Effectiveness of the Tribunal System in Sex Discrimination and Equal Pay Cases* (London: Cobden Trust).

Lindbolm, C. (1977) *Politics and markets* (New York: Basic Books).

Lockwood, D. (1958) *The Blackcoated Worker* (London: George Allen and Unwin).

London Equal Value Steering Group (LEVEL) (1987) 'A question of earnings – a study of the earnings of blue collar employees in London local authorities'.

London Equal Value Steering Group (LEVEL) (1987) 'Job Evaluation and Equal Value – a Study of White Collar Job Evaluation In London Local Authorities'.

Lehrer, S. (1987) *Origins of Protective Legislation for Women: 1905–1925.* (Albany, NY: SUNY Press).

Lynch, R. (1986) 'Organizing Clericals: Problems & Prospects', *Labor Research Review*, 8, 91–101.

Malveaux, J. (1985–6) 'Comparable Worth and Its Impact on Black Women', *Review of Black Political Economy*, 14(2–3), 47–62.

Malveaux, J. (1985a) 'The Economic Interests of Black and White Women: Are They Similar?', *The Review of Black Political Economy*, 14(1), 5–27.

Malveaux, J. (1985b) 'An activist's guide to comparable worth', *North Star* 1(1), 22–31.

Malveaux, J. (1984) 'Low wage black women: Occupational description, strategies for change'. (Unpublished paper, NAACP Legal Defense and Education Fund).

Malveaux, J. (1982) 'Recent trends in occupational segregation by race and sex'. (Paper presented to the Committee on Women's Employment and Related Social Issues, National Academy of Sciences).

Mansbridge, J. J. (1986) *Why We Lost the ERA.* (Chicago: University of Chicago Press).

Martinez Morning News-Gazette (1972) 'CC Clerical Employees Vote Strike: County, Union Still Continue Negotiations'. June 20, 1.

Maxwell, P. (1988) 'The Impact of Equal Value Legislation in Northern Ireland' paper (presented at conference sponsored by the Public Administration Committee. Bath University).

Maxwell, P. (1989) 'The Impact of Equal Value Legislation in Northern Ireland' (shorter version of the above), *Policy and Politics*, 17(4), 295–300.

Mazmanian, D. A. and Sabatier, P. (1983) *Implementation and Public Policy* (Glenview, IL: Scott, Foresman and Company).

McKeown, P. (1988) 'Tipping the Scales', *Marxism Today*, September, 1988.

McKibben, R. (1988) 'Limited Pay Growth Thwarts Nursing', *American Nurse*, 20(5), 3.

Meehan, E. M. (1985) *Women's Rights at Work* (London: Macmillan).

Melosh, B. (1982) *'The Physicians's Hand'*, *Work Culture and Conflict in American Nursing* (Philadelphia: Temple University Press).

Milkman, R. (1985) 'Women workers, feminism, and the labor movement', in Milkman, R. (ed.), *Women, work, and protest: A century of U. S. women's labor history* (Boston: Routledge and Kegan Paul, pp. 300–22).

Miller, R. (1980) 'Hospitals', in Somers, G. (ed.), *Collective Bargaining: Contemporary American Experience* (Madison, WI: Industrial Relations Research Association).

Millward, N. and Stevens, M. (1986) *British Workplace Industrial Relations 1980–84* (London: Gower).

Minneapolis Star (1974) 'State-job sex bias suspected', 15 October, 7C.

Minneapolis Star (1977) 'Study says state's job policy full of sex bias', 23 March, 9A.

Minneapolis Star and Tribune (1982) 'Group says "female" jobs pay less than "male" jobs', 22 January, 1A.

Minneapolis Star and Tribune (1982) 'Quie vetoes bill establishing "job creation" conference', 24 March, 6B.

Minneapolis Star and Tribune (1983) 'Squabble in the sisterhood', 20 March, 2C.

Minneapolis Star and Tribune (1983) 'County pays women less, study indicates', 8 June, 12B.

Minneapolis Star and Tribune (1983) 'State closing gender gap on salaries', 26 July, 1A.

Minneapolis Star and Tribune (1983) 'Legislation requested to equalize public wages', 23 September, 17A.

Minneapolis Star and Tribune (1984) 'Civil rights panel to study major program changes', 6 January, 3A.

Minneapolis Star and Tribune (1984) 'School clerical workers fight equal pay issue', 22 February, 4B.

Minneapolis Star and Tribune (1984) 'Minnesota's comparable worth plan was the first in nation, and "it works",' 29 April, 1B.

Minneapolis Star and Tribune (1984) 'Comparable worth raises concerns', 31 July, 1B.

Minneapolis Star and Tribune (1984) 'Perpich loses spot on group's board', 1 August, 13A.

Minneapolis Star and Tribune (1984) 'Disagreement over methods stalls city's pay equity project', 16 August, 20A.

Minneapolis Star and Tribune (1984) 'A Hennepin County comparable worth study', 24 August, 8B.

Minneapolis Star and Tribune (1984) ' "Comparable worth" a loony idea, says rights panel chief', 17 November, 1A.

Minneapolis Star and Tribune (1985) 'Local governments tackle issue of comparable worth', 14 March, 1Y.

Minneapolis Star and Tribune (1985) 'Comparable-worth bill passes', 10 May, 20B.

Minneapolis Star and Tribune (1985) 'Durenberger set to introduce comparable worth legislation', 15 May, 10A.

Minneapolis Star and Tribune (1985) 'State's comparable worth law a model', 6 September, 1A.

Minneapolis Star and Tribune (1986) 'School district approves comparable pay plan', 30 April, 6B.

Minneapolis Star and Tribune (1986) 'County study finds inequities in women's pay', 14 November, 7B.

Minneapolis Tribune (1976) 'State panel on women's pay is backed', 6B.

Minneapolis Tribune 'Study: Women suffer job bias', 8 November, 1B.

Minneapolis Tribune (1977) 'Economic status of women profiled', 17 April, 17E.

Minneapolis Tribune (1979) 'Women's council strives to continue record of success', 5 February, 2B.

Minneapolis Tribune (1979) 'Women in Minnesota still lag in pay', 11 June, 10A.

Minneapolis Tribune (1980) 'Union, feminist leaders see bias in pay differences', 26 August, 1A.

Minneapolis Tribune (1981) '230 secretaries strike in area school district for custodian salaries', 1 July, 6A.

Minneapolis Tribune (1981) 'Some on women's economic council object to social issues', 19 November, 8D.

Minnesota Department of Employee Relations (no date) *Salary Plan, Effective July, 1988,* supplied by Nina Rothchild, Commissioner of Employee Relations.

Minnesota Department of Employee Relations (1986) *Pay equity in Minnesota local governments* (St. Paul, MN).

Minnesota Department of Employee Relations (1985) *Biennial work force report.* (St. Paul, MN).

Moore, R. and Marsis, E. (1983) 'What's a Woman's Work Worth?' *The Progressive,* 47, (12), 20–22.

Morris, T. (1986a) *Innovation in Banking* (London: Croom Helm).

Morris, T. (1986b) 'Trade Union Mergers and competition in British banking', *Industrial Relations Journal,* 17, 129–40.

Mueller, C. M. (1987) 'Collective Consciousness, Identity Transformation, and the Rise of Women in Public Office in the United States'. In Katzenstein, M. F. and Mueller, C. M. (eds.), *The Women's Movements of the United States and Western Europe* (Philadelphia: Temple University Press).

National Committee on Pay Equity (NCPE) (n.d.) *Bargaining for pay equity: A strategy manual* (Washington, D. C.: NCPE).

National Committee on Pay Equity (NCPE) (1989) *Pay equity activity in the public sector 1979–1989* (Washington, D. C.: NCPE).

National Committee on Pay Equity (1988) *Survey of State-Government Level Pay Equity Activity* (Washington, D. C.: NCPE).

National Committee on Pay Equity (NCPE) (1987a) *Pay equity: An issue of race, ethnicity, and sex* (Washington, D. C.).

National Committee on Pay Equity (NCPE) (1987b) *Briefing paper on the wage gap* (Washington, D. C.: NCPE).

National Committee on Pay Equity (1984) *The Cost of Pay Equity in Public and Private Employment* Washington D. C.: NCPE).

National Joint Council for Local Authorities' Services (NJCLAS) (1990) *Circular No. 319,* (London: NJCLAS, 2 August).

National Joint Council for Local Authorities' Services (NJCLAS) (1987) *Review of Grading Structure, Assimilation and Assessment,* (London: NJCLAS, August).

National Union of Public Employees, Northern Ireland Division (1986) *Review,* (Belfast: NUPE).

Needleman, R. (1988) 'Women workers: A force for rebuilding unionism', *Labor Research Review* (11), 1–14.

Nelson, B. J. (1985) 'Comparable worth: A brief review of history, practice, and theory', *Minnesota Law Review,* 69, 1199–1216.

Nelson, B. J. (1985) 'Popular misperceptions of comparable worth policies and their political consequences'. (Presented at the Western Political Science Association meetings, March).

Nelson, B. J. (1984) *Making An Issue of Child Abuse: Political Agenda Setting for Social Problems* (Chicago: University of Chicago Press).

New Earnings Surveys of Great Britain and Northern Ireland (1989) (London: Department of Employment).

Newman, W. (1986) 'Statement of Winn Newman and Associates, Washington D. C.'. in *Comparable Worth: Issue for the '80's. A Consultation of the US Commission on Civil Rights Vol 2 Proceedings* (6–7 June, 1986) (Washington, D. C.: Civil Rights Commission).

Newman, W. and Vonhof, J. (1981) ' "Separate but Equal" – Job Segregation and Pay Equity in the Wake of Gunther', *University of Illinois Law Review,* 2, 269–331.

O'Donovan, K. and Szyszczak, E. (1988) *Equality and sex discrimination law.* (London: Blackwell).

The Pennsylvania Nurse (1987) 'PNA Reaches Sex Discrimination Settlement'. June: 1, 8.

The Pennsylvania Nurse (1987) 'PNA's Sex Discrimination Suit Against the Commonwealth Moves Closer to Court'. February: 1.

The Pennsylvania Nurse (1987) 'PNA Files Sex Discrimination Suit Against Commonwealth'. January: 4, 14.

Pennsylvania Nurses Association (1987) ' "Historic" Settlement Reached in PNA's Sex Discrimination Lawsuit". *Contact, Educational News of the Commission on Economic and General Welfare,* 15(3), 1, 3, 8.

Pennsylvania Nurses Association (1985) 'PNA Sex Discrimination Charges against the State of Pennsylvania', *Fact Sheet* (June 7).

Perry, F. E. (1984) *The Elements of Banking,* London Methuen & Co Ltd (4th ed).

Personnel Management (1987) 'Realising the dividends from positive action'. *Personnel Management,* (October) 62–67.

Phillips, A. and Taylor, B. (1986) 'Sex and skill'. In *Feminist Review* (ed.), *Waged Work: A reader* (London: Virago) pp. 54–66.

Povall, M. (1986) 'Equal Opportunities for Women in British Banking', *Equal Opportunities International,* 5(2), 27–44.

Prescott, P. (1987) 'Another Round of Nurse Shortage', *Image: Journal of Nursing Scholarship,* 19, 204–09.

Pressman, J. L. and Wildavsky, A. (1979) *Implementation,* 2nd ed. (Berkeley, CA: University of California Press).

Remick, H. (1984a) 'Dilemmas of Implementation: The Case of Nursing', in Remick, H. (ed.), *Comparable Worth and Wage Discrimination, Technical Possibilities and Political Realities* (Philadelphia: Temple University Press).

Remick, H. (1989b) 'Major Issues in a priori Applications'. In Remick, H. (ed.) *Comparable Worth and Wage Discrimination, Technical Possibilities and Political Realities*. (Philadelphia: Temple University Press).

Remick, H. (1981) 'The comparable worth controversy'. *IMPA Public Personnel Management Journal* 10(4), 371–83.

Reverby, S. (1987) *Ordered to Care, The Dilemma of American Nursing, 1850–1945*. (Cambridge, London, New York: Cambridge University Press), pp. 215–48.

Roback, J. (1986) *A Matter of Choice: A Critique of Comparable Worth by a Skeptical Feminist.* (New York: Priority Press, A Twentieth Century Fund Paper).

Roby, P. & Uttal, L. (1988) 'Trade union stewards: Handling union, family and employment responsibilities'. In Gutek, B., Stromberg, A. and Larwood, L. (eds), *Women and work: An annual review Vol. 3* (Newbury Park: Sage Publications) pp. 215–48.

Rubinstein, M. (1990) *Discrimination: A guide to the relevant case law on race and sex discrimination and equal pay*, 3rd edn (London: Eclipse Publications).

Rubinstein, M. (1984) *Equal pay for work of equal value: The new regulations and their implications.* (London: Macmillan).

Rupp, J. and Taylor, V. (1987) *Survival in the Doldrums: The American Women's Rights Movement, 1945 to the 1960s.* (New York: Oxford University Press).

Sacks, K. B. (1988) *Caring by the Hour: Women, Work and Organizing at Duke Medical Center* (Chicago: Univeristy of Illinois Press).

St. Paul Pioneer Press and Dispatch (1986) 'Council OKs Comparable Worth Pact', 10/17/86, 4C.

San Francisco Examiner (1986), 'Pay Equity Breakthrough', Feb. 2, 1986.

Sapiro, V. (1986) 'The women's movement, politics and policy in the Reagan era', in Dahlerup, D. (ed.), *The new women's movement: Feminism and political power in Europe and the USA* (London: Sage).

Scales-Trent, J. (1984) 'Comparable worth: Is this a theory for black workers?' *Women's Rights Law Reporter*, 8(1–2), 51–58.

Shreiner, T. (1985) 'How comparable worth plan works', *San Francisco Chronicle* (February 13).

Shrewsbury, C. M. (1984) 'Women in Minnesota politics: A preliminary sketch', in M. L. Gieske (ed.) *Perspectives on Minnesota Government and Politics* (Minneapolis, MN: Burgress Publishing Company).

Smith, J. P. (1979) 'The convergence to racial equality in women's wages' in Lloyd, C. et. al., (eds), *Women in the labor market.* (New York: Columbia University Press).

Snell, M. (1986) 'Equal pay and sex discrimination', in *Feminist Review* (ed.), *Waged work: A reader.* (London: Virago) pp. 12–39.

Sokoloff, N. J. (1988) *Between Love and Money: The Dialectics of Women's Home and Market Work* (New York: Praeger Publishers).

South East Region TUC (SERTUC) (n.d.) Women's Committee. *Still moving towards equality: A survey of progress towards equality in trade unions* (London: SERTUC).

Sparks, P. (1988) 'Gender Issues in the Nurturing Occupations: Focus on Nurses and Health Care Professionals'. Unpublished. On file at the School of Social Work (CUNY-Hunter College, New York).

Sparr, P. (1984) 'Re-evaluating Feminist Economics: Feminization of Poverty Ignores Key Issues', *Dollars & Sense*, 99 (September).

Spencer, M. (1990) 1992 and All That: Civil Liberties in the Balance (London: The Civil Liberties Trust).

Starr, P. (1982) *The Social Transformation of American Medicine* (New York: Basic Books).

Steinberg, R. (1990) *Report Concerning the Proposed Testimony of Dr. Ronnie Steinberg PHD (sic) Concerning the Appropriateness of the Respondent Hospital's Proposed Comparison System.* (Presented to the Pay Equity Hearings Tribunal for a Hearing between the Ontario Nurses Association and Women's College Hospital).

Steinberg, R. (1989) 'The unsubtle revolution: Women, the state and equal employment', in Jensen, J. *et al.* (eds.), *The feminization of the Labour Force* (New York: Oxford University Press), pp. 189–213.

Steinberg, R. (1987a) 'From Radical Vision to Minimalist Reform: Pay Equity In New York State, the Limits of Insider Reform Initiatives' (Paper presented at the Department of Sociology, Pennsylvania State University. April 10).

Steinberg, R. (1987b) 'Radical challenges in a liberal world: The mixed success of comparable worth', *Gender and Society*, 1(4), pp. 466–75.

Steinberg, R. (1984) 'A want of harmony', Perspectives on wage discrimination and comparable worth, in Helen Remick (ed.), *Comparable worth and wage discrimination: Technical possibilities and political realities* (Philadelphia: Temple University Press), pp. 3–27.

Steinberg, R. and Haignere, L. (1987) 'Equitable Compensation: Methodological Criteria for Comparable Worth', in Bose, C. and Spitze, G. (eds), *Ingredients for Women's Employment Policy* (Albany, NY: State University of New York Press).

Taylor, V. (1986) 'The Continuity of the American Women's Movement: An Elite-Sustained Stage'. (Presented to the Annual Meeting of the American Sociological Association, New York, September).

Tong, D. (1981) 'San Jose Mayor, Union Chief to Address Issues on TV', *Oakland Tribune*, July 7.

Towers, B. (1989) 'Running the gauntlet: British trade unions under Thatcher, 1979–1988.' *Industrial and Labor Relations Review*, 42(2), 163–88.

Townsend, P. (1979) *Poverty in the United Kingdom.* (Harmondsworth: Penguin).

Trades Union Congress (TUC) (1990) *TUC charter for women at work* (London: TUC).

Trades Union Congress (TUC) (1989) 'Comments of the TUC General Council on "Equal Pay . . . Making it Work – EOC Consultative Document" (London: TUC).

Trades Union Congress (TUC) (1989) *Equality for women within trade unions* (London: TUC, 1989).

Trades Union Congress (TUC), Equal Rights Department (1990) *Equal pay for work of equal value: Claims lodged with an industrial tribunal and negotiated settlements using equal value arguments* (London: TUC).

Treiman, D. R. (1979) *Job Evaluation: An Analytic Review*, An Interim Report to the EEOC. Washington D. C. : National Academy of Sciences.

Treiman, D. R. (1984) 'Effect of Choice of Factors and Factor Weights in Job Evaluation', in Remick, H. (ed.) *Comparable Worth and Wage Discrimination, Technical Possibilities and Political Realities* (Philadelphia: Temple University Press).

Treiman, D. R. and Hartmann, H. (eds.) (1981) *Women, Work and Wages: Equal Pay for Jobs of Equal Value* (Washington, D. C. : National Academy Press).

Tzannatos, P. Z., and Zabalza, A. (1984) 'The anatomy of the rise of British female relative wages in the 1970s: Evidence from the New Earnings Survey'. *British Journal of Industrial Relations, XXII* (2), 177–94.

U.S. Commission on Civil Rights (CCR) (1984) *Comparable Worth: Issue for the 80s* (Washington, D. C.: CCR).

U.S. Department of Education (1987) *Digest of Educational Statistics.* (Washington, D. C.: Government Printing Office).

U.S. Department of Labor (1989) 'Industry Wage Survey: Hospitals, Boston, MA, January, 1989', *Bureau of Labor Statistics Summary* (Washington, D. C.: Bureau of Labor).

U.S. Department of Labor (1987) 'Industry Wage Survey: Hospitals, August 1985'. (Washington, D. C.: Bureau of Labor).

U.S. Department of Labor (1983) 'Industry Wage Survey: Hospitals, October 1981'. *Bureau of Labor Statistics Bulletin*, No. 2204 (Washington, D. C.: Bureau of Labor).

U.S. Department of Labor (1980) 'Industry Wage Survey: Hospitals and Nursing Homes, September 1978'. *Bureau of Labor Statistics Bulletin*, No. 2069 (Washington, D. C.: Bureau of Labor).

U.S. Department of Labor (1971) 'Industry Wage Survey: Hospitals, March 1969'. *Bureau of Labor Statistics Bulletin*, No. 1688 (Washington, D. C.: Bureau of Labor).

US Department of Labor (1967) 'Industry Wage Survey: Hospitals, July 1966', *Bureau of Labor Statistics Bulletin*, no. 1553 (Washington, DC: Bureau of Labor).

Verba, S. (1967) 'Some dilemmas in Comparative Research', *World Politics*, 20, 111–27.

Vogt, R. (1972) 'Decision Due Monday; CC Employees' Talks at Impasse', *Contra Costa Times*, 22 June, p. 1.

Walby, S. (1986) *Patriarchy at Work* (Cambridge: Polity Press).

Walker, J. (1969) The Diffusion of Innovations among the American States', *American Political Science Review*, 63, 880–900.

Wallace, P. (1980) *Black Women in the Labor Force* (Cambridge: MIT Press).

Willborn, S. (1989) *A Secretary and a Cook: Challenging Women's Wages in the Courts of the United States and Britain* (Ithaca: ILR Press, Cornell University).

Withers, C. and Winston, J. (1989) 'Equal Employment Opportunity', in *One Nation Divided* (Washington: Citizen's Commission for Civil Rights, 1989).

Index